Adobe®
BUSINESS CATALYST®

DESIGN FULL-FEATURED WEBSITES
WITHOUT THE HASSLES OF DEVELOPMENT

Tommi West and John Ulliman

D1710288

Adobe

Adobe Business Catalyst
Design full-featured websites without the hassles of development
Tommi West and John Ulliman

This Adobe Press book is published by Peachpit.
For information on Adobe Press books, contact:
Peachpit
1249 Eighth Street
Berkeley, CA 94710
510.524.2178
510.524.2221 fax

For the latest on Adobe Press books, go to: www.adobepress.com
Peachpit is a division of Pearson Education.
To report errors, please send a note to: errata@peachpit.com

Editor: Rebecca Gulick
Copy Editor: Liz Welch
Technical Reviewer: Pau Rodriguez Masgrau (Clubcard, LLC)
Production Coordinator: Becky Winter
Interior Design and Compositor: Danielle Foster
Cover Design: Charlene Charles-Will
Proofreader: Patricia Pane
Indexer: Valerie Haynes Perry

ISBN-13: 978-0-321-80957-5
ISBN-10:   0-321-80957-2

9 8 7 6 5 4 3 2 1

Printed and bound in the United States of America

Dedications

Tommi West

My husband David has been a constant source of inspiration and encouragement
throughout this project. I am so thankful for his endless love and enthusiasm.
I dedicate this book to him and his amazing brain.

John Ulliman

I'd like to thank my wonderful wife Andrea for her love, support, and especially
her patience.

Acknowledgments

Thanks to Danielle Beaumont, Group Product Manager, and Adam Broadway,
Adobe Product Evangelist, at Adobe Systems, Inc.

Thanks also to Damon Hampson, Marketing Manager, and Nancy Davis, Editor-in-
Chief, at Peachpit/Adobe Press. Thanks to Liz Welch for her excellent copyediting
services. And to Mario Gudelj and Pau Rodríguez Masgrau for their tech-editing help
and Business Catalyst skills.

And a very special thanks to Victor Gavenda, Rebecca Gulick, and everyone at
Peachpit/Adobe Press who helped make this book possible.

Contents

Introduction to Adobe Business Catalyst   vii

CHAPTER 1   **Creating Your First Free Trial Site**   1

Signing Up and Logging In   2

Reviewing the Trial Site   3

Exploring the Features in the Admin Console   6

CHAPTER 2   **Accessing Site Content**   15

Using the Website Area of the Admin Console to Manage Pages   16

Using Adobe Dreamweaver to Manage Page Content   21

CHAPTER 3   **Working with Templates**   29

Understanding Templates   30

Examining the Elements of the Template Used in the Trial Site   31

Managing and Applying Templates in the Admin Console   32

Applying Templates to New Pages in Dreamweaver   35

Editing Templates in Dreamweaver   39

Editing Menu Items in Dynamic Menus   44

CHAPTER 4   **Configuring, Inserting, and Customizing Modules**   47

Examining Module Functionality Displayed on the Live Site   48

Editing the Data Displayed in Modules   49

Customizing the Appearance of Modules with Layouts in the Admin Console   52

Inserting Modules into Web Pages with the Admin Console   56

Using the 1-Click Insert Menu to Insert Modules   59

Customizing the Behavior and Display of Modules   61

Inserting Modules into Web Pages with Dreamweaver   63

Adding a Link to the FAQ Search Page from the FAQ page   66

Customizing Data by Updating Module Layout Files in Dreamweaver   66

Understanding the Workflow for Setting Up Features with Modules   69

CHAPTER 5   **Building Web Forms to Gather Visitor Data**   **73**

Examining the Contact Form on the Trial Site   75

Accessing Form Data in the Dashboard of the Admin Console   77

Understanding Workflows   79

Editing Web Forms   82

Adding Web Forms to Web Pages in Dreamweaver   85

Using the Module Manager to Insert Web Form Module Tags   89

Creating Web Forms with the Web Form Builder   90

Adding Web Forms to Pages with the 1-Click Insert Menu   94

Overview of Working with Web Forms   96

CHAPTER 6   **Setting Up an Online Store**   **99**

Examining the Online Store on the Trial Site   100

Using the Admin Console to Edit and Configure the
Online Store   103

Customizing Layouts to Control the Appearance of the
Online Store   112

Adding a Product Search Form to the Store's Home Page   123

Setting Up Shipping Options   125

Configuring Payment Gateways   128

Working with the eCommerce Tools to Build Online Stores   130

CHAPTER 7   **Understanding Customer Management and the
Site's Database**   **133**

Configuring Web Forms to Generate Cases   135

Updating the Steps in a Workflow   138

Working with Cases   139

Adding Notes and Tasks   142

Searching for Cases   144

Managing Approvals in Workflow Steps   146

Using Workflows to Facilitate Business Goals   148

Examining How Secure Zones Gather Data   148

Setting the Landing Page of a Secure Zone 152

Updating the Header to Add a Logout Link 154

Testing the Changes to the Site 155

CHAPTER 8 Marketing with E-mail Campaigns 157

Examining the Newsletter Signup Form on the Trial Site 159

Working with Subscribers and Recipient Lists 160

Creating and Inserting Subscription Forms 165

Editing Web Forms to Add an Option to Subscribe
to a Newsletter 166

Creating and Sending E-mail Campaigns 168

Tracking E-mail Campaign Statistics 175

Creating a Recipient List to Target a Segment of the
Customer Database 177

CHAPTER 9 Creating Custom Content Types with Web Apps 183

Building a Sample Web App 185

Populating Web App Items 191

Inserting Web Apps on a Page 193

Adding Search Functionality to a Web App 196

Creating Web Apps Populated with Visitor Data 198

Inserting the Web App Item Submission Form on a Page 200

Testing the Web App Item Submission Form 203

Workflow for Building Web Apps 207

CHAPTER 10 Analyzing Performance and Revenue with Reports 209

Accessing Report Summary Information 212

Generating and Saving Custom Reports 216

CHAPTER 11 Upgrading Sites and Managing Domain Names online 1

Creating User Accounts and Setting Permissions with Roles online 2

Upgrading the Trial Site online 11

Finalizing Sites to Prepare for Launch online 15

Best Practices for Building Trial Sites and Backing Up Data online 17

Index 222

NOTE: Available
for download from
peachpit.com

Introduction to Adobe Business Catalyst

The Internet has completely transformed the way products are marketed and sold. Technology is evolving very quickly and businesses are constantly reinventing themselves. Customers want more for their money. They have learned to shop around to find the best value. They compare reviews to purchase the highest-rated items. As the expectations of potential buyers continue to increase, it is up to businesses to engage customers in new ways. It's not enough for a business to simply have a searchable site. Static web experiences and stale product catalogs do not inspire online sales.

Successful e-commerce websites require a new level of sophistication. In addition to offering secure and simple payment transactions, they must be able to track site activity and collect visitors' information, and to market products to potential customers. Business owners need the tools to easily access this critical data, use site analytics to optimize their inventory, add promotions to increase product sales, and target existing customers using strategic marketing campaigns to encourage repeat purchases.

It's important to create a portal that facilitates two-way communication. Site features such as blogs, comments, and forums allow visitors to become involved with a business. The exchange of feedback and personalization generates a buzz of interest. Visitor interaction draws new customers to participate with a site, just as a lone person walking down the street is drawn to investigate the store with a crowd of shoppers inside.

As a web developer, your goal is to produce this online presence for business owners. And it makes sense to use a system that is scalable and flexible. It should be easy for you and your clients to update and maintain the site. A high-traffic site with constantly rotating inventory, timely sales promotions, and immersive features is critical to building a sustainable business model.

The site launch is no longer the moment of handoff when you move to the next project and your client's site becomes frozen. A freshly published online business is the beginning of an ongoing partnership between you and your clients. They reap the rewards of your consultation services to help them review their site data and optimize their store, while you enjoy a predictable monthly revenue stream.

In this book, you'll learn how to use the Adobe Business Catalyst Platform to build successful online businesses. You'll find hands-on, step-by-step instructions that cover all the aspects of creating a modern and effective online sales mechanism. You'll discover how easy it is to combine your unique designs and layouts with your client's project requirements to deliver a custom website. You'll also see how to improve a live site's performance to increase online sales and exceed your client's expectations.

NOTE: Please visit peachpit.com for an additional chapter of this book. To access it, register for a free account at http://peachpit.com, and then register this book using its ISBN number (0321809572). You'll then be able to download Chapter 11: Upgrading Sites and Managing Domain Names.

Understanding Adobe Business Catalyst

The Adobe Business Catalyst Platform is a hosted CMS (Content Management System) that includes all the features needed to create online businesses—from displaying simple photo galleries to developing shopping carts. You can use your web-design skills to build complex websites quickly and efficiently. The pages use industry-standard HTML, CSS (Cascading Style Sheets), and JavaScript code. Programming experience is not necessary, and you don't need to purchase additional software. All you need to get started is a browser with an Internet connection.

TIP: If you usually work with Adobe Dreamweaver to create websites, you can download and install the free Business Catalyst extension for Dreamweaver to perform many of the same development tasks from within the Dreamweaver workspace. Additionally, you can create Business Catalyst templates (DWT files) using Dreamweaver.

The prebuilt features, known as modules, make it easy to set up site functionality. Using an online interface, you add features to a page, exactly where you want them to appear in the design. You enable and configure the settings to control how the modules appear and behave. The module toolset facilitates your development process while making the system extremely flexible. It enables you to focus on designing the site and how it will look, rather than setting up the back-end database or programming how the site works.

This solution is a fully integrated, all-in-one CMS. If you've investigated using other CMSs, you know that the setup process usually involves installing and maintaining many different systems. Attempts to make a variety of systems work together and share data can be frustrating. This is where the Adobe Business Catalyst Platform shines. Because it is a unified system, the pieces are integrated and you don't have to worry about conflicts or performance issues. All of the interactive features, including web-form submissions, customer contact data, order information, and site traffic reports are stored in a central database.

Examining Strategies for Online Businesses

Before building an online business, it is helpful to search online and compare various online stores to see how they are set up. When you first visit a site, notice your initial impression of the presentation and its design. Pay attention to the overall performance and how long the pages take to load. Explore the site to see if the navigation is intuitive. Look for error messages and broken links. Try searching for a product within a store catalog. Put some items in the cart to experience the checkout process. Click the Back button and see what happens. It is important to analyze these details to learn why some online store projects fail.

Customers are drawn to websites with clean designs and clear instructions. A common mistake is to put too much content on the home page. Visitors may never get past the first page if they cannot tell what the site sells or how to proceed. When working with your clients, establish two or three primary actions that the visitor should perform on each page, and then rank them by priority:

1. Click the featured product link and purchase an item in the online store.
2. Sign up to receive the monthly newsletter.

Limit the goals for each page to three or less. Design the page to ensure that the top-priority actions are the most visually prominent items.

Customers look for secure pages before entering their credit card information. If the page doesn't use an HTTPS URL prefix, they may decide not to enter their credit card information in the form fields. If the site presents errors or issues with the Secure Sockets Layer (SSL) certificate, many people will leave the site immediately.

The Business Catalyst interface includes the ability to create secure pages. It is not necessary to purchase or renew an SSL certificate because an HTTPS version of the site is included automatically with the site hosting. Since the pages of a shopping cart are secure and customers never leave the site during the transaction process, they feel more confident about entering their payment information.

Building successful online businesses

The process of running an online business is a lot like running a brick-and-mortar store; many of the methods for increasing revenue are applicable. As you consult with your clients, get them to share their knowledge of sales techniques. They can provide valuable insight into reaching their target audience. Refine the proven strategies for improving sales in their retail store and apply them to get similar results in their online business.

For example, when a business needs to move a large quantity of inventory, they create a prominent display near the front door with an inviting sales price. Window shoppers see the discount and it entices them to purchase the item. Some sales include bulk discounts, such as buy two items and get the third item free. In a best-case scenario, the shopper may decide to purchase additional items before checking out.

You can take these suggestions and use them to update the site. Create a featured item graphic and place it prominently on the home page. Put the featured product in the virtual "storefront" so that potential customers are aware of the sale. Add promotional discount messaging in the product page and in the shopping cart pages that reminds customers of the opportunity to buy two items and get the third item free.

Print advertising is expensive. The Adobe Business Catalyst Platform includes many integrated features to promote online businesses without incurring costly printer and shipping expenses. For example, you can place a newsletter signup form on the site to collect the e-mail addresses of potential customers. Their contact data is stored in the database, along with any purchases, web-form inquiries, or other interactions they perform on the site. You can use the integrated e-mail campaign service to target specific customers and distribute sales promotions. You can also create loyalty programs to encourage repeat sales and let customers know that you appreciate their business.

Think about the websites that you investigated. When you added an item to the cart but then left the site, did you ever hear from the business again? Wouldn't it be more effective if you received an e-mail message from the business a week later that mentions the item you put in the cart (but did not purchase) is now on sale? Think of the sales opportunities that present themselves when the site data is automatically collected and easily accessed—facilitating the distribution of promotions.

Key areas to focus on when analyzing an online business model

When you meet with a potential client about building their site, determine whether their business would benefit from the features included in the Adobe Business Catalyst Platform. Although this seems obvious, it is important; not every business model is a good fit.

Companies that sell products or services will get the most out of the solution. The system is specifically geared toward setting up an online catalog and facilitating payment transactions. The products could be physical objects that require shipping or digital files that are downloaded from the site after purchase. The system includes everything you need to set up tax codes and shipping options.

Web forms can be configured to contact business owners or sales teams via e-mail or text message. This is an excellent approach to use if the business offers services that require immediate attention. Short Message Service (SMS) message notifications ensure that the team on call can respond to website service requests in a timely manner.

NOTE: You can assign cases to different roles (sets of users) to ensure that each support request is assigned to the best person to respond to the customer's inquiry.

The back-end interface (accessed only by your development team and the business owners themselves) includes the ability to manage support requests and respond to customer cases. Each support case is assigned its own unique case number. E-mail communications sent between the business and customers are tracked and time stamped to ensure that every issue is resolved and no one slips through the cracks.

The combination of customer management data reporting and online support features enables the business to provide customer service using minimal team resources.

Your clients can also access the back-end interface to make content changes to the site without using HTML or CSS code. The browser-based tool is intuitive to use, and they can type right into the fields that you set as editable. You can also enable the Announcements feature so that clients can add recent company news. This approach eliminates the bottleneck situations that can occur when the web designer is the only person who can perform updates. While not every client has the time or inclination to manage their own site content, this feature is very empowering for some businesses that want a greater sense of control and need to update their sites frequently.

Secure zones enable registered visitors to enter their credentials and access password-protected areas of the site. They can be used to share exclusive information with members, such as premium content and downloadable files. Private forums or client deliverables can be distributed through secure, non-searchable sections of the site. You can configure secure zones to be free or require payment for access as an additional way to generate revenue. You can also create secure zones to share confidential information with customers by displaying their account information and order history.

When you configure an online store, you have complete control over the payment gateways used to process transactions. The options are extremely flexible, because you can configure the currency to accept international payments. And you can set up payment gateways that support recurring payments to sell subscriptions, such as Authorize.Net, eWay, PayPal, and Sage Pay.

However, there are businesses that may not need these features. A static brochure site that is designed to simply make it easier for customers to find contact information and a store location may not utilize the tools.

Additionally, this solution is best suited for small to medium-sized businesses. Although it offers many time-saving features, such as the ability to batch import inventory to update product catalogs, it was not designed to accommodate an online store that sells tens of thousands of items.

When you evaluate potential clients, consider the key benefits that the Adobe Business Catalyst Platform offers:

- All-in-one hosted solution
- Flexible design layouts that utilize templates to streamline production time
- Customizable online store product catalogs and shopping carts
- Interactive site features, including web forms, blogs, and forums
- A central back-end database that stores all the site's data
- Integrated e-mail marketing campaign creation, distribution, and tracking
- Robust reporting features that enable data access on a granular level

Using This Book

If you are a designer who has previously only created static websites or a developer who has created dynamic websites and is looking for a new system, this book is geared toward you.

You'll learn how to integrate the features in the Adobe Business Catalyst Platform to build an interactive online business. You'll get an in-depth understanding of what's possible so that you can confidently consult with your clients. This book assumes that you already run a successful web design and development business.

Although the projects you build with Business Catalyst are dynamic websites, you do not need prior experience programming with server-side scripting languages. You should have an understanding of web-design concepts, as well as some prior knowledge of working with HTML, CSS, and JavaScript code.

The Adobe Business Catalyst Platform offers free trial sites. The instructions provided in this book describe how to build a sample site using one of the templates included with Business Catalyst and your own asset files.

How to contact the authors

Please send all inquiries and comments to:
Tommi West: info@tommiland.com
John Ulliman: info@onthewave.com

Mailing Address:
On The Wave
3136 Maxwell Ave
Oakland, CA 94619

Related Links

 Overview of Business Catalyst:
http://www.adobe.com/go/bc_feature_tour

CHAPTER 1

Creating Your First Free Trial Site

Contents

Signing Up and Logging In   2

Reviewing the Trial Site   3

Exploring the Features in the Admin Console   6

The Adobe Business Catalyst Platform offers free trial sites so that you can build projects and try the solution. And because the service is hosted, you can preview your live trial site right away. When you set up a trial site for your client projects, you choose a temporary subdomain for the site. This approach is handy because you can share the URL with your clients during the development process. After you design and deploy the site, your clients can review its features by interacting with the site online. Once your client approves the final version and you are ready to upgrade the site, you configure the actual domain name, set up the e-mail accounts, and open the online business to the public.

Signing Up and Logging In

Even if you've never created a Business Catalyst trial site before, you'll find the process quick and intuitive. It takes only a few moments and you don't have to enter payment information.

Begin by visiting the Business Catalyst website: www.businesscatalyst.com.

Click the free sign-up button in the header. When the trial site creation page appears, click Continue.

The Site Option page loads with a series of templates. Business Catalyst allows you to build blank sites and use your own unique designs—or create templates using Adobe Dreamweaver to build the site from scratch. You can also import existing client sites to use as the basis of a new trial site and to quickly re-create them in the Business Catalyst Platform.

For the purposes of building this sample project, you'll choose one of the templates included with the system to learn how the back-end works. You'll work with a pre-built site to focus on learning about the features in the Business Catalyst system, since you already know how to build web pages and format them with CSS styles.

To follow along with this project, select the template named Impressum Online Store and click Continue (FIGURE 1.1).

The Site Details page appears. At the top, enter the site name (the title that will appear in the browser chrome) and the temporary site URL, which is generally your client's business name or their existing domain name. In this sample project, you're creating a sample client site. As you follow along, you'll build this trial site for a fictitious client to learn how the system works.

FIGURE 1.1
The Impressum Online Store template displays a checkmark when it's selected.

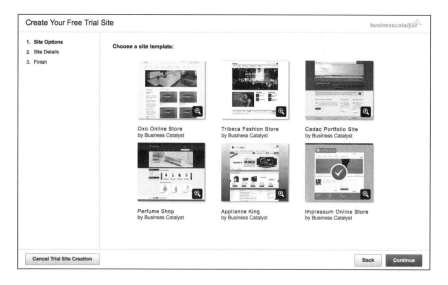

In the section that follows, enter your details:

1. E-mail Address
2. First Name
3. Last Name
4. Password
5. Country
6. Time Zone

Be sure to use a valid e-mail address and choose the time zone that is closest to your physical location. The time zone you select determines the data center that will host your site.

Next, read and confirm the end-user agreement by selecting the checkbox. Click the Create Trial Site button.

The Finish screen appears. As the trial site is created, a progress bar appears. When the trial creation process is complete, the page displays a confirmation message. Click the Login to the Admin area link (FIGURE 1.2). The Admin Console is the administration area where you'll build, manage, and deploy your site.

 NOTE: The system cannot host duplicate URLs. If the site URL you enter already exists in the system, the field background color turns red. If this occurs, enter a unique site URL for the sample client site.

Congratulations!

You have successfully created a new trial site. You will receive an email shortly with your login instructions.

Login to the Admin area

Preview your new site

FIGURE 1.2
Click the link to log in to the Admin area.

Before getting started, you should analyze the trial site as it appears right out of the box. Click the link in the overlay to preview the site in a new window.

Reviewing the Trial Site

At the moment, you have two browser windows open. The first contains the Admin Console for the site and the second contains the hosted, live version of the trial site you just created. Keep both windows open so that you can jump back and forth between them. When you're developing a site, you'll make changes in the Admin Console and refresh the live site to see the updates.

In this section, you'll take a few moments to see the prebuilt trial site that the system generated. It's based on the template of the sample site you selected. It includes many of the standard site features you'll set up when creating online businesses for clients.

In upcoming chapters, you'll learn how to edit the placeholder content provided in the template and customize the site using your own graphics. As you review the trial site, remember that you have complete control over the appearance of the finished sites you design; this is just a sampler of what's possible.

Home page

The home page displays the company branding and conveys the personality of the business (**FIGURE 1.3**).

FIGURE 1.3
The Home page of the trial site.

It includes features that are designed to gather visitors' data:

- Visitor registration, login forms, and order management
- Search functionality
- Primary and sublevel site navigation
- A newsletter signup form to subscribe visitors to a recipient list
- A contact form that enables customers to submit feedback and questions

Additional features enable the business to share information with visitors:

- A FAQ page that provides answers to common customer inquiries
- A news page that lists recent events and press releases
- An about page that defines the business and its mission
- A blog page that facilitates conversations with the online community

The main site design is defined using a template. Chapter 3, "Working with Templates," includes instructions to access, edit, and manage template files to create your own sites.

Online store

The online store displays a list of catalogs. Each catalog contains a set of products. Featured products highlight popular items to potential customers.

Click on a product's name or image to see a detailed view appear. While viewing a detail page for a specific product, the left column updates to display other recommended products.

In Chapter 6, "Setting Up an Online Store," you'll learn how to set up catalogs, products, and shopping cart functionality. Chapter 6 includes strategies to encourage impulse purchases and increase sales when developing online stores for your clients.

Blog page

A blog enables businesses to communicate directly with their customers. Businesses can post information and discuss topics in a format that is less formal than posting information on a web page.

Blogs are created using the Blog module. They can be configured to enable comment functionality so that visitors can post feedback about a blog post.

The right column contains links that help visitors navigate the blog archive. You can optionally choose to display these lists when you configure blogs.

Adding and configuring modules is described in detail in Chapter 4, "Configuring, Inserting, and Customizing Modules."

Forum page

Forums are more community-driven than blogs. Any registered visitor can create a new topic of discussion in a forum. In contrast, blog entries are posted by the business (although visitors may post comments if the comment feature is enabled). The threaded format is well suited to facilitate online conversations.

A site can have any number of forums, and each forum can contain unlimited topics. After a new topic is created, registered visitors can reply to the post.

The page also displays the date of the last post by default. If a forum is not very active, you can update the forum layouts to remove the last post date. You'll learn more about working with layouts to control dynamic data when you customize modules in Chapter 4.

If you'd like to try the forum, click the Forum link in the menu to visit the forum. Click the New Topic button and submit the form on the Forum Registration page to register as a new user. After creating a user account, use the New Topic form to enter placeholder text in the fields and submit the post. Your topic is immediately published. Click the topic name to see the details view of the post. Click Reply to add another post to the same thread.

Contact page

Like search functionality, contact forms are one of the features that clients often request. It's much more professional to add a contact form, rather than simply provide a link to an e-mail address on a Contact page. Form data is routed to the business team so that they can respond to customer inquiries. It's also stored in the central database, where it's easy for businesses to retrieve.

In Chapter 5, "Building Web Forms to Gather Visitor Data," you'll find instructions on creating, configuring, and customizing web forms using standard HTML and CSS code. Forms are a powerful feature that businesses can use to gather customer data and track support cases.

Exploring the Features in the Admin Console

The Admin Console is the backstage area that contains the tools you'll use to design and develop websites. It's where all the magic happens.

NOTE: If you closed the browser and the Admin Console is no longer displayed for your trial site, open a new browser window. Enter your site's URL in a browser with the /admin suffix, like this:

trial_site.businesscatalyst.com/admin

Log in to the Admin Console using your e-mail and password.

ENABLING ADMIN ACCESS FOR YOUR CLIENTS

Once the site is live, some of your clients may choose to take an active role in managing their online business, after you train them to use the interface. Other clients may prefer that you handle the site-updating responsibilities for them.

If desired, you can create an admin account for your clients. You can assign permissions to allow them to access some of the tools in the Admin Console. When they log in to their version of the Admin Console, they'll only see specific menu items, based on the features you enable for them. If you enable access, your clients can see site statistics and run reports. You can also train clients to update site content, if they're interested in participating in site maintenance activities.

If you haven't quit the browser since you created the trial site, switch to the other open browser window to view the interface. The welcome message is displayed and you can take the tour. When you're finished reviewing the tour, you should be in the Admin Console for your site.

Dashboard

The home page of the Admin Console contains the Dashboard, which provides an overview of the trial site's activity and statistics. Use the tools in this area to update your account details, access webmail, and schedule tasks.

In the Getting Started section, you can watch the video, read the FAQ, and visit Support Central to find answers and get up to speed quickly. The link to Support Central is also provided in the top-right corner of the Admin Console. It contains a vast knowledgebase of articles, a support forum, and helpful video tutorials.

Scroll down to view the weekly summary chart. Since you've just created the trial, there won't be any statistics to review yet.

After site launch, this area provides a graphical overview of the traffic, online sales, inquiries, and subscriptions over the past seven days. When the site is up and running, this will be the first place you look to check the site's performance and measure the success of the online store (FIGURE 1.4).

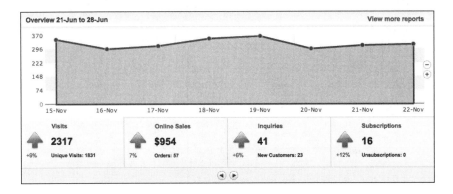

FIGURE 1.4
The site statistics are displayed in the Dashboard.

Scroll down farther to see the Live Feed. Site interactions, including form submissions, subscriptions, and purchases, are displayed as links.

Click the links in the Live Feed to jump directly to that record. Your clients can use this list to see which visitors are interested in the business offerings and use marketing strategies to convert them into paying customers.

The right column of the Dashboard contains other helpful links:

- News about the Business Catalyst Platform
- Upcoming tasks
- Campaign summary
- System usage statistics

Once you launch the site and it is ready for public consumption, you can use these areas to keep an eye on the daily progress and watch the business grow.

Website tools

The Website area contains the features you'll use to create, edit, and publish web pages. Use the tools here to create site navigation by setting up dynamic menus. It also includes some of the features used to create online communities (Blogs and Forums), syndicate site content (RSS Channels), and build password-protected areas of the site (Secure Zones).

The Web Pages page displays the site structure, including the folders that contain the CSS, images, and JavaScript files. The Home page (also called the Start page) is noted as the first page that will load when visitors access the site (FIGURE 1.5).

FIGURE 1.5
Review the Web Pages List page.

NOTE: The Business Catalyst Platform uses two domains for hosted trial sites: businesscatalyst.com and worldsecuresystems.com. The domains can be used interchangeably. After creating a trial site, you can access it using either domain name: trial_site. businesscatalyst.com or trial_ site.worldsecuresystems.com.

You'll also use this area of the interface to access InContext Editing. Using InContext Editing is intuitive. It doesn't require any coding or special software, because the pages are edited in a browser. And because you're editing the page directly, you can see how the text will wrap and how the changes you make will affect the live site.

Modules

Modules are prebuilt features that you can add to your site. These powerhouses of functionality are fully customizable. They are also completely configurable, so that you can control how they behave and the data they display. You can also update the appearance of modules to match the site's design.

The available modules are displayed in this area; click a module name to begin creating and configuring the feature (FIGURE 1.6).

FIGURE 1.6
Select the desired module to access the corresponding interface and set it up.

You can create features using modules and then insert them on pages. The system tracks everything for you, so that the modules you add are automatically linked to the site's central database. You never have to worry about updating the modules or checking for compatibility, because the modules are designed to work together seamlessly without conflicts.

e-Commerce

The main features you'll use to create an online business are available in the eCommerce tab. You'll build the catalogs to define the different sections of a store and then add products to populate each of the catalogs (FIGURE 1.7). You can update the appearance of the store using HTML, CSS, and layout files.

The online businesses you create can sell items globally, because you can set up payment gateways, currency, shipping options, and tax codes to target international markets.

FIGURE 1.7
Create new catalogs and manage them in the Catalogs List page.

Marketing features

Use the tools in the Marketing area to promote the business model and strategically target specific customers by sending them discount codes and sales promotions. You can create recipient lists by adding a newsletter signup form on the site, like the one on the Home page of the trial site. Or you may choose to import contacts from existing lists.

The built-in publishing system lets you design and send e-mail. Use this area to create new campaigns (FIGURE 1.8).

FIGURE 1.8
Access the Email Campaigns tools to create new campaigns, add recipients to lists, and design newsletter content.

The e-mail newsletters you send are tracked automatically, and the statistics are stored in the site's database. All of the online business sales and marketing information is available for review in a centralized location.

Customer database

The Customers tab contains the interface you and your clients can use to drill down into a specific record or sets of records in the database. You can search for a customer, support case, or order. The data is easy to access and customers' order history is easy to track within the system (FIGURE 1.9).

FIGURE 1.9
Use the search functionality in the Customers tab to find a specific customer in the database.

This vital contact data enables business owners to stay in touch with their customers. They can ensure that every support case is resolved and every inquiry is answered.

Reports

Your clients are more likely to access the features in the Reports tab than any other area of the Admin Console. They can view the charts to see the site performance at a glance. They can also use the reporting tools to check specific statistics (FIGURE 1.10).

FIGURE 1.10
View the Reports Summary to check the site performance.

Report information displays in real time, so clients can check the influence of their marketing efforts and keep their fingers on the pulse of their business.

File Manager

The File Manager is located to the far right side of the site navigation. This helpful area enables you to connect via FTP to the host server to manage the site's files.

Using the links at the top, you can create, delete, and upload files that are not web pages. Click on an image to see its thumbnail in the right sidebar, along with the path, size, and dimensions of the file. You can use this area to resize, delete, or preview the image in a browser.

NOTE: In addition to using the File Manager, you can use any third-party FTP client or an HTML editor (such as Adobe Dreamweaver) to connect to the host server and access the site's file structure.

Admin menu

Access the Admin menu on the top-right side of the window. Use the links in this menu to manage, configure, and customize the site.

You can perform administrative tasks, such as managing users and roles. You can also set the site's domain name and update site templates.

This is an area that you will use exclusively; your clients won't access these options.

Partner Portal

The link to the left of the Admin menu enables you to access a whole new area of the interface called the Partner Portal. Without even realizing it, when you create your first trial site in the Business Catalyst Platform you are also automatically generating a free Partner account. This account includes the ability to access the Partner Portal to manage your own web business, in addition to using the tools you've seen so far to build websites.

NOTE: The Admin Console and the Partner Portal are the two sections that make up the integrated interface of the Business Catalyst Platform.

To better understand the two areas, you could consider a tailor's business in a brick-and-mortar building. In this comparison, the Admin Console is the room in which the sewing of garments takes place—where clothing is fitted and constructed. The Partner Portal is analogous to the back room, where the office manager performs bookkeeping tasks and generates invoices.

When you first click the link to visit the Partner Portal, the welcome screen appears. Enter your web design business name in the provided field.

The goal here is to define the Partner Portal as your private area (as opposed to the Admin Console area, which might be accessed by your clients). The Partner Portal contains the tools that help you manage your client sites and run your web business.

Later, when you check your e-mail, you'll find a message in your inbox that welcomes you to the Partner Portal you just created. This message includes a link to access the

TIP: The name you enter here defines your free Partner account for the Partner Portal. Enter the name of your own personal design company (such as SuperSites) in this field, not the name of your client's business. It is an important distinction to make because you will continue using your Partner account as you create any number of trial sites. The name you enter for the Partner Portal must be different than the name you entered when creating the temporary URL for the trial site.

FIGURE 1.11
View information about your web business in the Dashboard tab of the Partner Portal.

Partner Portal directly. It also includes the login details, which are identical to the username (e-mail address) and password you used to set up the trial. One of the great things about this consolidated system is that you enter the same username and password to access the interface for all the sites that you create.

If you ever need to update your e-mail address, password, or other account details, click the Settings link in the top-right corner. This is also where you can find Partner Help.

Take a moment to explore the main areas of the Partner Portal. Click each tab, starting from the left side.

Dashboard

By default, every person who creates a trial site using the Business Catalyst Platform becomes a free Partner in the system. If desired, you can pay a onetime fee and upgrade your account to become a Standard or Premium Partner. If you upgrade your Partner account, you get special benefits, including the ability to make commissions on hosting fees and referrals (FIGURE 1.11).

Watch the videos in the Getting Started section to learn more about working with the Business Catalyst Platform. And check out the featured sites from other Partners in the Gallery section to get inspiration for your own site projects.

Clients

Use the tools in the Clients tab to manage your client sites. Click on the View link next to any item in the list to see the details for that site. You can quickly review a site's URLs, users, invoices, and system usage statistics. Once you've upgraded a site and published it, you can extend the items in the system usage statistics section if your client requires additional newsletters, disk space, or users.

In the Details section in the right sidebar, you can see the creation and expiration dates for the site. You can also see the time zone associated with it. Use the buttons in the sidebar to extend a trial site or upgrade a published site when your client is ready to take it live.

Resellers

When you upgrade your free Partner account to a Standard or Premium Partner account, you can earn a referral fee by referring other web developers to Business Catalyst. You can also accumulate commissions for hosting fees. Use this area of the Partner Portal to track those referrals.

Refer new Partners directly from within the system by clicking the button provided in this area.

Billing

This area is only applicable for Standard or Premium Partners. You can manage the income received from commissions in the first section.

The second section enables you to send invoices to your clients that have upgraded their sites and are paying monthly hosting fees. Because you can control the invoicing, you can optionally choose to integrate other web development fees into the monthly invoices that are sent to each of your clients. And you can use the consolidated billing to track the status of the invoices that were sent and paid in one convenient location.

Tools

The Partner Resources section of the Tools area is filled with helpful training materials and related services. Use these resources to get detailed information about pricing and review the Getting Started Guides.

In the right sidebar, you can download the free Business Catalyst extension for Adobe Dreamweaver, so that you can connect to your site and update it from within the Dreamweaver workspace.

The other sections linked in the left sidebar are not applicable unless you upgrade your Partner account. Premium Partners can use the tools in these sections to send out system announcements and weekly messages to their clients. They can also customize trial site templates and e-mail newsletter templates. Additionally, they can configure the online editor in the Admin Console to customize how it appears when clients log in and update site content.

Also be sure to check out the Training and Community tabs located on the far right side of the navigation bar. The Community area contains the interface to share your sites in the Gallery; this feature is only available to Standard and Premium Partners, but free Partners can view the uploaded sites.

The Training area contains additional video tutorials. The core set is available to free Partners. You can also sign up to attend weekly live training sessions to ask questions and get support from the Business Catalyst team.

Create Site

Now that you've become a free Partner, you'll use this area of the Partner Portal to create additional trial sites under your account in the future (FIGURE 1.12). Do not create them using the Free Sign Up button provided on the Business Catalyst site because you'll get a message stating that your e-mail address is already registered to an existing Partner account.

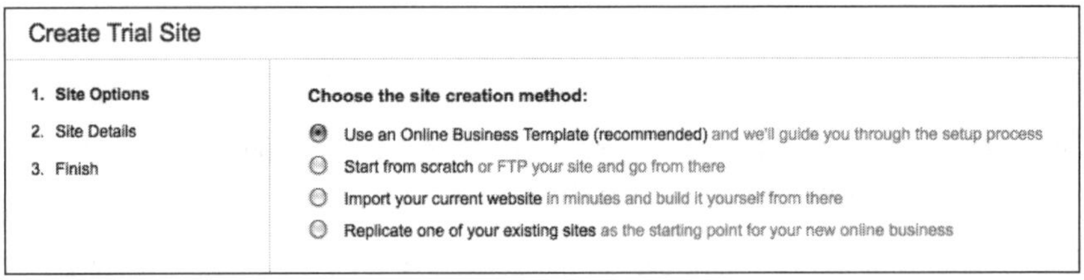

FIGURE 1.12
Use your Partner account to log in and create new trial sites in the Partner Portal.

Create Trial Site	
1. Site Options	**Choose the site creation method:**
2. Site Details	⦿ **Use an Online Business Template (recommended)** and we'll guide you through the setup process
3. Finish	○ **Start from scratch** or FTP your site and go from there
	○ **Import your current website** in minutes and build it yourself from there
	○ **Replicate one of your existing sites** as the starting point for your new online business

As a free Partner, you can create an unlimited number of free trial sites and pitch them to prospective clients. If you haven't finalized the contract or finished developing the site yet, you can extend the expiration date of trial sites until a site is approved and ready to be launched.

This is a fitting place to end the exploration of the Partner Portal. You've come full circle in the site-creation process. You are now an official Business Catalyst Partner and can begin focusing on building and configuring the trial site.

Returning to the Admin Console

To jump back to the Admin Console, click the Back To Admin link in the top-right corner. As a Partner, you can quickly jump back and forth between these two areas. If you choose to set up access to the Admin Console for your clients, they won't see the link to access your Partner Portal area.

In the next chapter, you'll begin using the tools in the Admin Console to update the content in the trial site.

Related Links

 Business Catalyst website:
www.businesscatalyst.com

 Getting Started with Your First Business Catalyst Trial Site:
http://www.adobe.com/go/bc_partner_account

 Introduction to Your Online Business:
http://www.adobe.com/go/bc_online_business

CHAPTER 2

Accessing Site Content

Contents

Using the Website Area of the Admin Console to
Manage Pages   16

Using Adobe Dreamweaver to Manage Page Content   21

There are several methods you can use to access and update web page content. Use one method (or a combination of all three) to build and revise a site.

In a real-world project, you'll use the Admin Console to work with the modules and set up dynamic data (because these features are only available in the Business Catalyst online interface). You can also use the Admin Console to make quick changes to the live site, because the editing features are easy to access. When you build the templates and pages, you'll use an HTML editor such as Adobe Dreamweaver. It's optimal to use a fully featured coding environment when designing a site, editing layouts, and formatting the site with CSS.

In this chapter, you'll use the tools provided in the Admin Console to change text and update images in the trial site. You'll also download and install the Business Catalyst extension for Dreamweaver to connect to the host server via FTP and update the site.

Using the Website Area of the Admin Console to Manage Pages

Log in to the Admin Console and click the Website tab. This area contains the features you'll use to create, edit, delete, and publish web pages. This toolset is always available online so you can update the site from any browser with an Internet connection, in case you are on-site with a client or away from your workstation.

While the Web Pages submenu is selected, the default Basic View displays a list of your existing pages. If you click the link in the top-right corner to switch to the Advanced View, you'll see the list update to display each page's URL and a link to preview the pages in a new browser window. Click the links to toggle between the advanced and basic views.

Creating pages and editing page content in the online editor

You can click the options in the Action Box sidebar on the right side to create a new page and set up and manage URL redirects. Use the links in the Related sidebar to access the File Manager to upload and organize site assets and create a new template.

When you want to access the Web Page Details and edit the web-page content, click the corresponding filename in the list (FIGURE 2.1).

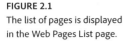

FIGURE 2.1
The list of pages is displayed in the Web Pages List page.

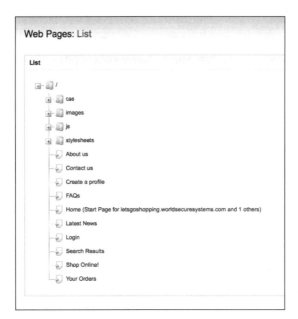

Begin by creating a new page and setting the page details:

1. Click the option Create A New Web Page in the Action Box sidebar.

2. If you want to save the page in a subfolder, use the Folder menu to select a new location. Otherwise, leave the menu set to /. The forward slash indicates that the page will be saved at the root level of the site.

3. Enter test.htm in the Page URL field of the Web Page Details section.

4. By default, the Page Name field is populated with the page URL you enter, without the file extension. The page name is also known as the page title, which is displayed in the top chrome of the browser window. The page name is also used to reference the page in the list displayed when you visit Website > Web Pages. For this example, use the default name that was added to the Page Name field, test.

5. The Release Date field is set to today's date by default. Note that you can set the page to publish at a later date if desired. You can also update the Expiry field to set a date in the future when the page will automatically be unpublished from the live site.

6. The Enabled checkbox is selected by default. If you decide to make a page temporarily unavailable on the live site (but don't want to delete it), deselect this checkbox.

7. The default template is automatically applied. In most cases, you'll use the same template as you build pages to create a consistent site design. However, you can reset the page to use a different template, or no template, at any time. Different sections of a site can use different template files.

> **TIP:** Although the system does not require a file extension when defining page URLs, it is a best practice to enter consistent extension suffixes in the Page URL field. Choose either .htm or .html and create all new pages in a site using the same file extension.

A NOTE ABOUT TEMPLATES

The sites you create in the Business Catalyst Platform are designed using templates. Templates are essentially standard HTML pages that include all the elements common to the other web pages in the site, including branding, company logo, site navigation, customer login form, the header, and the footer.

When you edit a web page, you only add or edit the unique page content that appears inside the template's frame. The template itself is edited separately—you won't see the template content displayed in the online editor of the Web Page Content section.

In Chapter 3, "Working with Templates," you'll learn how to create, edit, and manage template files.

When you're finished adding the Web Page Details, click the arrow icon next to the header to collapse the section.

The menu options in the Action Box sidebar enable you to do the following:

- Add modules to a web page
- Add the page to a navigation menu
- Preview the page in a browser
- Set the page as the Start Page (also known as the index page)
- Make the page secure (which adds the page to a secure zone)
- Syndicate the page for publication using RSS
- Add metadata to the page
- Set the workflow approval process
- View the web-page usage statistics
- Archive the page and roll back to the previous version
- Access the audit log

Editing page content in Design view

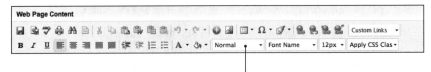

NOTE: When working in a browser, always save (or click Save and Publish) to save your changes before closing the browser window. However, if you navigate away from the page, you can often click the Back button, return to the online editor, and save the page without losing your changes.

Scroll down to the Web Page Content section. When you create a new page, this field is blank because only the content that will appear on the page is displayed.

This section contains the online editor, which displays the formatting tools across the top of the field. Use these tools to manage the page content.

Follow these steps to add some text content to the new page:

1. Click inside the Web Page Content field and type Test Page.
2. Select the text. In the toolbar, use the menu to the right of the paint bucket icon (which currently says Normal) to set the text as Heading 1 (FIGURE 2.2).

    The text formatting updates to use the default H1 style.

FIGURE 2.2
Use the tools in the online editor to format the header and paragraph text.

Web Page Content

Set the selected text to a paragraph
style with the formatting menu.

3. Click directly below the header you just created and type a paragraph of text, with several lines of placeholder text, like this:

    This is how a test page looks in the site. This is an example of a paragraph on a page. This text is formatted as paragraph text.

4. Select the text. Use the same formatting menu to set the text formatting to Paragraph.

5. Click immediately after the paragraph text and press Enter (Windows) or Return (Mac) to set the cursor on the next line below the paragraph.

6. Locate the Image Manager button in the toolbar; it's the icon that displays the sun over the mountains, to the right of the blue cross button. Click the Image Manager to open it.

7. A new window opens displaying the Image Manager. Click the Upload Files link. In the top menu, choose the /images/ folder.

8. Click the Select button and browse to select an image from your hard drive (FIGURE 2.3).

FIGURE 2.3
Use the Image Manager to select the image file to upload.

9. Click the Upload button. A confirmation message indicates that the file was successfully uploaded.

10. Select the image in the list of files. The right sidebar displays a preview of the image, its path, file size, and dimensions (FIGURE 2.4).

11. Click the Insert button to add the selected image to the page.

FIGURE 2.4
The details of the image are displayed in the sidebar.

Editing page source code in HTML view

As you edit pages, you can switch back and forth between the Design view and the HTML view. Click the tabs below the content field to switch back and forth between the two editing modes.

Follow these steps to edit the source code:

1. Click the HTML tab to view the code for the page. Notice that the <h1>, <p>, and <img> tags were inserted automatically when you edited the page content in Design view.

2. Click before the first line of code and type an opening div tag:

```
<div>
```

3. Click below the last line of code and type a closing div tag:

   </div>

   Below the Web Page Content, three buttons are displayed:

   - Save
   - Save And Publish
   - Delete

   If you click Save, the recent changes to the page are saved without publishing the page to the live site. (This creates a working copy of the page, which you can choose to update, publish, or delete later.) If you click Save And Publish, the edited page is uploaded to the host server. And if you click Delete, the page is removed from the site entirely after you click OK in the confirmation dialog box.

4. Click the Save And Publish button. A confirmation message indicates that the page was published to the live site.

5. Click the link in the Action Box sidebar to preview the page in a new browser window.

   The page loads and you can see the content you added, surrounded by the design elements of the default template that's used in the trial site.

Updating the site using InContext Editing

Now return to the Admin Console. Click the left subnavigation link to access InContext Editing.

InContext Editing doesn't require any coding or special software. Because you can edit the page directly, you can tell how the text will wrap and how the edits you make will affect the live site. You and your clients can edit the site content within the page while it's displayed in a browser window.

The InContext Editing page displays a Welcome message. If desired, you can select the option Don't Show This Dialog Again. To learn more about InContext Editing, click View Tutorial.

Click the Start Editing button to close the Welcome message and begin editing the page.

The editable regions of a page are indicated with dark dashed lines. You can click inside an editable region to select some text and begin making changes. It's just like editing text in a word processing program.

NOTE: If you want to edit a different page in the site, click the links on the home page to browse to the page you want to edit. If the page is an orphan and doesn't have any links to it from the home page, edit the URL in the browser's address bar to access an orphaned page.

Follow these steps to update text content:

1. The home page of the site is displayed by default. In the Our Company section of the footer, click the About Us link to load the About page in the editor.

2. Scroll down to the container that displays the header "An Online Store Out of the Box" (FIGURE 2.5). Click before the header text and type About Our Company.

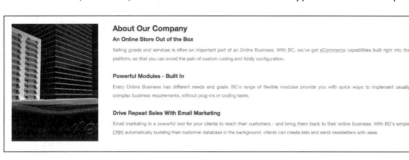

FIGURE 2.5
Click inside an editable region to make changes.

3. With the text you just typed selected, use the menu options in the top of the window to set the font, size, style, alignment, or indent attributes of the text.

Also explore the process to update images:

1. Select the skyscraper image and click the Insert Images button in the editing toolbar. The menus next to the toolbar change to display the tools you can use to update and upload images.

2. To insert a new image, click the page to set its location. Use the interface to select the location and filename of the file to upload it.

When you're finished making changes, you can click the Save, Save And Publish, or Discard button at the bottom of the window.

Visit the home page of the trial site to see your recent changes displayed.

Using Adobe Dreamweaver to Manage Page Content

You can also make updates to your site using Dreamweaver, which is handy if you're already familiar with working in that environment.

You can use the free Business Catalyst extension for Dreamweaver to connect to your site and make many of the site changes from within the workspace.

Installing the Business Catalyst extension for Dreamweaver

There are two methods you can use to set up the Business Catalyst extension for Dreamweaver.

Option 1: To install the extension from within Dreamweaver, follow these steps:

1. Launch Dreamweaver.

2. Choose Window > Business Catalyst to open the Business Catalyst panel.

3. Click the Get The Extension button.

   Your default browser launches and the Business Catalyst extension page loads.

4. In the right sidebar, click the Download button to get the extension.

5. A dialog box appears with the message "You have chosen to open the BusinessCatalyst.mxp file. Would you like to save this file?" Click Save File.

6. The file downloads to your local machine. Double-click the MXP file. This causes the Adobe Extension Manager to launch automatically.

7. Read the extension disclaimer, and then click Accept. The confirmation message confirms that the Business Catalyst extension has been installed. Click OK. Quit the Adobe Extension Manager.

8. Quit and then relaunch Dreamweaver. Choose Window > Business Catalyst to see the new extension installed in the Business Catalyst panel.

Option 2: To download the extension from the Partner Portal, follow these steps:

1. Quit Dreamweaver, if it is currently open.

2. Click the link in the top-right corner of the Admin Console to visit the Partner Portal.

3. Click the Tools tab. In the right sidebar, click the link to download the extension.

4. After the extension file finishes downloading, double-click it to open the MXP file. The Adobe Extension Manager launches automatically.

5. Read the extension disclaimer, and then click Accept. The confirmation message confirms that the Business Catalyst extension has been installed. Click OK. Quit the Adobe Extension Manager.

6. Launch Dreamweaver. Choose Window > Business Catalyst to open the Business Catalyst panel. The extension is now installed.

Logging in to a site with the Business Catalyst extension

When you're working in Dreamweaver, you can choose Window > Business Catalyst whenever you need to reopen the Business Catalyst panel.

The extension in the panel displays a login screen. Use these steps to log in:

1. Enter the same username (e-mail address) and password that you used to log in to the Admin Console.

2. Enable the checkbox next to the option Stay Logged In.

3. Click the Login button (FIGURE 2.6).

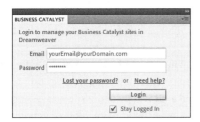

FIGURE 2.6
Enter your credentials in the Login screen of the Business Catalyst panel.

A progress bar displays briefly as Dreamweaver contacts the server and connects to your site. If the panel displays the message that it cannot connect, check your Internet connection. If you're connected to the Internet, try reentering your username and password again.

If you have misplaced your password, click the link Lost Your Password? and check your e-mail messages to find instructions on how to reset your password.

Connecting to a site with the Business Catalyst panel

After you've successfully logged in, the panel updates to display your name and provide a menu of your Business Catalyst sites. Use these instructions to choose a site and set up the site definition within Dreamweaver:

1. Use the Select A Site menu to select the name of the site you want to edit. Choose the name of the trial site you created for a fictitious client, not the Partner name you entered to access the Partner Portal.

2. After you've defined the site in Dreamweaver, the dot to the right of the site's name will turn green. However, there's a onetime process you must follow the first time you connect to a site within Dreamweaver. Before the site is defined, the dot to the right side of the site's name is hollow. If the site name displays a hollow dot, the Business Catalyst Quick Site Setup wizard automatically appears.

3. Enter the same username (e-mail address) and password that you used in step 1 to log in to the Business Catalyst panel. Click Login (**FIGURE 2.7**).

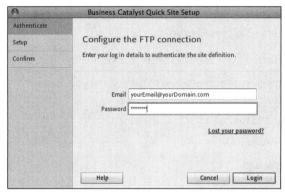

4. The Setup screen appears. Click the folder icon to the right of the Local Root Folder field. Use the window that appears to create a new, empty folder on your desktop. This is the folder that will hold a local copy of the site files, so it's a good idea to name the folder the same name as the trial site. After selecting the folder, click Select (Windows) or Choose (Mac). The path to the local root folder is displayed in the field. Click Setup (**FIGURE 2.8**).

5. A confirmation window appears, indicating that the site setup is complete. By default, the Download Locally checkbox is enabled. This setting means that when you click Done, Dreamweaver will download all the site files from the host server into the folder that you specified in step 4. If for some reason you don't want to download the files now, you can deselect this option and download the files later using the Files panel. Click the Done button to complete the setup and initiate the download process.

6. The Background File Activity window appears, along with a prompt: "Are you sure you wish to get the entire site?" Click OK.

7. When the site has finished downloading, the Background File Activity window displays the message "File activity complete." Click Close.

Editing site content with Dreamweaver

After you've defined a site in Dreamweaver, you won't have to use the Quick Site Setup wizard again. You'll be able to follow this workflow to begin editing pages:

1. Launch Dreamweaver. Open the Business Catalyst panel.

2. If you enabled the option to stay logged in, you'll already be connected to your site. But if not, enter your username and password and click Login.

3. Use the Select A Site menu to select the name of the site you want to edit. For these instructions, be sure to select the name of the trial site from the list. Do not select the name of the Partner account that you entered the first time you accessed the Partner Portal.

4. Begin working with the trial site by double-clicking the files in the Files panel. Use the same workflow you use when editing non–Business Catalyst sites.

Using the Files panel, you can create pages, update the site, and make revisions to the site structure, using the familiar Dreamweaver workspace and the HTML editing features in the Document window.

In addition to accessing the files in the Files panel and editing pages, you can use the Business Catalyst panel to insert Business Catalyst modules into pages. In Chapter 4, "Configuring, Inserting, and Customizing Modules," you'll learn how to configure modules and insert them using both the Admin Console and Dreamweaver.

Updating the images in the slide show

Swap out the existing image files in the template's slide show with images that exist on your computer:

1. In an image-editing program such as Adobe Fireworks or Adobe Photoshop, crop four image files to 943px wide by 288px high. Export them in JPEG, GIF, or PNG file format and save them in the images subfolder of the site's local root folder.

2. In Dreamweaver, open the Files panel and click the arrow to the left of the local root folder to see all of the site files. Double-click the home.htm file to open it in the Document window. By default, the screen is split vertically to show both Code view and Design view.

3. When you review the page in Design view, you cannot immediately see the slide-show images. Scroll horizontally to the right until the image of sneakers is displayed in the window. Click the image.

4. The corresponding slide-show code is highlighted in the Code view. Locate the line of code that defines the four images in the slide show:

```
<ul class="gallery">
<li><img src="images/img-1.jpg" alt="some-image" /></li>
<li><img src="images/img-2.jpg" alt="some-image" /></li>
<li><img src="images/img-3.jpg" alt="some-image" /></li>
<li><img src="images/img-4.jpg" alt="some-image" /></li>
</ul>
```

5. In the first line of code that defines the first image, replace the filename with the name of the file you copied to the images folder. Also update the alt tag with a descriptive alternate text for the image, like this:

```
<ul class="gallery">
<li><img src="images/shopping_image1.jpg" alt="Store shelves" /></li>
```

6. Repeat step 5 and update the remaining three lines of code with the filenames of the custom images you saved in the images folder and the corresponding alt tag text. When you're finished, your edited code will look similar to this:

```
<ul class="gallery">
<li><img src="images/shopping_image1.jpg" alt="Store shelves" /></li>
<li><img src="images/shopping_image2.jpg" alt="Shopper" /></li>
<li><img src="images/shopping_image3.jpg" alt="Store interior" /></li>
<li><img src="images/shopping_image4.jpg" alt="Merchandise" /></li>
</ul>
```

7. In Code view, scroll down to locate the second unordered list that displays the links and titles for each element in the slide show:

```
<ul class="switcher">
<li><a href="#">Item name 01</a></li>
<li><a href="#">Item name 02</a></li>
<li><a href="#">Item name 03</a></li>
<li><a href="#">Item name 04</a></li>
</ul>
```

8. Replace the placeholder titles (Item name 01, Item name 02, etc.) with descriptive names that match the alt tags you added previously, like this:

```
<ul class="switcher">
<li><a href="#">Store shelves</a></li>
```

```
<li><a href="#">Shopper</a></li>
<li><a href="#">Store interior</a></li>
<li><a href="#">Merchandise</a></li>
</ul>
```

9. Save the page and choose Site > Put to push the page up to the live server. When prompted "Put dependent files?" click Yes.

Updating the Welcome text above the login form

Explore the editing workflow by making more changes to the trial site:

1. Continue editing the home.htm file. Scroll down the page design to locate the existing text in the left-side login area that says:

   Welcome!

   This is your home page. This site contains a members-only section so your customers can log in and access secure content. To log in and see how it works, use the following credentials: Username: **guest** and Password: **guest**.

2. In Design view, click between the last character (e) of Welcome and the exclamation mark. Update the Welcome! header to add a longer header:

   Welcome to our new company site!

3. Select the paragraph of text located below the header and above the login field. Enter the following replacement text (FIGURE 2.9):

   We are pleased to announce the launch of our new online store. We are now open 24 hours a day to serve you.

   If you are already a registered customer, please sign in.

FIGURE 2.9
Edit the text in the Login area of the home page.

4. Save the page again and choose Site > Put to push the changes live. (Alternatively, you can right-click on the filename in the Files panel and choose Put from the menu that appears.) This time, since you've already uploaded the four new image files when you put the page last time, you can click No at the Put Dependent Files? prompt.

NOTE: When you edit sites with Dreamweaver, you may be familiar with using File > Preview In Browser to view a local version of the page. However, for this project it is a best practice to view the live version of the trial site in a new browser window. Always save and put the site files after making changes. Then, switch to the browser and click Refresh to see the live site display the recent updates. Because the trial site is already uploaded to the host servers, always put the files and view the live site instead of previewing the local files or using the Live View feature.

Testing the live site updates

After editing the images and text content of the site, view the changes that you made by publishing the pages and viewing them on the live host server.

Follow these steps to view the home page of the live site on the host server:

1. After making a change, save the page and choose Site > Put (or click the Put button) to upload the edited file. You can also right-click (Control-click) on a filename in the Files panel and choose Put from the menu that appears. If you updated images, CSS, or other related associated files, click Yes at the Put Dependent Files? prompt.

2. Launch a browser. Enter the URL to visit your trial site. The URL will look something like this:

   my_trial.businesscatalyst.com

3. The browser loads the home page with the recent changes displayed.

4. Test the updated slide show by clicking the titles to view the custom images that you uploaded to the host server.

As you can see from these examples, you can use Dreamweaver to connect to your Business Catalyst sites and edit them within the familiar HTML editing workspace.

Related Links

 Managing Your New Business Catalyst Site's Content:
http://www.adobe.com/go/bc_key_concepts

 Making Changes to Your Website Content:
http://www.adobe.com/go/bc_update_site_content

CHAPTER 3

Working with Templates

Contents

Understanding Templates	30
Examining the Elements of the Template Used in the Trial Site	31
Managing and Applying Templates in the Admin Console	32
Applying Templates to New Pages in Dreamweaver	35
Editing Templates in Dreamweaver	39
Editing Menu Items in Dynamic Menus	44

When you design the appearance of sites built with the Business Catalyst Platform, you'll use template files. Templates contain the recurring parts of the design that are displayed on every page, such as the header, footer, logo, and site navigation.

Every Business Catalyst site uses at least one template file. If you make multiple templates, it's a best practice to set one of the templates as the default. Every new page you create uses the site's default template automatically, unless you set the page details to use a different template. (In rare cases, you can choose to create a page that doesn't use a template at all.)

In this chapter, you'll learn how to create, edit, and apply templates using both the Admin Console and Dreamweaver.

Understanding Templates

The word *template* in web design has some negative connotations. Some designers equate templates with inflexible page designs or boring rectangular page layouts. However, in Business Catalyst templates are completely customizable.

For the purposes of learning the system, you'll use one of the prebuilt templates that's included with the site-creation process. As you practice editing this fictitious client site project, remember that we don't recommend using the prebuilt templates for your actual client sites. However, the prebuilt templates are useful for quickly creating a sample site and testing the Business Catalyst features.

Once you've finished working with this test site and have a better understanding of how the system works, you'll start fresh by creating a brand-new trial site. You can upload your own templates or import existing site designs as you build new sites for prospective clients. In your custom designs, you can create many different templates to define the appearance of each section. You have complete control over the layout, the structure of each template, and the resulting design.

Template files consist of standard HTML and CSS code. Each template file contains a single editable region where the unique page content is placed. When the browser renders the page, the template loads and the page's content is displayed inside. The editable region is defined with a single tag:

{tag_pagecontent}

TIP: When you build Business Catalyst templates in Dreamweaver, choose Insert > Template Objects > Business Catalyst Editable Region to insert the {tag_pagecontent} code. Take care not to choose the generic Editable Region option when making templates for Business Catalyst, because the code used to define the editable regions is different.

Templates have many benefits. Because the site's appearance is separated from the site functionality, you can redesign the site by updating a single file. The site uses the same template file to render the pages, which ensures that they're consistent and easy to navigate. Template elements are cached in browsers, so the site performance is optimized. Not only do templates compartmentalize the design to facilitate site changes, but they also simplify the creation of new pages. When you create or edit a web page, you only work with the content for that page. You and your clients can easily access individual pages and make changes without affecting the design of the entire site.

If you use Adobe Dreamweaver to edit sites, you are probably familiar with creating DWT files. You'll use a similar workflow to build the DWT files used as templates for Business Catalyst sites. The only real differences are the tags used to define the template's editable region and the use of a single editable region, rather than defining multiple editable regions within each template file.

Examining the Elements of the Template Used in the Trial Site

Before you begin creating a new template from scratch, it's helpful to look at a live site and identify the elements that are included in the template. Generally speaking, you'll add any common elements that appear on all the site pages to the template file to consolidate them in a central location.

Reviewing the trial site's home page

Use a browser to visit your trial site. The site address will look something like this:

http://trial_site.businesscatalyst.com

Starting from the top of the home page, a thin bar contains several navigation links:

- Log In
- Create New Profile
- View Orders
- Shopping Cart Summary

Below that, the header area displays the company logo and horizontal site navigation. You can use the Dynamic Menus module in Business Catalyst to create these menu bars quickly and efficiently.

A search field appears at the top right. One of the many benefits of building dynamic sites is the ability to create sites with searchable content. Customers appreciate the ability to search for the items they want; it ensures that site content is easy to find.

The regions of the page are defined using standard div tags. All of the items in the header above the slide show are included in the template.

Because the slide show is displayed only on the home page of the site, it marks the beginning of the unique page content and isn't included in the template. Although you won't see it if you view the source code of the page rendered in the browser, this is the area of the template that contains the tag to define the editable region:

{tag_pagecontent}

The home page begins with the slide show. In Chapter 2, "Accessing Site Content," you edited the HTML code of the slide show's unordered list tags to customize the content. The functionality of the slide show is provided by code in a linked JavaScript file.

This example illustrates the type of custom code you can add to your pages, either by hand-coding in the Admin Console or writing the code with an HTML editor such as Dreamweaver. When adding site features, you aren't limited to using the modules included with Business Catalyst.

Scroll down to the white area below the slide show. This section is also unique to the home page and isn't included in the template file. The left side features a login form that enables registered visitors to access a password-protected area of the site. The right side displays a signup form that allows visitors to subscribe to the company newsletter. These forms gather the potential customers' contact information, which is then stored in the site's database.

Directly below the forms, the blue footer spans the bottom of the page. The footer is included in the template content. The footer and the bottom navigation links are displayed on all of the site's pages. As you can see from this example, a template is like a shell that surrounds the unique page content displayed inside. Although you can choose to place the editable region tag in any location, it's most commonly placed in the middle of the template so that the elements of the template surround the unique content added to each web page (FIGURE 3.1).

FIGURE 3.1
This diagram illustrates how template content surrounds unique page content.

As you update the template file, you'll return to this browser window to refresh the page and see the changes. Keep this window open so that you can switch back and forth between the Admin Console and Dreamweaver as you follow along with these instructions.

Managing and Applying Templates in the Admin Console

The trial site you're working with uses one prebuilt template file called Main template.dwt.

You'll begin your exploration of working with templates in the Admin Console by opening a web page you created in Chapter 2 and seeing how to apply a specific template file to define the appearance of that page.

Applying a template to a web page

In this section, you'll see how easy it is to apply a template file to a web page within the Business Catalyst interface.

If the site has multiple templates, you can choose which template is applied to each page in the site. Follow these steps:

1. Open a new browser window and log in to the Admin Console.

2. Choose Website > Web Pages to view the list of pages in the site.

3. Click the file named test. This is the page you created previously.

4. The Web Page Details page loads to display the details for the test.htm page. Click the arrow icon next to the Web Page Details header to expand the panel.

    Notice that the Templates menu was automatically set to use the default template. In this example, the Main template is the default template for this site (FIGURE 3.2).

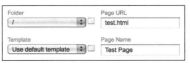

FIGURE 3.2
Use the Templates menu in the Web Page Details page to apply a template to the page.

5. Pull down the Templates menu to see the full list of templates in a site. In this sample site, there's only one template file (named Main). Don't change this setting; in most cases, the pages will be set to use the default template.

For this example, it doesn't matter whether the Templates menu is set to use the default menu or the Main template file, because they are the same file. If the majority of the pages are using the same default template, it simplifies the task of redesigning the site later. As you'll see in the next set of steps, you can create new templates and then choose which template is set as the default.

Accessing and creating new templates

The template files in the Admin Console are kept in the template section of the interface, separated from the web pages of a site.

Follow these steps to access the list of templates and manage them:

1. Use the Admin menu in the top-right corner to choose Admin > Manage Site-Wide Templates (FIGURE 3.3).

2. The Templates List page loads, displaying the list of existing templates (FIGURE 3.4).

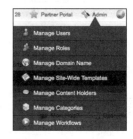

FIGURE 3.3
Use the Admin Console to manage templates.

FIGURE 3.4
The list of templates is displayed.

The trial site currently has one (default) template, named Main. In the Action Box sidebar, notice that you have the option to create a new template, using the same workflow you use to create new web pages.

If you click the Enable Tablet & Phone Support (Multiscreen) option at the top of the page, two additional blank templates are added to the site to support display on mobile devices and tablets. If enabled, detection code will be added to your site and will display the site using the template that matches the visitor's device, rather than displaying it with the existing Main template. If you choose to use this option, be sure to edit the two new templates; otherwise, the site will look blank when viewed on tablets or phones.

3. Click the link for the Main template. The Template Details page appears. Click the arrow button next to the header to expand the Template Details (FIGURE 3.5).

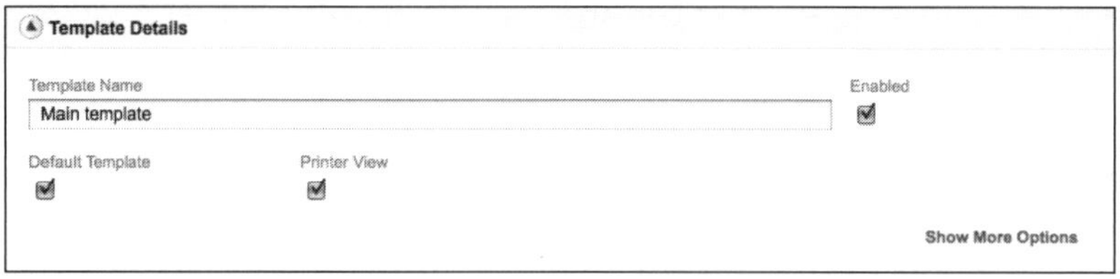

FIGURE 3.5
The Template Details page.

TIP: When you build sites with more than one template, it's a best practice to always set one of the site's templates as the default template using the Default Template checkbox in the Template Details page. When you create features using modules, many of the module pages are created dynamically and they use the site's default template to set the design of dynamic pages when they're rendered. This ensures that the module pages will match the other web pages in the site.

4. By default, the Enabled option is selected. Later, if you want to remove this template from the site (but not delete it), you can deselect this checkbox.

5. Leave the Default Template checkbox selected. The trial site is configured to use the Main template file as the default template.

6. Click the arrow button to collapse the Template Details. Scroll down to review the template displayed in the Template Content field of the online editor (FIGURE 3.6).

7. Take a moment to review the content of the template in both the Design and HTML tabs of the online editor. When you review the source code in the HTML tab, notice that the {tag_pagecontent} tag is used to define the location of the unique page content.

The layout for this template file is fairly complex. This type of content is difficult to update within the limitations of the online editor, so it's best to avoid editing the template file here. However, if you need to make very minor text changes, you can edit the document in the Template Content window and then click the button to save and publish the changes to the live site.

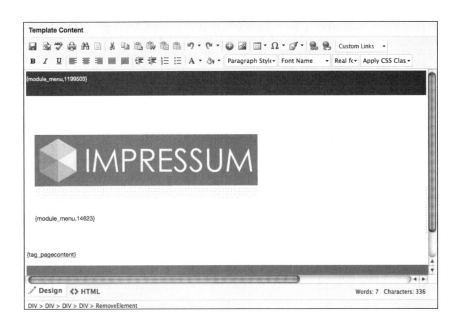

FIGURE 3.6
The online editor displays the
template content.

It's important to take extra care when editing template files. Always make a backup copy before making major changes. We recommend using Dreamweaver or an HTML editor because templates are critical to displaying a site's design. If you make a mistake and publish a broken template, the issues are immediately reflected on every page of the live site based on the template.

Now that you've seen how to access, create, and manage templates in the Admin Console, you'll switch over to Dreamweaver and learn how to access and edit DWT files in the WYSIWYG workspace. The HTML editing features in Dreamweaver make it easy to locate and update the CSS styles. Using Inspect mode and the CSS Styles panel, you'll make changes to the code and swap out the logo in the template.

Applying Templates to New Pages in Dreamweaver

You'll begin working with templates in Dreamweaver by creating a new web page that's applied to a specific template file. The template you select when creating the page defines the appearance of that page.

You'll use the options in the New Document dialog box to choose the template from the list of templates. Just like the Admin Console, Dreamweaver connects to the site and lists the template files available for use.

TIP: When you manage your site using both the Admin Console and Dreamweaver, it's a good idea to always synchronize your site in Dreamweaver before you begin editing any of the site pages. That way, you are sure that any pages you changed or added in the Admin Console are automatically updated in the Files panel. Similarly, after making any changes in Dreamweaver, always put the updated files to upload them to the host server and view the updates on the live site. If you follow this workflow, you'll be sure that both sets of files in Dreamweaver and the Admin Console interface are synchronized at all times.

Creating a new web page while applying a template

In this section, you'll create a web page in Dreamweaver that's attached to an existing template file in the Business Catalyst site.

Follow these steps:

1. Launch Dreamweaver. Connect to your site in the Business Catalyst panel.

2. Choose File > New to access the New Document window.

3. In the left column of the New Document window, choose Page From Template. In the Site field, the name of the trial site should already be selected. In the Template for Site field, select the Main template if it is not already selected (**FIGURE 3.7**).

FIGURE 3.7
The New Document dialog box in Dreamweaver.

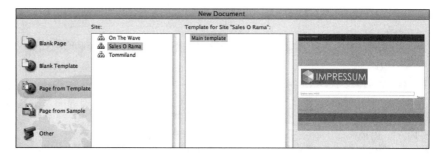

4. Click Create to close the New Document window and create the HTML file.

5. The untitled page appears in the Document window. Choose File > Save to save it within the site's local folder. For this example, name the file policy.htm and save it at the root level of the site.

6. Click the Split button in the top-right corner to view both the Code and Design views simultaneously in the Document window.

CREATING NEW PAGES IN DREAMWEAVER

Whenever you create a new page in Dreamweaver, always save the page inside the site folder before editing it, as described in the previous steps. By saving the page, you're specifying where the page exists in the site hierarchy. This practice ensures that you'll avoid issues when inserting images or adding links to other pages and files in the site.

Adding placeholder content to the new web page

The new Policy page displays the template assets in Design view of the Document window. If you look in the Code view, you'll see that the code for the template content is grayed out. Only the unique page content is editable on this page. This is similar to the behavior in the online editor of the Admin Console, which only displays the unique page content when you're editing pages. Any changes you make to this page occur within the template's editable region.

Follow these steps to update the page content:

1. In Design view of the Document window, click inside the editable region named ContentArea that contains this placeholder text:

   {tag_pagecontent}

2. Look in the Code view to see that your cursor is within the placeholder text that is highlighted here. The text is surrounded by the comment tags that define the template's editable region:

   ```
   <div id="main">
   <!-- InstanceBeginEditable name="ContentArea" -->
   {tag_pagecontent}
   <!-- InstanceEndEditable -->
   </div>
   ```

3. In Code view, select the entire {tag_pagecontent} placeholder text and press the Delete key to remove it from the page. While your cursor is still within the editable region of the code, type the following:

   ```
   <div class="main-holder">
   <div class="content">
   </div>
   </div>
   ```

4. Click the Refresh button in the Property inspector or click the Design view. The page design updates to show that the page area now displays a white background. This occurs because the CSS styles include a rule that sets the background color of items with the class main-holder to white. This change makes it easier to work with the template, because the text content you'll add in the next step is displayed on a white background.

5. Back in Code view, click after the opening `<div class="content">` tag, before the two closing `</div>` tags. Enter the following tags to populate the Policy page with text content:

`<h1>Return policy</h1>`

`<p>Lorem ipsum dolor sit amet, consectetur adipiscing elit.`
`→ Sed tempus imperdiet enim. Pellentesque et quis.</p>`

`<ul>`

`<li>Nam elementum congue varius.</li>`

`<li>Nam vulputate tincidunt felis.</li>`

`<li>Rutrum sollicitudin elit id sodales.</li>`

`<li>Morbi est vitae enim sceleris tempor.</li>`

`</ul>`

6. Click the Refresh button or the Design view. The page design updates in Design view to display the newest changes (**FIGURE 3.8**).

FIGURE 3.8
Enter the content to build out the Policy page.

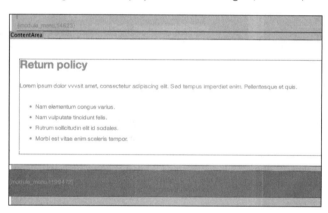

7. Save the page by choosing File > Save.

8. Upload the page by choosing File > Put (or right-clicking on the filename in the Files panel and choosing Put in the menu that appears).

Alternatively, you can select the policy.htm file in the Files panel and click the Synchronize button in the top of the Files panel. (It's the second button from the right side, with the two curved arrows that create a circle.) Click Preview and then OK to put the policy.htm file and update it on the remote server.

Editing Templates in Dreamweaver

In the beginning of this chapter, you learned how to access the area of the Admin Console that contains the templates for the site. In this section, you'll learn how to access the same files using the Dreamweaver workspace.

You'll make a minor change to the template content by adding a copyright notice in the footer. You'll also add a CSS rule to the external style sheet file that's linked to the template. Remember to tread lightly—the changes you make to the template file affect all the other pages in the site that are linked to it. Make a local backup copy of the site before editing these files.

Accessing and updating template files in Dreamweaver

Follow these steps to open the DWT file and make changes to the template:

1. In the Files panel, click the arrow next to the Templates folder to expand it.
2. Double-click the Main Template.dwt file to open it in the Document window (FIGURE 3.9). The logo image is partially obscured in Design view due to the CSS style formatting.

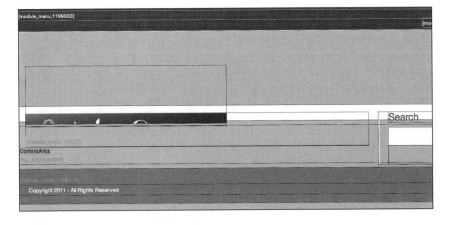

FIGURE 3.9
The Main template is displayed in the Document window.

3. Look in Code view and notice that the source code for the template is editable. When you open the template file directly, you can change the template content.
4. Take a moment to review the Code view and Design view. Notice that module features, including site navigation and the shopping cart summary, are displayed with module tags. In Chapter 4, "Configuring, Inserting, and Customizing Modules," you'll learn how to configure and add modules to display dynamic data on the site.

5. Click the Inspect button at the top of the Document window to enable Inspect mode. This action automatically also enables Live View. Inspect mode allows you to identify specific areas of the code and jump to them quickly.

6. In Design view, hover over the module tag in the footer. Your site's unique menu ID will be different, but the tag will look something like this:

   {module_menu,1199472}

7. While the colored bar highlights the bottom module tag, right-click or Control-click on the element to bring up the Inspect menu. Choose Inspect.

8. The Code view updates to display the corresponding code for the footer and the menu module:

   ```
   <div id="footer">
   {module_menu,1199472}

   </div>
   ```

9. In Code view, click after the module tag and before the closing div tag for the footer (FIGURE 3.10). Enter the following code:

   ```
   <div class="copyright">
   Copyright 2011 - All Rights Reserved
   </div>
   ```

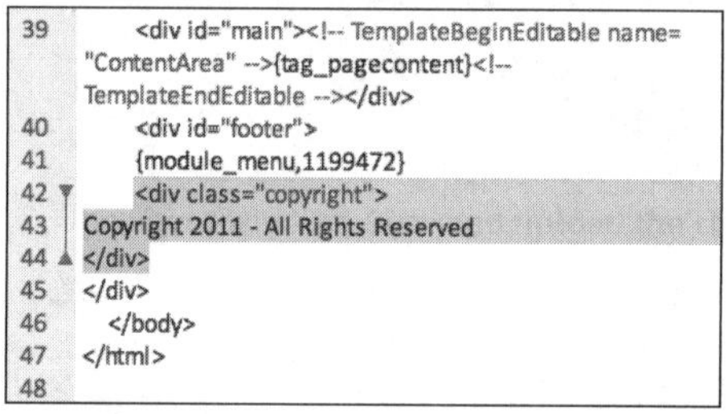

FIGURE 3.10
The copyright message is displayed in a div in the footer of the page.

```
39      <div id="main"><!-- TemplateBeginEditable name=
     "ContentArea" -->{tag_pagecontent}<!--
     TemplateEndEditable --></div>
40      <div id="footer">
41      {module_menu,1199472}
42      <div class="copyright">
43   Copyright 2011 - All Rights Reserved
44   </div>
45   </div>
46      </body>
47   </html>
48
```

10. Click the Refresh button in the Property inspector or in Design view to see the new div with the copyright message displayed in the footer of the template. It's in the correct location, but it needs some formatting.

11. Click the New CSS Rule button in the bottom of the CSS Styles panel.

12. In the New CSS Rule Definition dialog box that appears, enter the class name for the style in the Selector Name field:

    .copyright

    In the bottom of the dialog box, use the Rule Definition menu to define the rule in the all.css style sheet.

13. Click OK. The CSS Rule Definition dialog box appears. Add the following styles to the .copyright class:

    color: #FFF;

    padding-left: 20px;

14. Save the template. The Update Template Files dialog box appears. Click Update to update all the pages that are based on the template. When the Update Pages message displays Done, click the Close button.

15. Put the template file to upload it to the server. When the dialog box asks if you want to put the dependent files, click Yes to upload the all.css file to the css folder as well as upload the Main template.dwt file to the Templates folder.

16. Switch to the browser window that displays the live site. Click Refresh to see the home page load with the new copyright message in the footer. Click some of the links to see that the copyright message now appears on every page that uses the template file.

The features in the Dreamweaver workspace facilitate the process of finding code and creating CSS rules. You can follow the same workflow you use when building other site projects to edit your Business Catalyst sites.

Updating the logo in the template

Using the HTML editing features in Dreamweaver, you'll locate and update the CSS code in the external style sheet to customize the logo in the template. You'll use Inspect mode to jump right to the code and then access the rule in the CSS Styles panel to set the path to the new logo image.

Before you begin this section, prepare an image file to use to replace the existing Impressum logo. Use an image-editing program to create an image that is 410px by 120px. Export the file as a PNG file and save it as **logo_new.png** in the images folder of your site.

Now that the new logo image is saved inside the site folder, you can swap it out:

1. Click the Inspect button to enable Inspect mode.

2. In Design view, hover over the existing Impressum logo. Right-click or Control-click and select the Inspect option from the menu that appears. The path to the logo file is displayed in the Current tab of the CSS Styles panel (FIGURE 3.11).

TIP: In addition to the css folder, there's a stylesheets folder at the root level of the site that contains the modulestylesheet.css file. This CSS file must remain in the stylesheets folder to work. Do not move it or rename the stylesheets folder or its filename. The modulestylesheet.css file contains the rules that control the appearance of features built with modules; it's linked to every page in the site. Before making any changes to it, create a backup copy of the original, in case you need to revert.

TIP: In addition to using the Inspect mode in Dreamweaver, you can install the free Firebug add-on for the Firefox browser. Once the Firebug utility is installed, view the live site in Firefox and use it to inspect the elements of the page and preview the code. Both strategies are especially useful when editing templates and pages that you didn't create, because you can identify the names of the classes referenced in the CSS styles.

FIGURE 3.11
The CSS Styles panel displays
the link to the logo image file.

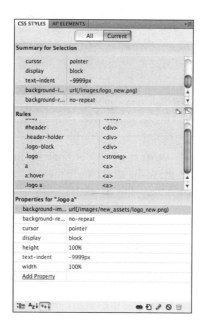

3. If you look in the Code view, the logo code is highlighted with the existing company name and link to the home page:

    `<a href="/home">IMPRESSUM</a>`

4. In Code view, replace the existing company name with a different fictitious client name, like this:

    `<a href="/home">Sales O Rama</a>`

5. While your cursor is still in the Code view, click the Current tab of the CSS Styles panel to see the rules applied to the current style: .logo a. The list of rules is displayed in the Properties pane of the CSS Styles panel.

6. The first rule sets the background image for the .logo a style. Select the background rule and click the Edit Rule button (the pencil icon) to launch the CSS Rule Definition dialog box.

7. Because you selected the background rule, the Background category is displayed by default. Click the Browse button next to the background-image field and browse to select the logo file named logo_new.png in the images folder. Click Select (Windows) or Choose (Mac) to update the path to the background image.

8. Click OK to close the CSS Rule Definition dialog box.

9. Choose File > Save All. Click Update in the dialog box that asks "Update all files based on this template?" When the Update Pages dialog box displays Done, click the Close button to close it.

10. Choose Site > Put to upload the template page. At the prompt Put Dependent Files?, click Yes to also upload the all.css file and the logo_new.png image file.

11. Switch to the browser window that displays the live site. Click Refresh to see the home page load with the new logo image. Click some of the links to see that the updated logo now appears on every page of the site (FIGURE 3.12).

FIGURE 3.12
The new logo is displayed on the live site.

Identifying the module tags in the template

Return to Dreamweaver. Because the template file contains the elements of the site that are displayed on every page, it's the ideal location to place the site menus. The menu links are consistently displayed on all the pages, which means visitors can navigate the site intuitively.

You can choose to create the navigation for a site and customize it to match the site's design. You can add a series of links directly into the template or use the Dynamic Menu module included with Business Catalyst to generate the site menus. If you use modules, you can update the appearance of the menus using standard HTML and CSS styles, just as you can format the text links you create.

In this example, the template file is using two different module tags to display navigation menus at the top and bottom of the page (FIGURE 3.13).

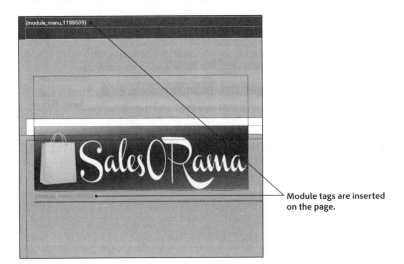

Module tags are inserted
on the page.

FIGURE 3.13
Module tags display the site navigation.

NOTE: You can insert existing module tags into pages and templates using Dreamweaver. However, the Business Catalyst panel in Dreamweaver does not include the ability to configure modules.

Take a moment to locate the two module tags in the template. One module tag is located in the header and the other is in the footer. These module tags are used throughout Business Catalyst pages to indicate where data content will be displayed.

Editing Menu Items in Dynamic Menus

Because modules can only be configured in the Admin Console, you'll quit Dreamweaver and switch over to working in the Business Catalyst interface.

Follow these steps to access and edit dynamic menus:

1. Open a new browser window and log in to the Admin Console.

2. Choose Website > Dynamic Menus to access the Dynamic Menus List page (FIGURE 3.14).

3. Review the list of existing menus. The trial site has five menus that are created and configured to display navigation on the site:

   - Footer menu

   - Header menu

   - Main menu

   - Webshop menu

   - Webshop menu 2

   You can create unlimited menus for a site using the Dynamic Menus module.

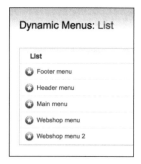

FIGURE 3.14
The list of menus is displayed in the Dynamic Menus List page.

4. Each one of the items in the list is a link. Click the Footer menu link to access the Menu Details page for that menu. Click Next to see the individual menu items for the Footer menu (FIGURE 3.15).

5. Take a moment to review the menu items and subitems. Each item has a label. As you click each label in the tree structure hierarchy, the fields in the center of the page update to display the details about that menu item.

   If the menu item has a link, the path is included in the Item URL field. The Parent menu sets the submenu's location.

   If you want to temporarily remove a menu item (but not delete it), you can deselect the Enabled option to deactivate the selected menu item.

6. In the tree structure hierarchy, select the Order & Payments menu item, directly below the Root level. Click the New Item button at the bottom of the page.

7. Enter the label name Return policy in the Item Label field.

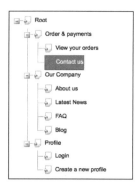

FIGURE 3.15
The footer menu items are displayed in a tree structure hierarchy.

8. Click the small white box icon below the Item URL field. The Link Manager window appears. Click the arrow icon below the Select Web Page field and scroll down to locate the web page you created named Policy. Select the Policy page and click Select to add the link.

   Notice that in addition to adding menu links to web pages, you can click the link categories at the top of the Link Manager to add links to dynamic features in the site (FIGURE 3.16).

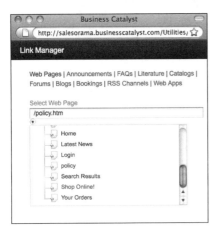

FIGURE 3.16
Select the policy.htm page in the Link Manager.

9. Use the Parent menu to select Order & Payments. This setting creates a menu item that is a subitem in the Order & Payments section of the footer menu.

10. Click Save Item. The tree structure hierarchy updates to display the new menu item named Return Policy as a subitem of the Order & Payments section. A confirmation message states that the item details are saved.

11. Switch to the other browser that displays the live site. Refresh the page and you'll see that the Order & Payments section of the footer menu now contains a new link to the Return Policy page. Click the link to see the policy.htm page load.

TIP: Right-click on the menu items in the tree structure hierarchy to manage the menu item names and reposition them within the structure of the menu.

CUSTOMIZING THE APPEARANCE OF DYNAMIC MENUS

If desired, you can modify the appearance of the Dynamic Menu layout. Using CSS styles, you can format the menu and customize the elements of the menu to match your site's design. Enable the Assign your own CSS to menu item option to access the fields for the menu states.

Business Catalyst lets you add styles directly to the states of the menu by editing the code directly in the Admin Console.

When working with templates, you can use the Inspect mode feature in Dreamweaver as described previously. Inspect the template code to identify and update the CSS rules that have been applied. You can also use the Firebug add-on for the Firefox browser to inspect the live site and discover which rules to update to affect the appearance of menus created with the Dynamic Menus module.

CHAPTER 4

Configuring, Inserting, and Customizing Modules

Contents

Examining Module Functionality Displayed on the Live Site   48

Editing the Data Displayed in Modules   49

Customizing the Appearance of Modules with Layouts
  in the Admin Console   52

Inserting Modules into Web Pages with the Admin Console   56

Using the 1-Click Insert Menu to Insert Modules   59

Customizing the Behavior and Display of Modules   61

Inserting Modules into Web Pages with Dreamweaver   63

Adding a Link to the FAQ Search Page from the FAQ page   66

Customizing Data by Updating Module Layout Files
  in Dreamweaver   66

Understanding the Workflow for Setting Up Features
  with Modules   69

Modules are prebuilt features in Business Catalyst. They enable you to manage many parts of the site content by facilitating the display of dynamic data stored in the site's database. When site data is displayed through module features, it consolidates the data in a central location and makes it easier to update.

Using the Admin Console, you can add new data to modules once they are set up (**FIGURE 4.1**). Click the Modules tag to view the list of modules.

FIGURE 4.1
Access modules on the
Module List page of the
Admin Console.

The process is so easy that some clients may choose to take a more active role in running their site and managing the data that's used to populate the features driven by modules. This setup is ideal: you manage the configuration of the features and control the module's appearance, and your client can update the module's content without the possibility of breaking the site functionality or changing the design.

Examining Module Functionality Displayed on the Live Site

The FAQ page is a good starting example. By posting store policies and guidelines online with the FAQ module, businesses can reduce the number of customer contacts and support cases. Visitors enjoy interacting with the FAQ list and are less likely to use the contact form to ask questions if they can find their answers online.

In this section, you'll review the FAQ module in the trial site to see how it behaves and displays data of frequently asked questions:

1. In a browser window, visit the trial site. The home page loads. In the Our Company section of the footer menu, click the FAQ link.

2. The FAQ page loads, displaying the list of FAQ data in the module interface. The frequently asked questions are displayed as a collapsed list of linked questions (**FIGURE 4.2**).

FIGURE 4.2
The list of questions is displayed as links on the FAQ page.

3. Click the question "What is your refund policy?"

   The answer displays below the question text, along with a comment form (FIGURE 4.3).

FIGURE 4.3
After clicking a FAQ question, you'll see the corresponding answer.

Editing the Data Displayed in Modules

When you're setting up dynamic site features, there are two distinct ways you control the modules:

- Managing the data in the module
- Customizing the feature to define how it displays on the page

In this section, you'll learn how to update the data in a module to revise the content displayed by the FAQ.

Accessing module data in the Admin Console

Follow these steps to update the data in one of the existing FAQ items:

1. Log in to the Admin Console and choose Modules > FAQs. The list of FAQ items appears (FIGURE 4.4).

FIGURE 4.4
The list of existing FAQs is displayed in the FAQs List page.

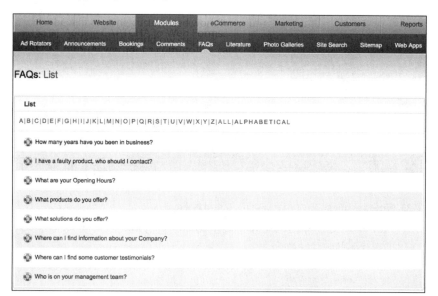

2. Click an existing FAQ item to edit it. Select the "What is your refund policy?" item.

3. The FAQ Details are displayed.

4. Select the existing placeholder answer text. Use the online editor to update the text content with different text, like this:

   You can return an item within 90 days of purchasing it for store credit. You can also choose to exchange the item for another item in the store.

   To learn more, read our Return Policy.

5. Select the text Return Policy. Use the Custom Links menu to view the list of site content and expand the Web Pages section. Select the policy page in the list of web pages to add the link to the Policy page (FIGURE 4.5).

6. Scroll down and click Save.

➕ **TIP:** By default, the questions in the FAQ are displayed alphabetically. If you want specific FAQ items to appear at the top of the list of questions, enter a numeric value in the Weighting field in the FAQ Details. Items with higher numbers in the Weighting field display above items with lower numbers.

For example, a weighting value of 100 will display above a weighting value of 50. The weighting value controls the sorting order of the dynamic data. This behavior differs from other CMS weighting systems. For example, in Drupal the lighter (lower) numbers are displayed on top.

Use the Custom Links menu to add a link to the Policy page.

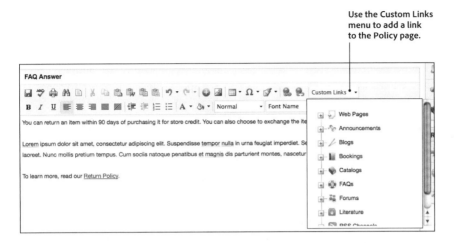

FIGURE 4.5
Use the online editor to format the FAQ answer text.

If you switch back to the browser window that contains the live site and refresh the FAQs page, you can test your work. To see the content that you just updated, select the "What is your refund policy?" question. Notice that the list expands and the answer text you entered appears on the page. Click the link in the answer text to load the Policy page.

Next, you'll learn how to add a new FAQ item to the existing list of questions:

1. Switch to the browser window that displays the Admin Console. Choose Modules > FAQs.

2. In the Action Box sidebar, click the option Create A New FAQ.

3. The FAQ Details page appears with fields where you can enter the new question (FIGURE 4.6).

> **NOTE:** The Templates menu defines the template used to display the FAQ item. All new items use the default template automatically, so you only need to change this setting if you want to assign a unique template to create a special page design for the FAQ section of the site.

FAQ Details

FAQ Question	Release Date	Enabled
	20-Jul-2011	☑

Template	Weighting	Expiry Date	
Use default template		1-Jan-9999	
			Show More Options

FIGURE 4.6
The FAQ Details page includes the fields to create a new FAQ item.

4. Enter the following text in the Question field:

   Where are you located?

5. Scroll down to the online editor and enter the answer in the FAQ Answer field:

   Sales O Rama is located in San Francisco, California.

6. Scroll down and click Save.

If you want to check your work, you can switch to the browser with the live site and refresh the FAQ page. You'll see the new FAQ question appear in the list of questions.

Customizing the Appearance of Modules with Layouts in the Admin Console

You have complete control over the design of features built using the Business Catalyst modules. In this section, you'll learn how to update their appearance to define the way they're displayed on the page.

To design module features, you update the module's layout files. These files use standard HTML and CSS code and contain tags to indicate where the dynamic data is displayed. By editing the layout files, you can set rules to make the features match the site's design. You can also choose precisely which data to display and where it will appear within the feature.

Many modules have more than one layout file to control each feature's various views. For example, a module feature may have a list view that's shown when the page first loads, which is controlled by the list layout file. And then a second layout file, called the details layout file, controls how the module feature appears when the visitor clicks on an item in the list to see the details for that individual data item.

Editing the List layout

In this section, you'll change the List layout to affect how the list view appears when the FAQ feature first loads. The current display of the FAQ questions look a little crowded. To fix that, you'll add a div container with a simple line break at the end of each item to add space between the items in the list.

Follow these steps to access and edit the List layout file:

NOTE: By clicking the Admin link, you can see all the options available, which is helpful when you're first becoming familiar with the interface. However, once you're more familiar with the options, you can simply use the Admin menu and select the same items in the menu that appears.

FIGURE 4.7
The list of Administration options is displayed in the Administration List page.

1. Switch to the browser window displaying the Admin Console. Click the Admin menu link in the top-right corner to see the Administration List page (FIGURE 4.7).

Administration options ——

2. Click the More Customization Options icon. The Customize Home page appears. Click the FAQ Layouts icon to access the FAQ layouts (FIGURE 4.8).

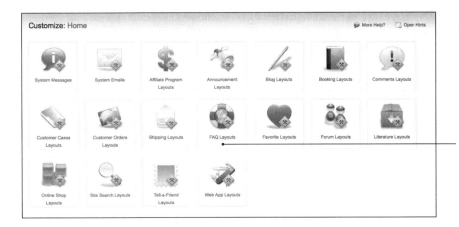

FIGURE 4.8
The list of modules is displayed in the Customize Home page.

Click the FAQ Layouts icon to customize the layouts of the FAQ module.

3. The FAQ Layouts page appears. Select the List layout from the menu at the top of the page to edit the layout that affects the appearance of the FAQ list of questions before the visitor clicks on them (FIGURE 4.9).

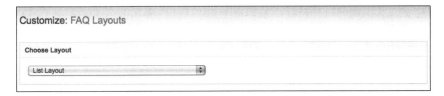

FIGURE 4.9
Choose the List layout in the menu at the top of the FAQ Layouts page.

4. The online editor currently displays the data tag to display the answer for the question: {tag_question}.

5. Update the HTML code in the online editor to add some formatting that wraps around the FAQ question module tag, as shown here:

```
<div class="faq-question">
{tag_question}<br />
<br />
</div>
```

The tags and formatting you enter are repeated for each FAQ item in the list (FIGURE 4.10).

6. Click Save to save the changes to the List layout.

NOTE: In addition to accessing layouts using the Customize Home page, you'll find that many modules also include an option in the sidebar to customize the layouts in the module configuration pages. Immediately after adding data to the module, you can jump to the area of the interface to access the module's layout files.

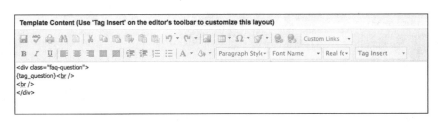

FIGURE 4.10
Enter the HTML tags to control the appearance of the FAQ questions.

To see how the recent changes to the List layout affect the display, switch to the browser window with the live site. Refresh the FAQs page to see the FAQ question list appear. Notice that the updated list has more space between each item, because the <br /> tag you added to the List layout is repeated between each question.

Editing the Detail layout

In the next section, you'll update the Detail layout to affect how the detail view appears when the answer for a selected FAQ item loads. The Detail layout defines how the feature appears after the visitor interacts with the module by clicking on a linked item in the list.

Follow these steps to edit the Detail layout file:

1. Switch to the browser window displaying the Admin Console. The FAQ Layouts page is still displayed.

2. Use the Choose Layout menu to select Detail Layout. The page updates to display the default appearance of the Detail layout (FIGURE 4.11).

FIGURE 4.11
By default, the Detail layout page includes the comment form.

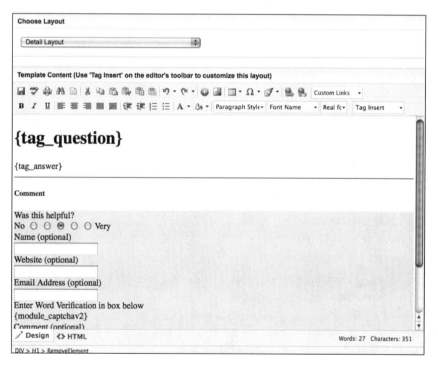

3. In this scenario, imagine your client requests that you disable the comment functionality that allows visitors to add feedback about the items in the FAQ. In the online editor, update the appearance and behavior of the Details layout by removing the comments tag. Click the HTML tag to see the source code. Locate `<div class="comment-form">` and select the code up through the closing `</form > </div>` tags. While the entire comment form is selected, press Delete to remove it from the layout (FIGURE 4.12).

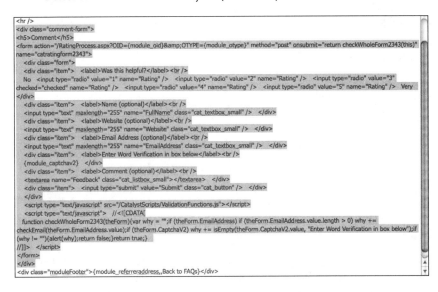

FIGURE 4.12
Select the source code for the Comment form and delete it.

4. Click Save.

Switch to the browser window that displays the live site. Refresh the FAQs page to load the updated layout files. This time, if you click any of the questions, you'll notice that when the answer appears, the comments form is no longer displayed.

The FAQ feature is looking better after customizing the module. And you've completed the client's request to remove the comment functionality from the FAQ page. However, there's another change to make. It isn't necessary to display the Back To FAQs link since the answers display on the same page. Follow these steps to remove it:

1. Switch to the browser window displaying the Admin Console. The FAQ Layouts page is still displaying the Detail layout.

2. In the online editor, select and delete this tag:
   `{module_referreraddress,,Back to FAQs}`

3. Next, you'll use the Tag Insert menu to add a new tag attribute. Click after the `{tag_answer}` tag and press Enter (Windows) or Return (Mac) to move down to the next line. Type last updated: (be sure to include the colon).

TIP: In this example, you removed the comments tag to delete an element of the module. You can also add new functionality and display different data elements by using the Tag Insert menu in the online editor. The Tag Insert menu displays only the tags that are applicable to the current layout file you're editing.

While your cursor is located at the end of the previous line, use the Tag Insert menu in the online editor to select the lastupdatedate tag from the list of possible tag attributes. The tag that displays the last updated date is inserted (FIGURE 4.13):

last updated: {tag_lastupdatedate}

FIGURE 4.13
The Detail layout contains the tags that define how the data is displayed.

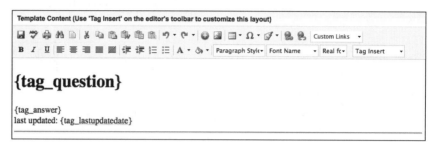

4. Click Save.

To see how you've altered the FAQ feature by editing the layout files, switch to the browser window with the live site. Refresh the FAQs page to reload the updated layouts. Click a question link to see the corresponding answer appear. Notice that the Back To FAQs link is no longer displayed. Below the answer, the last updated date is displayed in the location where you inserted the date tag.

Tag attributes are powerful because you can see the data stored in the site's database and choose which elements of each feature that you want to display in the module feature. And by editing layout files, you can precisely define where each piece of dynamic data is displayed within the design.

Inserting Modules into Web Pages with the Admin Console

In this section, you'll learn how to add a module that you've created and configured to a page of the site. Just as with the tag attributes in layout files, you can place your cursor on a page and insert the module tag to place the feature where you want it to appear alongside the other elements on the page. You'll also see how to customize the behavior of the module that's displayed during the insertion process.

Begin by reviewing the FAQ page and see how the module has been added using the module tag:

1. Switch to the browser window displaying the Admin Console. Choose Website > Web Pages.

2. The list of pages appears. Click the FAQs page to see the details for that page. The Web Page Details page loads (FIGURE 4.14).

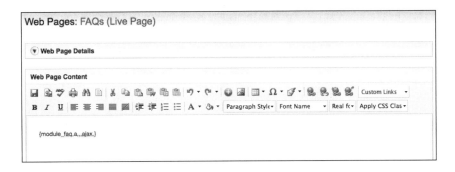

FIGURE 4.14
The Web Page Details page displays the FAQ module tag.

NOTE: Although the FAQ feature is not currently displayed on the web page, the data for the module still exists in the database. It's an important distinction that you can set up and store module data without displaying it on the live site.

3. The FAQs page currently displays the module tag that inserts the FAQ feature. Delete the tag in the online editor.

4. Scroll down and click Save And Publish.

To get a better grasp of how the module tag works, switch to the browser window with the live site. Refresh the FAQs page to see that the FAQ feature is no longer displayed on the page.

In the next section, you'll review the various methods you can use to insert a module on a web page.

Inserting modules while editing web pages

The first method of inserting modules is accomplished while editing web pages in the Web Page Details page. When accessing a specific page, you can choose to insert module tags. This workflow is helpful when you're already populating a page with content and you want to add modules to the page design.

Follow these steps to insert a single FAQ data item on a page:

1. In the Admin Console, choose Website > Web Pages. The list of web pages is displayed. Click the FAQs page to edit it.

2. The Web Page Details page appears. Scroll down to view the page content in the online editor. Click your cursor at the desired location on the page. For this example, the page is empty so simply click in the Web Page Content field.

3. Click the Module Manager icon (the blue cross button) in the toolbar of the online editor. When the Module Manager appears in the right sidebar, click the FAQs item to expand it (FIGURE 4.15).

4. The FAQs category in the Module Manager has three options:

   - Display List Of FAQs

   - FAQs Search Box

   - FAQs Search Results

   Click the first option, Display List Of FAQs.

FIGURE 4.15
Click the FAQs option in the Module Manager to see the suboptions.

5. The Module Manager updates to display a Select Display Criteria menu. The menu includes the following options:

- Individual Item
- All Items
- All Items In A Category Classification
- Latest Items
- Individual Random item

Insert an individual item on the page by selecting the first item in the menu, Individual Item.

6. The Module Manager updates to display a second menu, Choose Item. Use this menu to select the name of the item to insert. In this case, choose the item you edited earlier: "What is your refund policy?"

When you select an individual item from the menu, the Module Preview area below updates to show you how the data item will appear when you insert it (FIGURE 4.16).

FIGURE 4.16
Select the individual FAQ item in the Choose Item menu.

7. Click the Insert button to add the module tag to the FAQ page. The module tag that displays an individual FAQ item looks similar to this (displaying a different ID number):

{module_faq,i,44834}

8. Close the Module Manager by clicking the red close button in the top-right corner. The panel in the right sidebar disappears.

9. Scroll down and click Save And Publish.

A confirmation message indicates that the page was successfully published. Switch to the browser window that displays the live site and refresh the page. This time, the FAQs page only displays the "What is your refund policy?" individual item.

If you click the individual FAQ question, you'll notice that a new page loads to display the corresponding FAQ answer. This differs from the original behavior of the trial site; the answer was displayed on the same page when you tested it before. Later in this chapter, you'll learn how to customize the behavior of modules to display answer data on the same page by customizing the module's attributes to use Ajax functionality.

10. Return to the window with the Admin Console. Select the module tag in the online editor and delete it. (You'll insert the FAQ module tag again in the next section.) Scroll to the bottom and click Save And Publish to save the page.

Inserting modules using the Module Manager has two advantages:

- If you're already editing a page, you can insert any module type—without leaving the online editor on the Web Page Details page.
- The Module Manager includes the ability to insert a module tag that displays a specific individual item or an individual random item on a page.

Using the 1-Click Insert Menu to Insert Modules

As you create and configure modules, you'll notice that most of the modules include an option in the Action Box sidebar that enables you to choose an existing web page in the site and add the module to it. In this workflow, you move seamlessly from the module creation and setup to directly placing the module on a page (without having to access the page from the Web Page section of the Websites tab in the interface).

For example, if you've edited a FAQ item in the FAQ Details page, the Action Box sidebar includes an option to add the current module to a web page.

Follow these steps to insert the list of FAQ items in a web page:

1. In the Admin Console, choose Modules > FAQs. The list of FAQ items is displayed in the FAQs List page. Select any of the items to access the FAQ Details page. Click the link Add Item To A Web Page in the Action Box sidebar (FIGURE 4.17).

2. The 1-Click Insert menu appears, displaying a list of all the pages in the site. Scroll down through the list and select the name of the page you want to edit. For this example, select the FAQs page.

   The window updates to display the contents of the FAQs page in the online editor. The page is currently empty because you deleted the module tag in the previous section.

3. If the FAQs page contained other content, you could place your cursor at a specific location on the page to set where the FAQ module appears. Since the page is blank, just click in the field.

   Use the 1-Click Insert menu to select the individual module item or a specialized set of module data. The following options are available:
   - Insert Only This FAQ Item
   - Insert All FAQ Items
   - Insert The Latest (Most Recent) FAQ Item
   - Insert A FAQ Search Box
   - Insert All Items That Are Classified Within A Category: FAQ

Click the link Add Item To A Web Page.

FIGURE 4.17
After creating the module, you can insert it on a page.

UNDERSTANDING CLASSIFICATION

By classifying items into categories, you create taxonomy to display different items on pages. You can add and assign categories to specify sets of related content, so that they can be displayed together dynamically. For example, you can specify subsets of information, such as news for the entire company or news about a specific product.

First, add the categories that pertain to the topics of the site. Then, as you create new items, assign the categories to each item.

Choose Admin > Manage Categories to access the area of the interface where you can add and control categories for a site.

4. Select the option Insert All FAQ Items. The module tag that displays the list of FAQ items looks like this (FIGURE 4.18):

    {module_faq,a,}

FIGURE 4.18
Use the 1-Click Insert menu to insert the module tag.

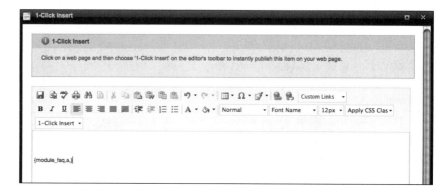

5. Scroll down and click Save And Publish. The updated page is published to the live site. Click the X in the top-right corner to close the 1-Click Insert window.

A confirmation message appears indicating that the item was published successfully. To see the updated page, either switch to the browser window that displays the live site or click the link in the confirmation message to preview the web page.

Refresh the FAQs page to see the entire list of FAQ items. If you click any of the items in the list, the corresponding answer appears in a new page.

Inserting modules with the 1-Click Insert menu has two advantages:

- The workflow is efficient; after creating and setting up modules, you can immediately insert them on pages.

- The 1-Click Insert menu makes it easy to quickly add a specific module type to multiple pages in the site.

Customizing the Behavior and Display of Modules

When you inserted an individual FAQ item and the list of FAQ items on the page, the feature was displayed at the location where you clicked the page, at the cursor's insertion point. Additionally, the corresponding answers appear automatically when each question is clicked. However, when you first tested the FAQ page on the live site, the answers were displayed on the same page (below the list of FAQ items). After deleting and reinserting the FAQ module tags, the answers appear in a new page, instead of displaying on the same page.

In this section, you'll learn how to customize the behavior of the FAQ module display. To add the Ajax behavior, you'll update the module tag with the Module Manager on the Web Page Details page, because the 1-Click Insert menu doesn't offer this option.

Follow these steps to customize how the FAQ answers are displayed when a visitor selects a question:

1. In the Admin Console, choose Website > Web Pages. Select the FAQs page from the list of web pages. The Web Page Details page appears and the page is displayed in the online editor.

2. Select the existing module tag you inserted on the page using the 1-Click Insert menu. Press Delete to delete the tag. Leave your cursor at the same location.

3. Click the Module Manager icon (the blue cross button) to open the Module Manager in the right sidebar.

4. Click the FAQs category to expand it. Select the Display The List Of FAQs option.

5. The Module Manager displays the Select Display Criteria menu. Click the second choice: All Items. The Module Preview area updates to display a preview of the entire list of FAQ items.

6. Click the Customize link. Another set of options and menus appears.

   Use the Effect menu to select Ajax. This option adds the code that causes the answers to pop up on the same page, the way the FAQ list was displayed originally when you first reviewed the trial site.

   Leave the other default options, and click Insert (**FIGURE 4.19**).

FIGURE 4.19

Use the Customize settings in the Module Manager to set the Ajax effect.

+ TIP: The commas used in these tag attributes are just as important as the attribute values. The system uses both the commas and the tag attributes to define how the dynamic data is displayed. Visit Support Central and check the knowledgebase for more information on customizing modules with tag attributes.

7. The module tag is inserted on the FAQ page. This time, the tag looks like this:

    `{module_faq,a,,,ajax,}`

    Notice that the `ajax` attribute is added to the end of the module tag.

8. Scroll to the bottom and click Save And Publish.

Either click the option in the Action Box sidebar to preview the page in a new browser window or switch to the browser window that currently displays the live site. To review the recent changes, be sure to refresh the page. If the page doesn't display as expected, all changes to the page are archived in the system. Return to the Admin Console and click Archive And Rollback in the Web Page Details page to select a previous iteration of the page to revert back to the page before you changed it.

The FAQs page displays the entire list of FAQ items. If you click one of the items in the list, you'll see that the answer is displayed on the FAQs page, rather than loading in a new page.

Many modules have customization options that you can set to control a feature's display behavior. The Ajax effect you just added is one example. As you experiment with inserting modules into your sites, be sure to explore the options to learn the available options for each module.

UNDERSTANDING ATTRIBUTES IN MODULE TAGS

At this point, you've used two methods (the Module Manager and the 1-Click Insert menu) to insert three different module tags.

Take a moment to identify the various types of tags and how they display data.

First, you inserted an individual FAQ item:

`{module_faq,i,44834}`

Next, you inserted the list of FAQ items:

`{module_faq,a,}`

And finally, you inserted the list of FAQ items using the Ajax behavior:

`{module_faq,a,,,ajax,}`

The three module tags listed here specify the FAQ module. In the first tag, there are two tag attributes. The `i` attribute tells the system to display an individual item, and then the numeric ID specifies which item to display on the page.

In the second tag, the tag attribute after the comma is the `a`, which tells the system to display all the FAQ items in the list.

And in the third tag, a series of commas and the `ajax` attribute tell the system to display the FAQ answers with the Ajax behavior (expand the list and display the answer on the same page as the FAQ feature).

Inserting Modules into Web Pages with Dreamweaver

As mentioned earlier, you cannot configure module features in Dreamweaver. And the interface doesn't include the ability to populate the modules you create with data, the way you created a new FAQ item in the beginning of this chapter. However, once you've set up modules, you can use Dreamweaver to edit the site pages and design the page content. While you are building out the pages, you can also use the Business Catalyst panel in Dreamweaver to insert the module tags and control how the module layouts cause the modules to display.

Follow these steps to use the Business Catalyst panel in Dreamweaver to work with modules:

1. Launch Dreamweaver. Click the Synchronize button to sync the site files in Dreamweaver with the changes you made recently in the Admin Console. In the panel that appears, use the Synchronize menu to choose Entire Site. Set the Direction menu to Get Newer Files From Remote. Click Preview.

   The panel updates to display the list of newer files on the host server. Click OK to download (get) the newer files from the remote server.

2. In the Files panel, double-click the faqs.htm page to open it in the Document window.

3. The FAQs page loads. The page content contains the same module tag you inserted previously in the Admin Console:

   ```
   {module_faq,a,,,ajax,}
   ```

   To see how the module will render, click Live View. After you've finished reviewing the page, click Live View again to enable the editing features.

Using the Business Catalyst panel, you can insert the module tags directly into web pages. The panel enables you to add features to pages while using the HTML editing features in Dreamweaver to design the page and add other content.

Next, you'll set up a search page that enables visitors to look for specific FAQ items:

1. Choose File > New to access the New Document dialog box.

2. In the left side, choose the Page From Template option. Select the trial site in the Site list and then choose the Main template in the template list.

3. Click Create. A new, untitled page loads in a second tab in the Document window.

4. Choose File > Save. Save the page as FAQsearch.htm at the root level of the site directory.

5. In Design view of the Document window, click inside the editable region named ContentArea that contains this placeholder text: {tag_pagecontent}.

6. Look in the Code view to see that your cursor is within the placeholder text that is highlighted here. The comment tags that define the template's editable region surround the text.

```
<div id="main">
    <!-- InstanceBeginEditable name="ContentArea" -->
    {tag_pagecontent}
<!-- InstanceEndEditable -->
</div>
```

7. In Code view, select the entire {tag_pagecontent} placeholder text and press the Delete key to remove it from the page. While your cursor is still within the editable region of the code, type the following:

```
<div class="main-holder">
<div class="content">
  </div>
</div>
```

Click the Design view to refresh it. The editable region now displays a white background because the main-holder class includes a CSS rule to set the background color of the div container to white. This makes it easier to see the contents of the page.

8. In the title field at the top, enter a title for the page: FAQ Search page.

9. Copy the text you entered into the title field. In Code view, place your cursor before the two closing div tags.

Paste the title FAQ Search page into the editable region. While the text is selected, use the Format menu in the HTML section of the Property inspector to set the format of the selected text to Heading 1. In Code view, notice that <h1> tags are added to format the header text. In Design view, the text updates to show the H1 header styles.

10. In Design view, click your cursor after the header text. Press Enter (Windows) or Return (Mac) once, to create a line return (a set of <p> tags) below the header text. The cursor is positioned within the set of paragraph tags.

11. If it is not already open, access the Business Catalyst panel by choosing Window > Business Catalyst. Make sure you are logged in to the trial site and the trial site name is selected in the Select A Site menu.

12. In the Business Catalyst panel, the list of modules is displayed. Scroll down and click the FAQs category to expand it. Double-click the FAQs Search Box suboption to insert a search feature for FAQ items on the page at the cursor's insertion point (FIGURE 4.20).

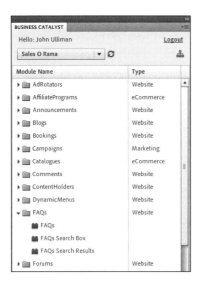

FIGURE 4.20
The list of modules is displayed in the Business Catalyst panel.

13. The Module Configure wizard appears. Click Insert (**FIGURE 4.21**).

FIGURE 4.21
The Configure Module wizard.

14. The Module Configure wizard closes and the search feature is inserted on the FAQ Search page.

15. Choose File > Save and then File > Put to upload the page to the remote server.

    In the Dependent Files dialog box that appears, click No. That option means that you'll only upload the FAQsearch.htm file.

    Switch to a browser. Enter the full URL in the browser's address bar to view the FAQ Search Page live site (**FIGURE 4.22**). The URL will look something like this:

    http://trial_site.businesscatalyst.com/FAQsearch.htm

FIGURE 4.22
The FAQ search functionality is added to the FAQ Search Page.

Adding a Link to the FAQ Search Page from the FAQ page

The new FAQ Search Page is finished, but at the moment the live site doesn't include a link to the new page you created. Currently, the only way to access the page is to type the page URL into a browser's address field. To make it easy to visit the FAQ search page, you'll edit the FAQ page and add a text link.

Follow these steps:

1. Return to Dreamweaver. Click the tab at the top of the Document window to edit the faqs.htm page. If you closed the page, double-click the faqs.htm page in the Files panel to reopen it.

2. In Code view, click just before the module tag. Type this line:

   ```
   <p>Try our new FAQ search feature</p>
   ```

3. Select the text "FAQ search feature." Use the HTML section of the Property inspector to add a link. Click the folder icon next to the Link field and browse to select the FAQsearch.htm page. Click Choose to add the path to the page in the link field.

4. Choose File > Put. In the dialog box that appears, click Yes to save the file before putting it.

5. The Dependent Files dialog box appears. Click No.

Switch to the browser window that displays the live site. To see the FAQ page again, click the link in the footer. Refresh the page to see the new link you just added. If desired, you can click the new link on the FAQ page to visit the FAQ Search Page.

Try testing the FAQ search functionality. For example, you can enter terms such as refund or offer in the search field. The corresponding search results appear on the page in the area below the search feature.

Customizing Data by Updating Module Layout Files in Dreamweaver

Earlier in this chapter you learned how to update the layout files using the Admin Console. Although it's possible to make small changes, we don't recommend using the online editor in the Admin Console to edit the source code. Generally speaking, you'll use the more robust HTML editing features in Dreamweaver to modify the HTML and CSS styles in layouts, to leverage the WYSIWYG interface and take advantage of code hinting, the Code Navigator, and the CSS Styles panel as you work. As you design the appearance of layout files, you can also insert tag attributes to control the display of data related to each module.

Follow these steps to modify layout files:

1. In Dreamweaver, open the Business Catalyst panel. Verify that the trial site is selected and you are logged in.

2. Open the Files panel. Locate the folder at the root level of the site named Layouts. Click the arrow icon next to the Layouts folder to expand it.

3. The Layouts folder contains a folder with the layout files for every module available in Business Catalyst (not just the modules used in the current site). Expand the folder named Faq to see the layout files for the FAQ module.

4. The FAQ module includes two layout files: one for the list view and the other for the detail view of the dynamic data. Some modules have fewer or more layout files, depending on their behavior. Double-click the list.html file in the FAQ folder to open it in the Document window (FIGURE 4.23).

FIGURE 4.23
Expand the Faq folder and open the list.html file.

Take a moment to review the source code in Code view. Although the layout.html file controls the display of dynamic data in the Business Catalyst system, it's really a normal HTML file. The only main differences are:

- The layout files must exist in the Layouts folder at the root level of the site (in the subfolder that corresponds to the module).

- The layout files must contain module tags that enable the system to insert data in the proper locations.

Notice that you can add standard HTML and CSS code into the layout files when you edit them to customize their appearance.

Whenever you open and edit layout files, the Business Catalyst panel updates to display the Tag Insert menu (FIGURE 4.24).

FIGURE 4.24
The Tag Insert menu appears
in the Business Catalyst panel.

The Tag Insert menu appears
below the list of modules
when a layout file is open.

The Tag Insert menu enables you to insert module tags within layout files as you work. It's a contextual menu: just like the Admin Console online editor, the Tag Insert menu only displays the tags that are applicable to the current layout you are editing.

5. In Design view, click in front of the existing module tag:

{tag_question}

Use the Tag Insert menu to choose the {tag_counter} tag. This tag attribute displays a number in front of each FAQ item in the List view, to create an ordered list.

After the new tag is inserted, the layout page now contains two tags:

{tag_counter}{tag_question}

6. Save and put the list.html page. Click No in the Dependent Files dialog box.

Switch back to the browser and view the live site. Click the FAQ link in the footer of the page to access the FAQs page. Click the link to visit the FAQ Search page. Notice that after searching, the FAQ list of search results now displays a numbered list of FAQ items (FIGURE 4.25).

FIGURE 4.25
The live site displays the FAQ
questions as a numbered list.

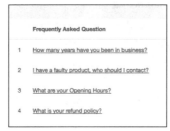

The changes you make to layout files affect all iterations of that module for the entire site. So, if you display a list of FAQ items on one page and an individual FAQ item on another page, keep in mind that the individual item would display the number 1 before the question link in the site's current configuration.

Understanding the Workflow for Setting Up Features with Modules

Now that you've explored the FAQ module, you've learned how to work with modules to add features to web pages, as well as how to customize a module's behavior and appearance. This list outlines the basic workflow:

1. When you create new features and configure modules, you must use the Admin Console.

2. Once the modules are set up, you can use both the Admin Console and Dreamweaver to insert the module tags to add the features to pages.

3. After the modules are inserted, publish the pages and test the basic functionality in a browser.

4. Finalize the way modules look and define the data that is displayed by updating the module layout files using Dreamweaver or the Admin Console.

Using modules to add new site features

Many of the other Business Catalyst modules work exactly the same way as the FAQs module. Try creating and configuring some of these features:

- **Ad Rotators.** The Ad Rotators module creates flexible messaging areas to display multiple items. Each time a page loads or is refreshed, a random item from the enabled set of content items is displayed. The content can be HTML, CSS, or Flash. If desired, you can add trackable links to each content item. The system tracks the clicks, enabling the business to identify which content items receive the most visitor interaction.

- **Announcements.** Use the Announcements module to create and post news about the business in chronological order. Each announcement includes a title and a description. When you configure announcements, you can choose to display an abbreviated version or the full version of the description.

- **Bookings.** You can configure the Bookings module to manage reservations and enable customers to save their space for an event. You can set limits on the number of spaces (if desired) and track the event's attendance. The Bookings module sends automatic e-mail reminder messages before the event date and can also send automatic messages after an event to help gather feedback and comments. Bookings are tracked in the system, just like orders, cases, and subscriptions.

- **FAQs.** The FAQs module is useful for displaying frequently asked questions or a glossary of terms on the site. As you discovered in this chapter, you control how the list of questions appears and you can create a search feature to enable visitors to find FAQ items based on matching keywords.

- **Literature.** The Literature module enables you to offer downloadable files on the site. You can also use the Literature module to share streaming media files with visitors. Literature items are tracked and the Admin Console displays statistics about the number of downloads and views.

- **Photo Galleries.** Use the Photo Galleries module to display sets of images with automatic navigation so that visitors can click through the gallery to see each image. If desired, you can add captions to photos. The Photo Galleries module automatically generates thumbnail images—you only have to create a folder containing the larger images that you want to display.

To research further, analyze and update live examples included with the trial site. Practice by customizing the trial site's existing modules, such as Announcements (the Latest News page), Blogs, Comments, and Forums. Each module uses its own set of layouts, so it's helpful to open them and become familiar with them. As you customize the appearance of modules, experiment by inserting or deleting tag attributes to see how you can control the display of data elements.

Or if you prefer, try adding new content by building Ad Rotators. Use images from your hard drive to populate the Photo Galleries module. Create new test pages and insert modules on the pages (directly from the module configuration page, using the Module Manager, or Dreamweaver).

WORKING WITH CSS TO CONTROL THE APPEARANCE OF MODULES

If you use the File Manager in the Admin Console, the Files panel in Dreamweaver, or a third-party FTP client to connect to the host server, you'll notice that there are two different folders at the root level of the site that contain CSS files.

The CSS folder contains a file named all.css. When you're editing styles to set the design for the rest of the site, you'll usually edit this file. The stylesheets folder contains modulestylesheets.css, which contains rules that control the appearance of modules.

Always keep both of these CSS files in their original locations. Do not move the files into other folders, rename the folders, or rename the files themselves. Before making any changes to any of the CSS files

(or the layout HTML files in the Layouts folder), always create backup copies and keep them on your local drive. That way, if you make a change and you need to revert, you can replace the file you edited with the original.

It's important to note that the rules located in modulestylesheets.css affect multiple modules. If you make changes to styles to update the appearance of one module, your edits may cause other modules to display differently as well.

It is a best practice to add comments whenever you make changes to these CSS files. Always test the live site after making any changes to the styles.

Related Links

 Setting Up Bookings:
http://www.adobe.com/go/bc_bookings

 Goodbye, Custom Coding:
http://www.adobe.com/go/bc_no_custom_coding

CHAPTER 5

Building Web Forms to Gather Visitor Data

Contents

Examining the Contact Form on the Trial Site	75
Accessing Form Data in the Dashboard of the Admin Console	77
Understanding Workflows	79
Editing Web Forms	82
Adding Web Forms to Web Pages in Dreamweaver	85
Using the Module Manager to Insert Web Form Module Tags	89
Creating Web Forms with the Web Form Builder	90
Adding Web Forms to Pages with the 1-Click Insert Menu	94
Overview of Working with Web Forms	96

Previously, you learned how the site's database stores and displays dynamic data in modules. The creation and display of module data enables you to create interactive features and develop compelling websites.

In this chapter, you'll take a look at how the Business Catalyst Platform gathers information submitted by visitors and stores it in the database. This is a powerful component of the online business, because the data obtained by interested visitors can be used in a variety of ways, including to:

- Generate an online community of like-minded people
- Track activities of specific customers to discover business trends
- Create recipient lists to send newsletters and e-mail campaigns
- Respond to product sales inquiries and schedule appointments
- Process online payment transactions
- Remind attendees about upcoming events and reservation bookings
- Enable registered visitors to log in to secure zones
- Send personalized anniversary greetings and annual service reminders
- Provide online help and manage customer support cases

Ultimately, these activities are used to convert visitors into customers.

Good communication is critical when interacting with potential customers. Web forms enable visitors to contact the business in a way that is more professional than simply providing an e-mail address. The user experience can include an online confirmation message and a personalized auto-reply e-mail message that is sent after each form submission.

The system makes it easy for your clients to access and track customer data, so that they can reply to inquiries in a timely manner. The Admin Console provides an overview of customer information in the Dashboard and includes an intuitive report system to locate specific records.

Web forms are completely customizable, facilitating the collection of data that is specific to a particular business. When you create a form for the site, you add the fields to define the data that is collected. You can add preconfigured fields, such as username, e-mail, and password. You can also make custom fields to tailor the input elements to match the theme of a site. Custom fields can capture data such as birth dates, gender, location, product models, and shoe sizes. Using reports, you can easily retrieve this information to learn more about your customers and their preferences. Businesses can use this specialized information to engage with their customers and connect with them on a more personal level.

You can also obtain feedback by including specific questions in your forms:

- Where did you hear about us?
- Would you like to subscribe to the newsletter?
- What time is most convenient to contact you?

When asking for personal data, it is a best practice to make the fields optional, rather than required, so that visitors do not feel overwhelmed. If you ask too many questions, they may decide not to submit the form at all.

All of the features in Business Catalyst, including web forms, are integrated into a single, centralized database. The data added to modules (as described in Chapter 4, "Configuring, Inserting, and Customizing Modules") is stored along with the customer data so that all the details of the site are easy to retrieve in the Admin Console.

To get started, you'll explore the trial site from the visitor's perspective, to see how the customer data is submitted. The template for the trial site includes a prebuilt contact form that you'll use in the next section to submit data and see how the system works.

FIGURE 5.1
The Contact page contains an HTML contact form.

Examining the Contact Form on the Trial Site

Every site should provide visitors with a method to contact the business. In the early days of the Web, the contact page typically included an e-mail address, telephone number, and snail-mail address. However, e-mail addresses are problematic because they may contain typographical errors. Messages might wind up in a junk folder or the Inbox of an employee who is out of the office.

Web forms are vastly superior to e-mail addresses because they can include notification workflows and route submissions to multiple addresses behind the scenes, to ensure inquiries are answered quickly. Additionally, contact forms can use image verification (CAPTCHA, which stands for Completely Automatic Public Turing Test to Tell Computers and Humans Apart) to prevent spambots from scraping sites to gather e-mail addresses for malicious purposes.

Because every inquiry is tracked within the system, the business can ensure that no messages go unanswered.

Visit the trial site in a browser. Click the Contact Us menu item to visit the Contact page and access the form (FIGURE 5.1).

Required fields of the form are marked with asterisks, and the code used to create the form includes form field validation. If you attempt to submit the form without providing the required data, an alert message is displayed (FIGURE 5.2).

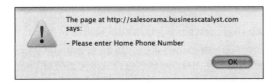

FIGURE 5.2
If you skip a required field, the form reminds you to enter the missing data.

Be sure to complete the form. You can enter bogus data if you'd like, but you can view the process more completely if you enter a valid e-mail address. If you use a real e-mail address and you check the account after submitting the form, you'll see an auto-responder e-mail message generated by the system.

When you submit the form, a Thank You page appears with a summary of the information that you submitted (FIGURE 5.3).

FIGURE 5.3
The form data is displayed on the page so that visitors can review their submission.

The summary is helpful because if visitors make a mistake when they enter their information, they may catch their error and resubmit the form immediately to correct it. It also emphasizes that their entry was successfully received, to promote a better user experience.

Now that you've entered some data in the contact form, you'll play the role of the business owner and see how the submitted form data is displayed in the Admin Console. You'll see how web forms are more than a message delivery system; they enable businesses to leverage customer data and convert inquiries into sales opportunities.

Accessing Form Data in the Dashboard of the Admin Console

Now that some activity has been recorded on the live site, you'll look at how submitted messages can be retrieved in the Admin Console. Follow these steps:

1. Open a new browser window and log in to the Admin Console.

   The Home page of the Admin Console displays the Dashboard with the summary of the site statistics (FIGURE 5.4).

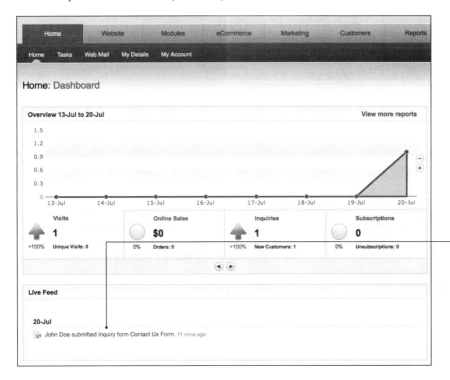

FIGURE 5.4
The Home page of the Admin Console contains the Dashboard.

The site activity is displayed in the Live Feed.

NOTE: In Chapter 11, "Upgrading Sites and Managing Domain Names," which is available for download from peachpit.com, you'll learn how to set up user accounts with access to the Admin Console so that your clients can log in. In that chapter, you'll also find out how to define which aspects of the Admin Console they can see, to control the areas of the site they can manage.

The Live Feed section of the Dashboard displays an up-to-the-minute record of all site activity. You can see all site interactions as they occur, including every form submission, every subscription, and every purchase. If you submitted the contact form when you reviewed the trial site, you'll see at least one entry here.

Remember that after you launch a site, your clients will log in to access this data in their own (limited) version of the Admin Console. They can use the Live Feed to see the site activity and run their business. The time-stamped entries enable them to see what is happening on the site at all times.

2. Click the link in the Live Feed that was generated automatically when you submitted the Contact Us form. The link takes you directly to the Customer Summary page, where the compiled customer data is displayed (FIGURE 5.5).

FIGURE 5.5
The Customer Summary page displays the customer data.

All of the details gathered from the form are included in the customer record and each customer is assigned a unique ID. Customers are tracked by unique IDs and their e-mail addresses, which enables a business to retrieve the entire log of form submissions entered by a specific person. By default, web forms include required fields for the name and e-mail address data, to identify each submission and assign the activity to the matching record.

FIGURE 5.6
Access cases in the Action Box sidebar while viewing the Customer Summary page.

Additionally, whenever a customer fills out a web form, a case is automatically created in the system. Each case also has a unique ID that enables business owners to follow up on support incidents and provide customer service. Cases are one of many aspects of site interaction that are tracked for each customer (FIGURE 5.6).

3. Click the Customer Cases option in the Action Box sidebar to view the case that was generated when you submitted the Contact Us form. Each case is date stamped and includes a link to view the data submitted in the form (FIGURE 5.7).

FIGURE 5.7
The Cases page includes links to access the case information for each incident.

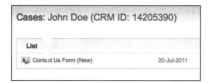

Your clients can use the workflow you just followed to access the submitted form data and manage each case as it comes in, to be responsive to customer inquires. The case management workflow follows this progression:

1. A customer submits a web form to ask a question or request a service.
2. Your client logs in to the Admin Console and views the Dashboard activity.
3. They click the link in the Live Feed to jump to the customer's summary.

UNDERSTANDING THE CONTACT DATA STORED IN THE DATABASE

Although the Admin Console refers to the contact data captured by forms as customer records, this is inaccurate. In reality, the system gathers and stores the contact data of all visitors who submit a form or sign up for a newsletter; in most cases, visitors who interact with a site have not necessarily purchased any items or services.

Contact data in customer records includes the following groups:

- Visitors

- Registered visitors (who created an account to log in to secure zones)

- Subscribers (who signed up to receive e-mail newsletters)

- Customers

For example, although a site may have gathered hundreds of customer records, only a fraction of those records reflect users who are paying customers. However, you and your clients can use the reporting system in the Admin Console to filter these groups to find the subset of contact data records related to customers.

It's also an important distinction that customer cases are not limited to providing support for customers who completed a purchase. In many cases, a business may respond to inquiries and track support incidents related to visitors and potential customers who have not yet completed a sales transaction.

4. They access the case by clicking the Customer Cases option in the Action Box sidebar.

5. In the list of cases that appears, they click the most recent linked entry.

6. The case is displayed. They read the form submission.

7. If desired, they can add notes or tasks to manage the case's resolution.

8. To reply, they can click the New Message link and send a message to the customer.

9. If the team sends correspondence regarding the case using the New Message link in the case area, the thread summary records the discussion in the system.

In Chapter 7, "Understanding Customer Management and the Site's Database," you'll learn more about how to manage users, access customer data, and customize the steps in workflows.

Understanding Workflows

Web forms collect the submission data and store it so that the interaction history and customer records are easily retrieved and managed by the business team in the Admin Console. But that isn't all that is happening behind the scenes.

Web forms can be configured to trigger workflows every time the form is submitted. A workflow is a process that you can set up to help automate and streamline business operations. For example, when a form is submitted, your client can receive a notification via e-mail and SMS. Workflows can also be configured as a reminder system with escalation rules to ensure that every case incident is resolved and nothing slips through the cracks.

Workflows are assigned to web forms as they are created. You can see the workflow assigned to the Contact Us form by viewing the form itself. To see the form elements and view the configuration of the form, you'll access the Web Form Builder.

1. Choose Modules > Web Forms to see the list of existing web forms displayed. Click the Contact Us form link to open the form in the Web Form Builder. Directly below the form's name, use the Click To Edit link to access the Web Form Details window (FIGURE 5.8).

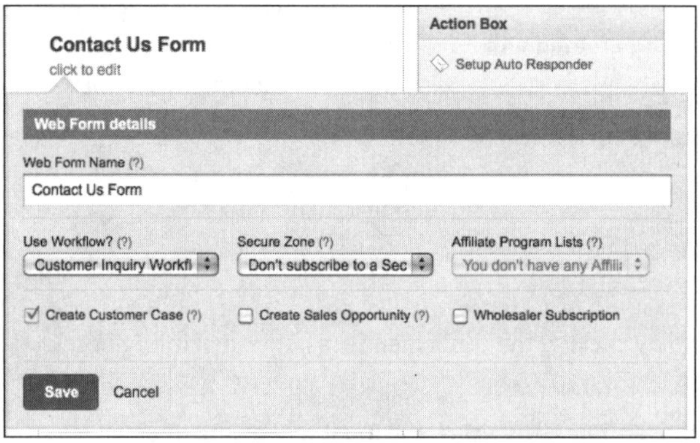

FIGURE 5.8
Workflows are set in the Web Form Details section of the Web Form Builder.

FIGURE 5.9
Access the workflow administration area by choosing Manage Workflows.

FIGURE 5.10
The two included workflows are displayed as links in the list of workflows.

Review the options in the Use Workflow? menu. You'll see that two pre-created workflow options are available:

- Content Approval Workflow
- Customer Inquiry Workflow

Leave the option set to Customer Inquiry Workflow; this option generates an automatic notification whenever a new form submission is received. Next, you'll take a look at the workflow section of the Admin Console to see how workflows can be configured.

2. In the Admin menu at the top of the page, choose the option Manage Workflows (FIGURE 5.9).

The two pre-created workflows that are included with the trial site are designed to help the business team approve content and respond to customer inquiries. These are the same options that were available as settings in the Web Form Details.

3. The list of workflows is displayed in the Workflows List page (FIGURE 5.10).

Click the Customer Inquiry Workflow link to open the Workflow Details page. Click Next to access the Workflows configuration page (FIGURE 5.11).

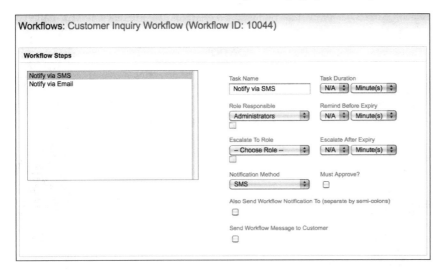

FIGURE 5.11
Set up notification steps in the Workflows configuration page.

Notice that the Customer Inquiry workflow currently includes two steps:

- Notify Via SMS
- Notify Via Email

Click on the workflow step Notify Via SMS. The Workflows configuration page includes fields to control several settings, but the most important is the first one: Role Responsible.

The Role Responsible menu is used to define which role (set of users—which may only consist of one person) will receive the notification for the selected workflow step. In this example, the SMS and e-mail notifications are sent to the Administrators role. Because you created the trial site, you are automatically added to the Administrators role.

Since your user account is added to the Administrators role, this means that the Customer Inquiry workflow is currently configured to send you notifications whenever the Contact Us form receives a submission.

If you used a valid e-mail address when you set up the trial site as described in Chapter 1, "Creating Your First Free Trial Site," check your Inbox to see the workflow notification message (FIGURE 5.12).

NOTE: When you set up user accounts for your clients and enable them to access the Admin Console, you can also create roles and add users to roles. This feature allows you to have unlimited flexibility in defining which person or sets of people receive workflow notifications and have permissions to access specific features within the Admin Console. You'll learn more about this process in Chapter 11, "Upgrading Sites and Managing Domain Names" which is available as a free download from peachpit.com.

FIGURE 5.12
The workflow generates a notification and the form details are sent in an e-mail message.

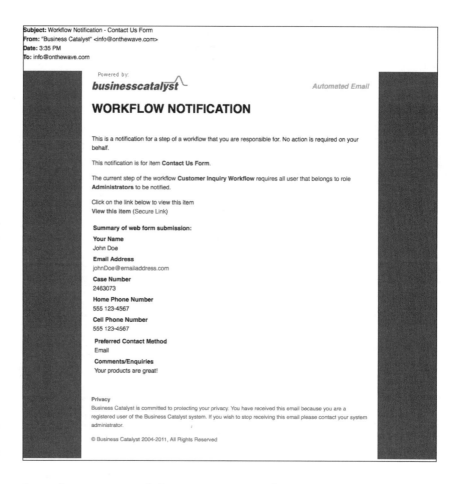

Subject: Workflow Notification - Contact Us Form
From: "Business Catalyst" <info@onthewave.com>
Date: 3:35 PM
To: info@onthewave.com

Powered by:

businesscatalyst   *Automated Email*

WORKFLOW NOTIFICATION

This is a notification for a step of a workflow that you are responsible for. No action is required on your behalf.

This notification is for item **Contact Us Form**.

The current step of the workflow **Customer Inquiry Workflow** requires all user that belongs to role **Administrators** to be notified.

Click on the link below to view this item
View this item (Secure Link)

Summary of web form submission:

Your Name
John Doe

Email Address
johnDoe@emailaddress.com

Case Number
2463073

Home Phone Number
555 123-4567

Cell Phone Number
555 123-4567

Preferred Contact Method
Email

Comments/Enquiries
Your products are great!

Privacy
Business Catalyst is committed to protecting your privacy. You have received this email because you are a registered user of the Business Catalyst system. If you wish to stop receiving this email please contact your system administrator.

© Business Catalyst 2004-2011, All Rights Reserved

TIP: To receive the SMS notification of the workflow, you must provide a valid cell phone number with text capabilities in your account information. To update the contact data for your user account, choose Home > My Details. Be sure to save the updated account information and then access the live site and submit the form again to trigger the workflow. Use your cell phone to check your text messages to see the SMS notification appear. As of this writing, the standard Pro Partner account includes 10 SMS notifications per month. So you may want to reserve SMS usage for workflows that require immediate attention.

Depending on your e-mail client, you may not see the message appear in your Inbox immediately. If you don't see the message, be sure to check your spam folder to see if the message was routed there.

Editing Web Forms

In the previous section on workflows, you reviewed the Web Form Details to learn how workflows are applied to individual web forms. You also interacted with the Contact Us form to see how it works in the default configuration of the trial site. Now, you'll learn how to edit the form elements to customize the data collected when a visitor submits the form. The Web Form Builder includes a wide array of fields, menus, and options that you can add to forms to gather the specific data applicable to an online business. Additionally, the Web Form Builder makes it easy to add, delete, edit, and rearrange the elements of each form.

1. Choose Modules > Web Forms to see the list of existing web forms appear. Click the Contact Us Form link to open the form in the Web Form Builder. A preview of the Contact Us Form is displayed in the center area (FIGURE 5.13).

FIGURE 5.13
The Contact Us Form is displayed in the Web Form Builder.

The Web Form Builder is a visual interface that enables you to create and edit forms. The forms you create are generated with standard HTML, CSS, and JavaScript code. You can adjust the appearance and style all the form elements the same way you update page elements in other, non–Business Catalyst sites.

2. Take a moment to review the existing form elements. As mentioned earlier, the name and e-mail fields are included by default (and are required fields) in every web form. This ensures that the system can match every form submission to an existing customer record (if a matching e-mail address exists in the system) or generate a new customer record.

All other form elements can be edited or deleted to change the data that's gathered by the form. You can also easily reposition the form elements within the form to rearrange them. For example, if you select the Cell Phone Number field element, you can drag it up or down within the preview area. When you release your mouse, the field snaps into place in its new location.

TIP: If you're familiar with programming in JavaScript, you can pre-populate hidden form fields based on data entered in other fields, add alert messages, and customize other behaviors in the form.

3. To delete a form element, click the Delete button (the red circle icon) in the top-right corner of the element that appears when you hover over it (FIGURE 5.14). For this example, delete the Home Phone Number field.

Click the Delete button to delete a form element.

Click OK in the confirmation window that appears to delete the form element.

4. If you'd like to edit a form element, hover over it and click the Edit button (pencil icon) to change the form element's label and required status. When a form element is set as required, a red asterisk is displayed to the right of the form element's label.

5. You can add new form elements by selecting the items in the left side of the Web Form Builder. The top portion of the Add New Items panel includes the tabs with different categories of the input items you can add to the form (FIGURE 5.15).

FIGURE 5.15
The Add New Items panel contains prebuilt form elements to add to the form.

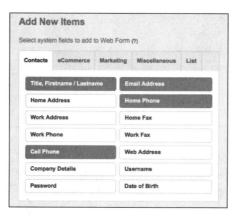

NOTE: When you make changes to a form with the Web Form Builder, there's no need to click a save button. Each change you make is saved automatically as you update the form. When you've finished editing a form, simply navigate away from the page.

The Business Catalyst Platform is an all-in-one solution, so the categories of form elements cover complex interactions with the other features of the site, including contact information, e-commerce, marketing, file attachments, image verification (CAPTCHA), and e-mail newsletters.

In the bottom portion of the Add New Items panel, you can create and add your own custom fields with unique labels. Choose from a wide assortment of form inputs, including fields, menus, lists, checkboxes, radio buttons, and datepicker calendars.

If you'd like to experiment with the options in the Add New Items panel to add custom fields to the form, you can update the existing Contact Us form. However, for this site project, the Contact Us Form is working as expected right out of the box.

UPDATING PAGES AFTER EDITING WEB FORMS

Whenever you make changes to an existing web form that has previously been inserted on a web page, you'll need to edit the page to delete and reinsert the form to ensure that the changes are reflected in the page of the live site.

Choose Website > Web Pages to access the page and then use the online editor to delete the existing form code and reinsert it. Or you can open the page in Dreamweaver and swap out the old form for the new form in the Document window.

Generally speaking, it's easier to edit code in the Dreamweaver workspace. In the next section, you'll open the Contact page and update the form's code using Dreamweaver. It's important to note that you can achieve the same goal in the Admin Console, so you can choose the tool that you prefer to work with when editing web pages.

Adding Web Forms to Web Pages in Dreamweaver

In this section, you'll replace the existing Contact Us Form with the updated version of the form that you edited in the Web Form Builder. You'll leverage the HTML editing features available in Dreamweaver to work with the source code. You'll also learn how to use the Business Catalyst panel and the Module Configure wizard to insert web forms on pages as you are editing them.

There are three methods you can use to add a web form to a page:

- Dreamweaver
- Module Manager
- 1-Click Insert menu

First, you'll explore the process using Dreamweaver. Later in this chapter, you'll learn how to use the Admin Console to insert forms. When you use the Module Manager, you can choose to insert forms as either HTML code or a module tag.

Deleting and reinserting web-form source code

First, you'll open the Contact page and find and remove the existing form in the source code. Follow these steps:

1. Launch Dreamweaver and log in to your site in the Business Catalyst panel, if you aren't already logged in.

2. Click the Synchronize button to sync the site files in Dreamweaver with the changes you made recently in the Admin Console. In the panel that appears, use the Synchronize menu to choose Entire Site. Set the Direction menu to Get Newer Files From Remote. Click Preview.

   The panel updates to display the list of newer files on the host server. Click OK to download (get) the newer files from the remote server.

3. In the Files panel, double-click the contact.htm page to open it in the Document window.

4. The Contact page loads. The page content contains the Contact Us Form. In Design view, click anywhere inside the form to select it. In the Tag Selector at the bottom of the Document window, click the <form> tag to select the entire form code (FIGURE 5.16).

FIGURE 5.16
The Tag Selector makes it easy to select the source code of the Contact Us Form.

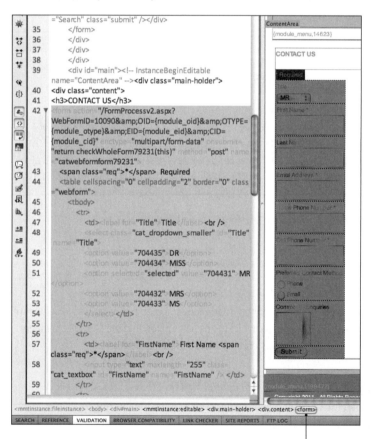

Click the <form> tag
in the Tag Selector.

5. While the form code is selected, press the Delete key to remove it. The cursor is automatically positioned at the perfect location to reinsert the new form.

6. In the Business Catalyst panel, scroll down through the list of modules and click the WebForms folder to expand it and see the list of subitems. Select the Web Forms option to insert a web form on the page.

7. The Module Configure wizard appears and displays a list of the site's existing web forms. Click the radio button next to the Contact Us Form and click Next (**FIGURE 5.17**).

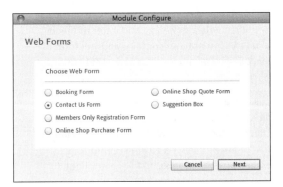

FIGURE 5.17
Select the form that you want to insert in the Module Configure wizard.

8. The Module Configure wizard updates to provide a text field to add the URL to the page in the site that will appear to visitors once they have successfully submitted the Contact Us Form. This is an optional feature that enables you to create a custom form submission confirmation page. If you want to use this option, create and publish a new page first, and then enter the absolute path (including the http:// prefix) in the provided field.

In this case, the trial site displays the default Thank You page after the form is submitted. So simply click Next on this screen and Insert on the final screen to add the updated Contact Us Form to the page at the location of the cursor's insertion point.

9. Save and put the page to upload the changes to the live site. In the Dependent Files dialog box that appears, click No.

If you want to see the recent changes and test the updated Contact Us Form, switch to a browser and visit the trial site. You can click the Contact Us link in the site navigation to access the Contact page and try resubmitting the updated form.

UPDATING THE CONTENT AND APPEARANCE OF SYSTEM MESSAGES

Business Catalyst includes prebuilt pages, called system messages, which are displayed by default in various parts of the site. These pages include a 404 Page Not Found page and the confirmation pages that appear automatically after visitors successfully subscribe to newsletters and submit web forms.

As described in step 8 earlier, there are areas in the system that enable you to create your own unique message pages that you set to appear in particular instances. In this scenario, you could create a new page and enter its link in order to redirect the form to a page in the site that contains another form or that displays a specific message. But you can also access and update the prebuilt system message pages that come with each site.

The system message pages provided by Business Catalyst are regular HTML pages, so you can edit the code to add CSS styles and edit the page content to display any message your client prefers. For example, you could include a sales promotion message that appears whenever a visitor submits a contact form, or a themed message on a ranch site's 404 Page Not Found page, like this:

Howdy Partner! This page has gone missing or was put out to pasture.

If you're working in Dreamweaver and you want to edit the default system message confirmation page that appears when visitors submit a form, use the Files panel to expand the Layouts folder. Open the SystemMessages subfolder and double-click the file named FormConfirmation-US.html to edit it in the Document window. Save and upload the changes to the server to update the live site.

If you're working in the Admin Console, you can customize the system message pages by choosing Admin > Customize System Messages. In the list of pages that appears, select the page named Web Forms Confirmation Page. Edit the page in the online editor and then click Save to update the live site.

Take a moment to explore all the system message pages that you can control in these locations, so that you can further customize a site. Also notice that you can access and edit system e-mail messages using a similar process.

Using the Module Manager to Insert Web Form Module Tags

The Module Manager in the Admin Console offers extra options when inserting modules that are not available in the Module Configure wizard in Dreamweaver. In this section, you'll learn how to insert a web form as a module tag to display it on the page.

Because web forms that are inserted as module tags are automatically updated in pages when they are updated in the Web Form Builder, this is a good strategy in projects where the form elements change frequently. Additionally, the module tag has the added benefit of streamlining the source code of the web page, because a single tag is used to display the web form rather than the HTML code that defines the form. Follow these steps when you want to use the Module Manager to insert a web form on a page:

1. In the Admin Console, choose Website > Web Pages to view the list of pages. The list of existing site pages is displayed. Click the name of the page you want to edit.

2. The Web Page Details page appears and the page is displayed in the online editor. Place your cursor at the location on the page where you want to insert the web form.

3. Click the Module Manager button (the blue cross icon) to open the Module Manager in the right sidebar. Select the Web Forms option to expand it and then click the Web Form suboption.

4. The Module Manager updates to display the Select Web Form To Insert menu. Using the menu, select the desired web form that you want to insert. The Module Manager updates again to display the insert options.

   If you want to insert the web form as a module tag, select the Insert As Module Instead checkbox and then click the Insert button (**FIGURE 5.18**).

5. The module tag is added to the page. Scroll down and click Save And Publish to push the updated page live.

It's a best practice to always test web forms after adding them to the live site, to make sure they work as expected and appear as desired on the page.

FIGURE 5.18
Check the checkbox to insert the web form as a module.

NOTE: At this point, you could simply click **Insert** to insert the HTML code for the form on the page.

INSERTING WEB FORMS AS MODULE TAGS

By default, web forms created in Business Catalyst are inserted as HTML source code. When you use Dreamweaver or the Admin Console to add the code to a page, the actual form tags (and form input tags) are inserted in the HTML code of the page.

In most cases, you'll use the process described in this section to add, edit, and delete code, because when you insert the form's source code you can edit the page to directly affect the appearance of the form with CSS styles. Usually, you'll want this level of control over the way the forms appear so that you can match the form with the site's design.

This approach does have one drawback. Every time you make changes to an existing form with the Web Form Builder, you'll need to edit the web pages to swap out the older version of the form's code with the newer code. As a result, you'll have to also reapply the CSS styles that you previously added to the web form.

If you plan on changing your form elements frequently, there is another method you can use. Rather than inserting the forms as HTML source code, you can insert the forms with a single module tag, which looks just like the tags you used to insert the FAQ feature in the previous chapter.

The downside of inserting web forms as module tags is that you cannot directly access the form's code on the page to make changes. Additionally, web forms can only be inserted as module tags in the Admin Console.

However, web forms that are inserted with module tags are automatically updated with the new form fields after editing the form in the Web Form Builder; it is not necessary to delete and reinsert web form module tags to update the changes on the pages.

Choose the method that works best for your project.

Creating Web Forms with the Web Form Builder

In the previous steps, you reviewed the Contact Us form that was included with the trial site to see how it works on the live site. You also explored how the form data is displayed to your clients within the Admin Console and how forms can be set up to send notification messages when a new form submission is received.

Next, you learned how to edit the form in the Web Form Builder and make changes to it. You saw how to delete the existing form code and reinsert it, and how to insert web forms with module tags.

It's important to note that there's nothing special about the Contact Us Form that is included in the trial site's template. It is a generic form just like the forms you can make from scratch. Remember, although you can insert the forms you create using both the Admin Console and Dreamweaver, you can only create and edit the forms themselves using the Web Form Builder in the Admin Console.

As you build sites for clients, you can create unlimited web forms and configure them to use any combination of form elements, along with the default required name and e-mail fields.

Creating a new page to insert the form

In this section, you'll create the Suggestion Box page that will be used to display the form.

1. In the Admin Console, choose Website > Web Pages > Create A New Web Page.

2. The Web Page Details page appears. Enter the page's filename in the Page URL field: suggestionBox.htm.

   Enter the page's name in the Page Name field: SUGGESTION BOX. Leave the Templates menu set to use the site's default template.

3. Click the HTML tab of the online editor and type in the following code to add a white background to the page:

   ```
   <div class="main-holder">
   <div class="content">
    </div>
   </div>
   ```

4. In the HTML tab of the Web Page Content field, enter the following text between the `<div class="content">` and the first closing `</div>` tag: We want your feedback! Click the Design tab and select the text you just entered. Use the Paragraph Style menu to set the text as Heading 1.

5. Click your cursor at the end of the header text and press Enter (Windows) or Return (Mac) once to add a new line break (FIGURE 5.19).

> **NOTE:** It's faster to use this shortcut by selecting the menu suboption rather than clicking the same option in the Action Box sidebar on the Web Page List page.

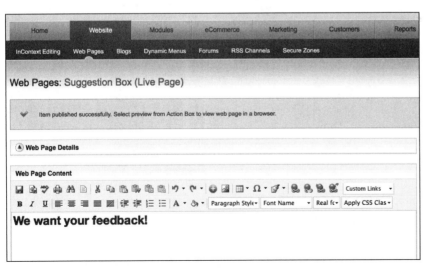

FIGURE 5.19
Add a header to the Suggestion Box page.

Later, you'll insert the Suggestion Box form at this location on the page.

6. Scroll to the bottom and click Save And Publish to save and publish the page.

Updating the site navigation with a link to the new page

TIP: It's faster to use the submenu options of the main Admin Console interface that appear when you roll over them. For example, you can choose Website > Dynamic Menus > Footer Menu > Add / Edit Menu Items to directly jump into the section. These menu suboptions are only displayed after you have previously visited a section in the Admin Console.

To make the new Suggestions Box page easy to access, you'll add a link to the new page you just created to the footer menu of the site. Follow these steps:

1. In the Admin Console, choose Website > Dynamic Menus. The list of existing Dynamic Menus is displayed. Click the Footer Menu to edit it and then click Next.

2. The Dynamic Menus Footer menu page appears. Enter the label for the new menu item in the Item Label field: Suggestion Box.

3. Click the box icon below the Item URL field to open the Link Manager. Click the down arrow icon below the Select Web Page field and select the new Suggestion Box page you just created. Click Select to close the Link Manager and add the link to the page in the Item URL field.

4. Use the Parent menu to choose the Our Company menu item. Scroll down to the bottom and choose Save Item.

5. The new Suggestion Box menu item is added to the Our Company section of the footer menu, at the bottom of the list (FIGURE 5.20).

FIGURE 5.20
Add the Suggestions Box menu subitem to the Our Company section of the footer menu.

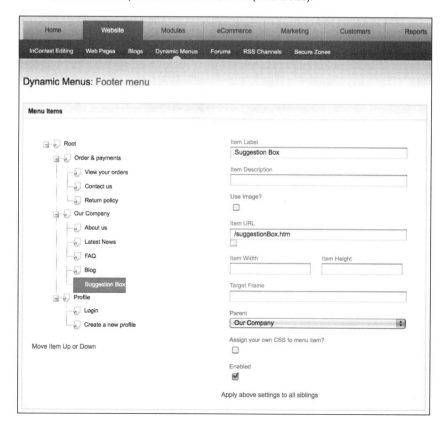

It's already in the perfect location for this project, but if you want to move the menu around to reposition it, you can right-click on the option and choose Move Up and Move Down. The footer menu in the live site is automatically updated when you click the Save Item button. If you'd like, you can switch to the browser window that displays the live site and refresh it. Click the Suggestion Box link in the footer menu to see the Suggestion Box page displayed.

Creating a new web form in the Web Form Builder

Now that the page is created and the new page has been linked from the menu, you are ready to create the Suggestion Box form.

1. Choose Modules > Web Forms > Create A New Web Form. The Web Form Builder page appears.

2. Enter the name of the form in the Web Form Name field: Suggestion Box.

3. In the Use Workflow menu, choose the option Customer Inquiry Workflow (FIGURE 5.21).

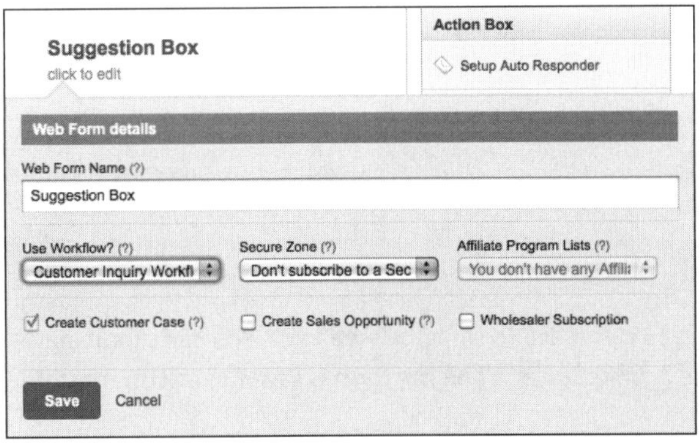

FIGURE 5.21
Set the workflow for the Suggestion Box form in the Web Form details section.

By adding a workflow, you're configuring the form to notify you (since it's currently set to notify all users in the Administrators role) whenever the form is submitted. Because this form is a Suggestion Box, you can test the behavior of receiving the notifications and using the case system in the Customer Summary section of the Admin Console to track and respond to customer suggestions.

4. Click Save to save the Web Form Details and close the window. The preview of the Suggestion Box form is displayed. By default, the name and e-mail address fields are already included and set as required.

5. Click the Text (Multiline) option in the Custom Fields section of the Add New Items panel. In the window that appears, enter the field name, Suggestions, and set the field as required. Click Save to add the new field to the form.

NOTE: Each form includes an auto-responder e-mail message that will send an auto-reply to the visitor who submits the form. You can edit the contents of the message as well as update the message's design. To access and edit the auto-responder message, click the Setup Auto Responder link in the Action Box sidebar.

6. Click the Checkbox (List) option in the Custom Fields section of the Add New Items panel. In the window that appears, enter the field name: Would you like an email sent to you if we implement your suggestion? In the Items field, type Yes. This time don't set the field as required. Click Save.

7. The preview of the form updates to show the recent changes (FIGURE 5.22).

FIGURE 5.22
The Suggestion Box form with the added form elements is displayed in the preview area.

Remember, there's no need to click Save to save the web form. You can simply navigate to another page of the Admin Console and the form is saved in its current state automatically.

Adding Web Forms to Pages with the 1-Click Insert Menu

NOTE: If you have navigated away from the Web Form Builder page, choose Modules > Web Forms. Select the name of the form you want to insert in the list of web forms that appears. The form is displayed in the Web Form Builder page and you can access the option to add the form to a page in the Action Box sidebar.

Previously, you used Dreamweaver and the Module Manager to insert web forms on pages. In this section, you'll use the third option by accessing the 1-Click Insert menu. This workflow is efficient if you've just built a form. Rather than navigating to the page in the Website section of the Admin Console, you can click the option in the sidebar of the Web Form Builder to add the form to a specific page immediately after creating it.

1. While you are in the Web Form Builder interface, choose the option in the Action Box sidebar to Add Web Form to a web page.

2. The 1-Click Insert window appears, displaying the list of web pages in the site. Scroll down and select the Suggestion Box page.

3. The Suggestion Box page loads in the online editor. Place your cursor at the location on the page where you want to insert the Suggestion Box form (on the line below the existing header text).

4. Use the 1-Click Insert menu to choose the option Insert This: Web Form. The HTML code for the form is inserted on the page (**FIGURE 5.23**).

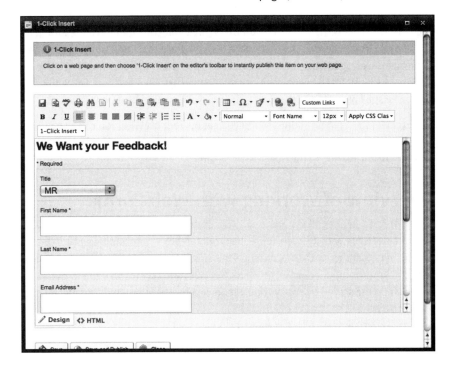

FIGURE 5.23
The Suggestion Box form code is inserted on the page at the cursor's insertion point.

The HTML form is inserted on the page in the online editor. If desired, you can make changes to the content of the page or click the HTML tab and edit the source code.

5. Scroll down and click Save And Publish to upload the changes to the live site.

To see how the Suggestion Box works, switch to a browser window that displays the trial site. Click the link in the Our Company section of the footer to visit the Suggestion Box page. Enter information in the Suggestion Box fields and submit the form to experience how the form works on the front end of the site.

Next, return to the Admin Console and click the Home tab to visit the Dashboard. The Live Feed includes a link that describes the recent activity (**FIGURE 5.24**).

FIGURE 5.24
The Suggestion Box
submission is listed in the
Life Feed section of the
Dashboard.

Click the link to view the Customer Summary page that corresponds to the e-mail address you used when you submitted the form. In the Action Box sidebar, click the Customer Cases option to view the list of cases, and then click the case link to see the form data displayed. If you want to reply to the customer, you could click the New Message link and send them an e-mail message within the system.

If you used a valid e-mail address when you set up your trial site, you can also check your Inbox to see the workflow notification message that was generated automatically when you submitted the Suggestion Box form.

Overview of Working with Web Forms

Web forms are an integral feature used in Business Catalyst sites to gather customer data and track site activity. Web-form elements can be customized to capture the specific data that's related to your client's business. You can also update the appearance of forms (using standard HTML and CSS code) and control how the forms behave behind the scenes to ensure your clients receive the submitted form data.

Adding e-mail and SMS notification to web-form functionality

If you want to configure a custom workflow notification system, configure the workflows first, before building and inserting web forms:

1. Set up user accounts for your clients.

2. Create the roles for different sets of users.

3. Add and configure the workflows to define who receives notification messages when a form submission is received.

4. Apply the workflow to the web forms as you build them.

In Chapter 7, "Understanding Customer Management and the Site's Database," you'll learn more about how to manage users, access customer data, and customize workflows.

Inserting web forms on pages of the site

After building a web form, you must insert it on a page and publish the page to make it available on the live site. Remember to add a link to the form page to make it easy for visitors to access it.

You'll follow three general workflows when working with web forms.

1: Build the web form first and then create and style the page that will display it

1. Build the web form in the Web Form Builder.
2. Create a page using Dreamweaver.
3. Use the Business Catalyst panel to insert the web form as HTML.
4. Edit the source code of the page and style the form with CSS using the editing tools provided in Dreamweaver.
5. Upload (put) the page to publish it to the live site.

2: Build the web form and then create the page that will display it—without styling the form

1. Build the web form in the Web Form Builder.
2. Create a page using the Website section of the Admin Console.
3. Use the Module Manager to insert the web form as either HTML or as a module tag.
4. Save and publish the page to make it available on the live site.

3: Create the page first and then build the web form

1. Create the page using either Dreamweaver or the Admin Console.
2. Build the web form in the Web Form Builder.
3. Use the 1-Click Insert menu to insert the form on the page as HTML.
4. Save and publish the page to upload it to the live site.

Updating the appearance and behavior of forms

After publishing the page that contains a form, always visit the live site and test the form. If you inserted the form as HTML, you can use the CSS Styles panel in Dreamweaver to style the form elements.

If you need to change the form elements after previously inserting the form on a page, update the form in the Web Form Builder. Then, edit the page in either Dreamweaver or the Admin Console to delete and reinsert the HTML code.

Remember, if you're using the Module Manager to insert the web form as a module, you can update the form elements in the Web Form Builder and the form is updated on pages automatically. However, you cannot access the source code to style the form if you insert the web form with a module tag.

Related Links

 Adding CAPTCHA to Web Forms:
http://www.adobe.com/go/bc_captcha

 Capturing Leads and Closing Sales:
http://www.adobe.com/go/bc_closing_sales

CHAPTER 6

Setting Up an Online Store

Contents

Examining the Online Store on the Trial Site	100
Using the Admin Console to Edit and Configure the Online Store	103
Customizing Layouts to Control the Appearance of the Online Store	112
Adding a Product Search Form to the Store's Home Page	123
Setting Up Shipping Options	125
Configuring Payment Gateways	128
Working with the eCommerce Tools to Build Online Stores	130

When you build a store using the Admin Console, you define every aspect of its organization. You create separate catalogs to contain sets of products and group related inventory items together. You can also tag the products with keywords to control how merchandise is displayed on the store's pages.

You have the ability to customize both the content and appearance of the online store. You choose the elements to include in product descriptions. You define how many products appear on each page and use your own templates to create a unique shopping experience.

The eCommerce tools provided in Business Catalyst are designed to make it easy to set up and manage a wide variety of stores. You can create small online stores that only sell a few items or larger stores that sell hundreds of products. The stores can sell e-products that are available for download or integrate with shipping vendors to deliver products of varying sizes and types internationally. Customers can book reservations online and schedule services. The configuration options are completely customizable so that you can choose the best approach for each business.

The Admin Console facilitates the process of configuring store functionality and the elements that are displayed on the store's pages. You set up everything based on the specifications provided by your clients. You control the List view of items in the store by editing the Individual Product Small layout file. And you update the Detail view of store items with the Individual Product Large layout file to control how a product's details appear when it is selected. You can add image galleries and videos to the product descriptions, if desired, to help customers compare items. You can also add new products individually or bring in an entire list of products as a batch import to populate the store. Once the store is ready for prime time, your client can log in to the Admin Console to run their own business by adding and updating products, fulfilling orders, and tracking sales with income reports.

The Business Catalyst Platform is a hosted solution that includes secure pages. There's no need to purchase and maintain SSL certificates. The system ensures that credit card data is kept private and payment data is handled safely and securely.

As the online business evolves, you can continue to make changes to the store. You can tweak a store's features to improve performance and update it to support your client's business model, display featured merchandise to highlight sale items, and add promotion codes and discount prices to encourage sales. The live site is always editable so that businesses can respond immediately to market changes. A well-maintained online store is an effective sales mechanism.

Examining the Online Store on the Trial Site

The trial site includes a prebuilt store right out of the box. Many of the store features are already set up, using placeholder content. In this section, you'll review the areas of the store and see how it works from a visitor's perspective.

In a browser, visit the live site. Click the Shop link in the top-level navigation to review the home page of the online store (FIGURE 6.1). Walking through this generic implementation of the store is a great way to learn how the eCommerce system works.

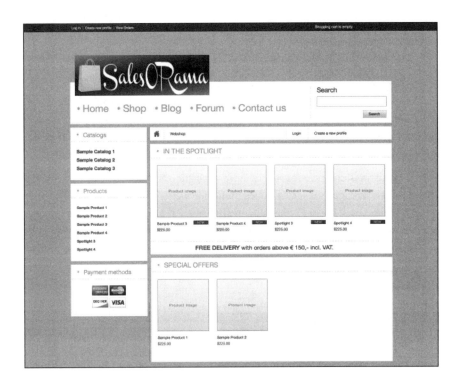

FIGURE 6.1
The home page of the online store.

The top-left column contains a list of catalogs. You can think of catalogs as departments in a store. Various sections of a store sell clothing, electronics, housewares, toys, and office supplies. Catalogs enable you to compartmentalize specific sets of items, thus making it easier for customers to find what they need and enable a business to display related merchandise.

For example, an online business that sells coats might have three different catalogs: men's, women's, and kids' coats. This organization allows customers to jump right to the products they want to purchase. The system is flexible, giving you complete control over the way catalogs are organized and how they are displayed. You can design each area of the store with a subject-specific theme to set the mood for various shopping experiences.

The next section in the left column displays a list of products. These are the individual items that populate each catalog. A men's coat catalog may contain any number of coats in varying sizes, styles, and colors.

The main area of this particular online store displays the featured product information, which can include attributes such as the product image, name, price, and indication whether it is new or a clearance item. This area is the equivalent of promotional sales shelves in retail stores. Featured items are prominently displayed to attract attention and drive sales.

Choose a product in the spotlight area and click the product's name or image to see the description appear. This is called the Detail view, which is controlled using the Individual Product Large layout file. In this example, the details include a larger image of the product, an interface to set the quantity and add items to the shopping cart, and descriptive text that entices the customer to buy it. Click the Add To Cart button to see how the shopping cart works. In the confirmation dialog box that appears, click OK.

Each page of the store includes special store navigation features such as the breadcrumb links at the top. You'll also notice that while viewing a product's detail page, the left column updates to display other recommended products. By tagging related items, you can suggest products that are similar to an item that has already caught the customer's interest.

Click the View Cart link in the top-right corner of the page to see the shopping cart (FIGURE 6.2).

FIGURE 6.2
The shopping cart displays the items prior to checkout.

When the shopping cart page loads, notice that the URL in the address bar of the browser displays the https:// prefix. That means the store's transaction pages are secure because they are transmitted via an encrypted 128-bit SSL protocol. Customers feel confident entering their credit card payment information on secure pages because the encryption protects sensitive data.

The shopping cart lists the items you've added to the cart. The store functionality is mostly working now, but if you click the Check Out button and complete the payment form with placeholder data, the form does not process the transaction when you click the Submit button.

Instead, the following error message appears, stating that an error occurred while processing the credit card because the payment gateway is not configured (FIGURE 6.3).

FIGURE 6.3
An error occurs because the payment gateway is not configured.

A payment gateway is a third-party service provider that processes payment transactions and protects customer's credit card details by encrypting the payment details. When the site is ready to launch, your clients can create accounts with their desired payment gateways and you can enter their account information into the Admin Console to enable online transactions.

In the next section, you'll review the store functionality from the Admin Console to learn how to use the interface to set up catalogs and products.

Using the Admin Console to Edit and Configure the Online Store

Now that you've explored the store from a customer's perspective, you'll see how to work with catalogs and products in the back-end interface. To start, you'll check out an existing catalog in the store.

1. Open a second browser window and log in to the Admin Console. Click the eCommerce tab. Take a moment to review the submenu items.

    The first two submenu items enable you to create and manage catalogs and products. Products are the actual items for sale (the store's inventory). Catalogs are organizational tools—like folders—that allow you to create sections in a store to display specific types of merchandise.

2. Choose eCommerce > Catalogs to view the Catalogs List page (FIGURE 6.4).

3. Click on any of the sample catalogs in the list to access the Catalog Details page.

FIGURE 6.4
The list of catalogs is displayed on the Catalogs List page.

You'll use this area to create and edit the information that pertains to each catalog. You can create unlimited catalogs and then choose to display them as desired. For example, if a store contains catalogs for men's, women's, and kids' coats, you could also create catalogs for Spring, Summer, Fall, and Winter. This enables you to display special sale pages in the store. To add or remove products from a catalog, click Next and use the interface on the next page to manage the products that are included in the catalog.

 NOTE: As you manage catalogs, remember that you can create as many catalogs as you'd like. When you remove products from catalogs—or even delete entire catalogs—you are not affecting the inventory of products. Catalogs are containers for sets of products that you use to make virtual departments in your online store.

Creating a new catalog

Follow these steps to create a catalog:

1. Use one of the following three methods to create a catalog:

    • Choose eCommerce > Catalogs > Create A New Catalog.

    • In the sidebar of the Catalogs List page, click Create A New Catalog.

    • In the sidebar of the Catalog Details page, click Create Another Catalog.

2. The Catalog Details page appears. In the Catalog Name field, enter Clearance Items. Set the Template menu to Use default template.

When you enter the catalog name, the URL above is generated automatically using the text you entered. However, the URL does not have to match the catalog name. Click the Edit button to access the field and enter a different URL: **special-offers**.

Notice that you could upload image files (using the File Manager, Dreamweaver, or an FTP client) and then choose an image for the catalog by clicking the square icon next to the Image field. In the trial site, the catalogs don't display image files, so leave this field blank for now.

Leave the Parent menu set to Root so that this catalog is created at the top level. Click Save to save the new catalog (FIGURE 6.5).

FIGURE 6.5
Enter the catalog information in the Catalog Details page.

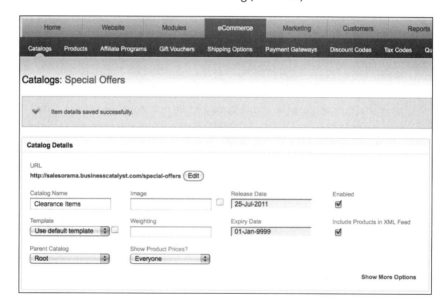

TIP: Use the single-arrow buttons to move individual products from one pane to another. Any products listed in the right pane when you navigate away from this page are automatically included in the catalog. To add all the products in the left pane to the catalog, click the double-arrow button that points to the right. If you make a mistake and want to start over (or remove all products from a catalog), click the double-arrow button that points to the left.

3. Click the Next button to access the next page, where you'll add products to the new catalog you just created.

In the left pane, select Sample Product 4 and click the top, right-pointing single green-arrow button. The page updates to display the Sample Product 4 in the pane on the right. That's all it takes to add a product to the catalog.

Repeat this process by selecting Spotlight 4 in the left pane. Click the top green-arrow button again to add it to the right pane too.

4. Once you've finished adding products to a catalog, you can simply navigate away or click the Back button to make changes to the catalog's details.

Managing products

In this section, you'll learn how to add a new product to the system manually. You'll find this knowledge handy when your client has several new items to add. This is an activity that you can optionally enable for clients so that they can manage their own products (if they're interested in maintaining the store themselves).

1. In the Admin Console, choose eCommerce > Products. The list of existing products appears (**FIGURE 6.6**). This is the same list you saw displayed earlier when adding products to a catalog.

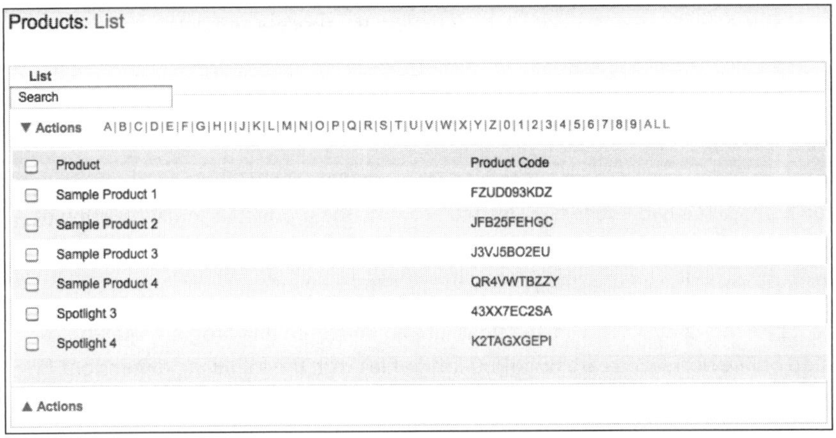

FIGURE 6.6
The list of products is displayed on the Products List page.

The names assigned to products are important because the products are listed alphabetically. It is helpful to adopt a naming convention as you enter products so that groups of related products line up in the list. If a store contains a significant number of products, you can navigate the list quickly by clicking the letter of the alphabet to see that section of the product list appear. To see the entire list of products, click All.

2. Click one of the product names in the list to select it. The corresponding product is displayed in the Product Details page. Each product contains basic information, including the following:

Product Name

- Small Image (usually displayed in the List view)
- Large Image (usually displayed in the Detail view)
- Release Date (the date the product is available on the site)
- Expiry Date (the date the product is removed from the site)
- Product Description

TIP: When the store is up and running, you don't have to delete an item to remove it from the store's virtual "shelves." Instead, you can select the product name in the Products List page and access the corresponding Product Details page. Uncheck the Enabled checkbox and click Save. The product information is still stored in the site's database, but it won't appear on the live site unless you return to the product details and enable it again.

FIGURE 6.7
Select all the products and use the Actions menu to delete them.

3. Click the option View All Products in the sidebar. Or you can click the Back button on your browser to return to the Products List page.

To start from scratch, you'll delete the existing products that were included with the trial site. Then, you'll create some new products to populate the store.

On the Products List page, select the top checkbox labeled Products. This selects all of the products in the list. (When you only want to delete a few products, you could also select each product individually in the list.)

While all the products are selected, use the top or bottom Actions menu to choose Delete. A confirmation message appears asking if you want to delete the selected items. Click OK to complete the process and delete the products (FIGURE 6.7).

Creating a new product

In this section, you'll add a new item to the store. Before beginning this process, you can prepare the two image files used to promote the product: a smaller version of the image is displayed as a list in the catalogs and a larger image is displayed when the customer clicks a product to view the product's details.

To follow along with these instructions, use an image-editing program like Photoshop or Fireworks to create two JPEG image files with the following dimensions (in pixels) to fit the design of the current trial site template:

- Large product image: 450 x 260
- Small product image: 153 x 153

Upload the two JPEG files to the live site using the File Manager, Dreamweaver, or a third-party FTP client. Or simply use the placeholder files included with the trial site template at these locations:

- /images/webshop/product-small.gif
- /images/webshop/product-large.gif

NOTE: If the online business sells merchandise in several countries, you can set product prices for each currency accepted by the online store. Use the Country menu to specify the country where the product will be sold.

When you build your client's sites with your own templates, you aren't limited to using these sizes. You can design the store pages any way you'd like. For this example, you'll populate the product data using the provided template file and predetermined image dimensions.

1. Use one of the following three methods to create a new product:
   - Choose eCommerce > Products > Create A New Product.
   - In the sidebar of the Products List page, click Create A New Product.
   - In the sidebar of the Product Details page, click Create Another Product.

2. The Product Details page appears. In the Product Name field, enter Pencils.

   Click the square icon next to the Small Image field and browse to select the small product image. Click the square icon next to the Large Image field and browse to select the large product image.

   If the product description you are adding is for an e-product (an electronic file that will be downloaded by the customer rather than physical merchandise that will be shipped), enable the checkbox in the Electronic Product section (FIGURE 6.8).

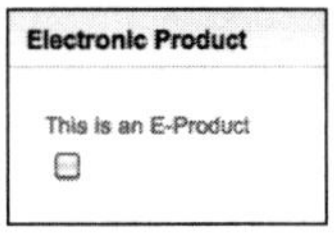

3. Enter some placeholder text in the Product Description field, like this:

   A variety pack of pencils in different sizes and shapes; each box includes 100 pencils and 100 erasers.

   If desired, you can use the formatting tools in the online editor to format the text (FIGURE 6.9).

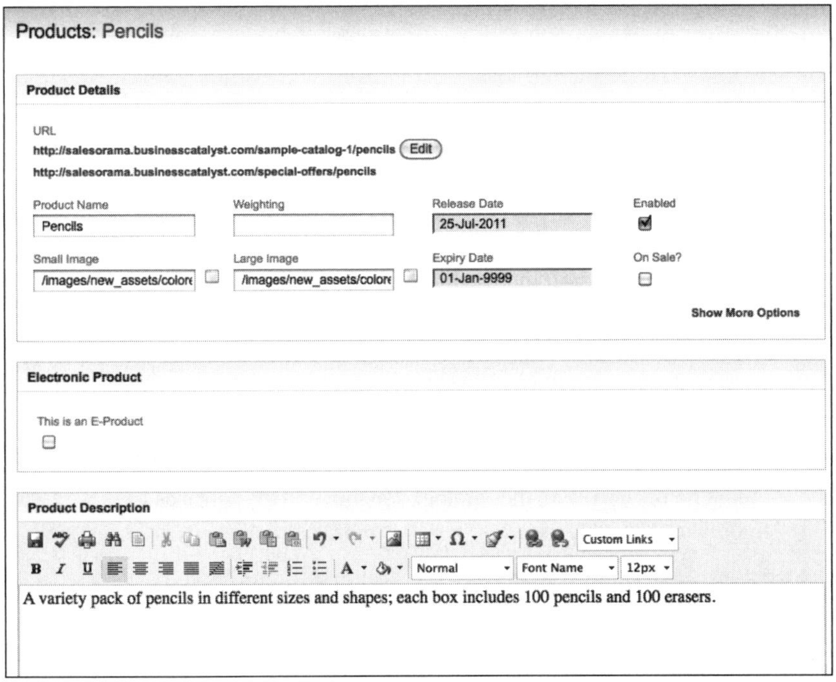

FIGURE 6.8
If the item is an e-product, enable the This Is An E-Product checkbox.

FIGURE 6.9
Enter the product information in the Product Details page.

While still in the Product Details page, scroll to the bottom and click Next. The page updates, displaying the fields where you can enter the price information for the product.

The Recommended Retail Price field is optional. Only enter a numeric value in this field if you want to display both the retail price *and* the sales price to customers when they view the product. This is another marketing strategy you can use to make your customers aware that the item on sale is a good value.

4. Enter the price that the customer will pay for the item in the Sell Price field using this format: 20.00.

5. Leave the other default settings and click Save Price (FIGURE 6.10).

FIGURE 6.10
Enter the price of the product
in the Sell Price field.

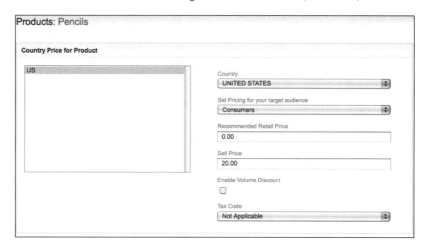

6. Click Next to access the next page of the Products section.

   The third and final page includes the interface that allows you to add the current product to one or more existing catalogs. You can always add products to catalogs later by editing the catalogs themselves, but this is an efficient way to add a new product to multiple existing catalogs.

7. Select the Sample Catalog 1 name in the left pane and click the top single right-pointing arrow button to move it to the right side. Repeat this operation to select and move the new catalog you just created, Clearance Items, to the right side as well. Now the Pencils product you just created is included in both the Sample Catalog 1 and the Clearance Items catalogs (FIGURE 6.11).

   There's no need to save; the catalogs you move to the right side are saved automatically on this page.

FIGURE 6.11
Add the current product to
catalogs by selecting the
catalog name on the left and
moving the catalog names to
the right side.

Products: Pencils

Add this product to catalogs by moving from left to right

| Sample Catalog 2 Sample Catalog 3 | | Sample Catalog 1 Clearance Items |

ADDING ADDITIONAL PRODUCT INFORMATION IN THE SHOW MORE OPTIONS DIALOG BOX

In many cases, you'll enter the basic product information to create each product you add manually. However, to set up inventory tracking or integrated shipping options (which use your client's shipping vendor account to calculate the shipping fees based on the weight and dimensions of each product), you can add additional product information by clicking the link Show More Options.

If you click the Show More Options link, a window appears with fields to add more product details to the site's database. By including these additional product attributes, the business can leverage more advanced store features (FIGURE 6.12).

For example, if you set up the optional feature to track inventory, the number of remaining products can be displayed in the online store layouts (in the List and Detail views) to display the quantity of items remaining in stock. This strategy is a helpful sales tool because as the number of available items decreases, it conveys a sense of urgency to customers. They realize they must purchase the item soon before it is sold out.

Shipping options are another consideration. If a store sells a single type of item (like T-shirts) that consistently cost the same amount to ship, the shopping cart can be configured to use a flat-fee rate such as $5.

Some online businesses sell a wide variety of merchandise and it's not practical for the business owner to predict the shipping fees necessary to fulfill orders. In these cases, your client can set up an account with shipping vendors (such as UPS, FedEx, or USPS) to manage the shipping costs.

In this scenario, additional product information (weight and package dimensions) is included with the product's details. This information can then be used to filter the shipping options at the time of checkout by weight, package size, or both. Based on the product information, the shipping cost is calculated and displayed in the shopping cart.

If the business has accounts with multiple shipping vendors, the product information can be used to calculate fees for several shipping methods. The shipping fees for each vendor are displayed at the time of checkout so that the customer can choose the desired shipping option before entering their credit card information and completing the transaction.

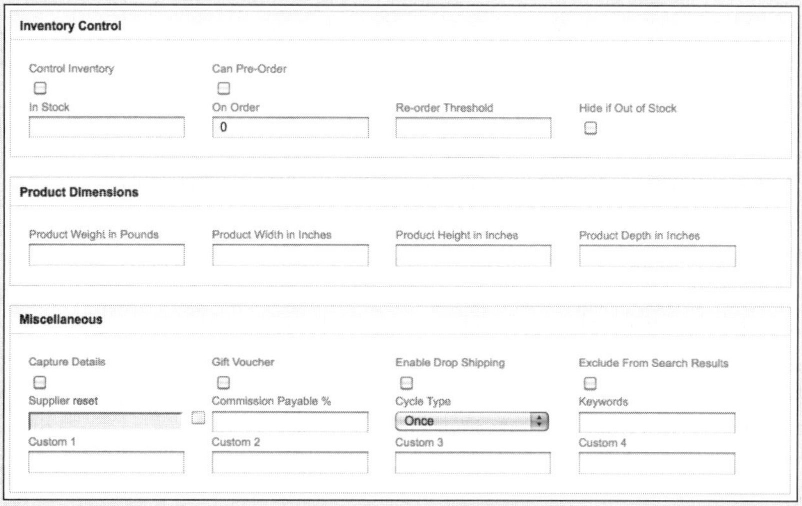

FIGURE 6.12 Show More Options includes optional fields that let you control inventory and enter product dimensions for shipping calculations.

ADDING TAX CODES

You can set up the relevant tax codes for the store so that they are applied as required during the checkout process.

Choose eCommerce > Tax Codes and enter the values on the Tax Codes List page.

If the business operates within the United States and sells products that require the application of state taxes in every state, you can click the link Add All USA State Tax Rates.

But be advised: If you click this option, the entire list of state taxes is added. You'll need to manually edit each US state tax individually to delete the ones you don't need—which is time consuming.

If the store you're configuring will ship products nationally and is required to charge state taxes in every US state, then this is a helpful feature. However, most companies only need to charge state taxes when processing transactions in the state where the business is located.

Identify the tax situation needed for each client; only click this option if the store requires the tax codes for all US states. Generally speaking, it is much easier to manually add the necessary tax codes than it is to edit each state's tax code one by one to remove them from the system.

Now that you've created a new catalog and added a new product to the store, it's a good time to review the live site and see the changes. Switch to the browser window that displays the trial site. If you click the Store link to access the store's home page, you'll see the list of catalogs on the left side has been updated to include the new Clearance Items catalog you added. Click the link to see that the new product, Pencils, is included in the catalog. If you click the Pencils product name or small image, you'll see that the Details page for the Pencils product appear. This page was generated dynamically using the online store layout files and the larger image file that you linked in the Product Details page.

If you'd like, you can interact with the store by adding the Pencils product to the cart. The new product you just added displays and works as expected. You can fill out the form and pretend to purchase the item, but you can't submit your payment information because the payment gateway for the site is not configured.

Copying products

When you are manually adding products to the store, you can duplicate an existing product and edit it rather than creating each product from scratch. This strategy makes the workflow more efficient because the prices are already entered. If the product that you copy is already added to catalogs, that information is copied as well. Copying products saves time because you can simply rename the new product and link the new small and large image files.

If you want to follow along, you can use the same two image files that you prepared in the previous section to create this new product. Or create two more JPEG image files with the following dimensions (in pixels):

- Large product image: 450 x 260
- Small product image: 153 x 153

1. Return to the Admin Console and choose eCommerce > Products. The list of products appears. Click the Pencils product to view the Product Details page.

2. Scroll down and click the Copy This Product option in the Related sidebar (**FIGURE 6.13**).

3. The page updates to display the Product Details page with a copy of the Pencils product.

4. Update the product URL by clicking the Edit button. Enter the new URL, toys, and then rename the product by typing Toys in the Product Name field.

5. Click the square icon next to the Small Image field and browse to select the small image of the product. Repeat this operation by clicking the square icon next to the Large Image field to set the image that appears in the Detail view of the store. Leave the checkbox next to the Enabled option selected (**FIGURE 6.14**).

FIGURE 6.13
Click the option to copy this product at the bottom of the sidebar on the Products page.

Product Details

URL
http://salesorama.businesscatalyst.com/sample-catalog-1/toys (Edit)
http://salesorama.businesscatalyst.com/special-offers/toys

Product Name	Weighting	Release Date	Enabled
Toys	20	25-Jul-2011	☑

Small Image	Large Image	Expiry Date	On Sale?
/images/new_assets/toys_	/images/new_assets/toys_	01-Jan-9999	☐

FIGURE 6.14
After copying a product, update the fields with the new product's details.

The Weighting field is optional. By default, products in the store display alphabetically by their product names. If this works for you, there's no need to enter any value in the Weighting field. However, if you want to affect the sort order so that the Zebra toy displays first—before the Aardvark toy—enter a numeric value in the field. The items weighted with the higher numbers display first; items with lower numbers display below. So if you create three products weighted at 5, 10, and 20, the items are listed on the store pages in this order:

20

10

5

6. Update the Product Description field with new placeholder text. When you finish updating the product details for this new product, click Save.

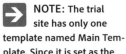

TIP: If your client has a large quantity of products to add to the store, you can batch-import them using a spreadsheet. This approach is much faster than manually adding each product as described earlier. In many cases, you'll import an entire inventory of products when first building the site to get the store up and running. Then, as your client expands their inventory to add new products, they can enter them manually.

There's no need to click Next to visit the last two pages in the Product setup unless you want to change the price of the product or the catalogs that contain it. If you'd like, practice creating a few more sample products by copying the Pencils or Toys products again. Edit the product details for each copy to populate the trial site's store. As you can see, the ability to copy existing, similar products and edit the product's details significantly speeds up the process of creating new products.

Customizing Layouts to Control the Appearance of the Online Store

In the previous sections of this chapter, you used the Admin Console to create and edit products and catalogs. As you add new items to the store, they appear automatically when you refresh the pages in the live site.

The appearance of the pages in the store is defined by two types of files:

- Templates (DWT files) define the outer design of the page (the header and footer content).
- Layout files (HTML files) define the design of the store in List and Detail views (and other views of the store) to specify the data that is displayed and the formatting of module elements.

Editing store layouts is similar to working with the FAQ layouts you edited in Chapter 4, "Configuring, Inserting, and Customizing Modules." You can access layout files by choosing Admin > More Customization Options (in the Admin Console), and they're located in the Layouts folder in the Files panel (in Dreamweaver).

NOTE: The trial site has only one template named Main Template. Since it is set as the default template for the site, every page of the site uses the template automatically, ensuring a consistent visual appearance.

In this section, you'll take a look at the layout files that are used to control the views of the online store modules (for catalogs and products) and learn how to edit them. As you saw in Chapter 4, you can edit the module layouts in both the Admin Console and Dreamweaver. You can also use both methods to edit and add tag attributes to define the specific data that's displayed in each view.

Editing store layouts in the Admin Console

It's a best practice to make backup copies of the site's layout files using Dreamweaver or an FTP client before you edit them. That way, if you edit the layout files past the point of no return, you can replace the edited versions with the files that you backed up.

There's a button at the bottom of each layout file titled Reset To Original. Be advised that this option resets the layout files to standard Business Catalyst layout files that aren't designed to work with the trial site's template. The reset button doesn't undo the changes you've made to revert each layout file as it was initially—and once you click the button to reset a layout file, there's no way to undo it.

IMPORTING PRODUCTS

When your clients have numerous products to sell, it's much more efficient to batch-import products to bring a large number of products into the system at once.

Select from one of the following methods to access the import template:

- Choose eCommerce > Products to access the Products List page. In the sidebar, click the Import Products option.

- In the Admin menu, choose Import Data. In the Import List page that appears, click Products.

The next steps involve downloading the template for your site:

1. The Products Import page appears. In the sidebar, choose the option Download Import Template File.

2. In the dialog box that appears, choose Open With Microsoft Excel and click OK.

   It's important to download the Import Template file and prepare it before importing the product data for a site. The template includes pre-created columns in the spreadsheet to ensure that the data is imported into the database correctly.

3. Read and follow all the instructions in the Excel file. Use Microsoft Excel to edit the XLS file and prepare it for import. Export the file after updating the file.

   After preparing the spreadsheet and adding the product information, you must export the file in Excel. You cannot import files that are in the XLS file format. The system supports the import of both comma-delimited and tab-delimited files. To ensure that there are no issues with commas that may appear in product descriptions, export the template from Excel as a tab-delimited file.

4. Return to the Products Import page in the Admin Console. Click the Browse button and navigate to select the tab-delimited file that you exported from Microsoft Excel.

5. Select the tab-delimited option. The File Type option you select must match the file type that you are importing.

6. Leave the other default settings and click Next. In the confirmation dialog box that appears, click OK.

7. The Products Import page updates to display the list of products to be imported. Review the list of products and click Import.

TIP: Always create a small batch of products to import to test the import process. Make sure that the data imports correctly before attempting to import a large set of data to the database. That way, if the data import process doesn't go as expected, you can easily delete the test products and start over.

You can access the store layouts in the Admin area of the Admin Console the same way you accessed the module layouts. Follow these steps:

1. Return to the Admin Console and choose Admin > More Customization Options. In the Customize Home page that appears, click the Online Shop Layouts icon.

2. The page updates to display the Online Shop Layouts page with the list of layouts. As you can see, many more layouts become available when customizing an online store compared to the FAQ module (FIGURE 6.15).

FIGURE 6.15
Choose a layout from the list of Online Shop Layouts.

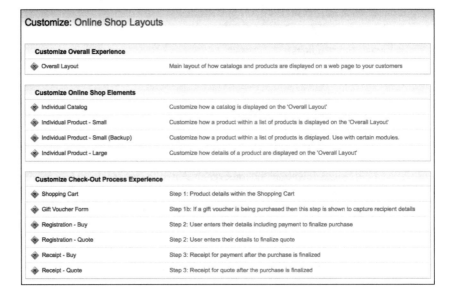

Using these layouts, you can customize every aspect of the online store to create a unique shopping experience. Each layout manages different views of the store, including the catalog List view pages, the Detail view of individual products, the shopping cart, and even the receipt sent to customers after they complete a purchase. Take a moment to review the list of 11 layouts to become familiar with all the areas you can edit within the store.

3. Click the top layout named Overall Layout to open it in the online editor.

   This layout is like a mini-template that controls the data displayed on the store pages. The module tags added to this layout are set up to define the contents displayed in the left sidebar in the live site. You can see the tags that define the list of catalogs and the recommended items (FIGURE 6.16).

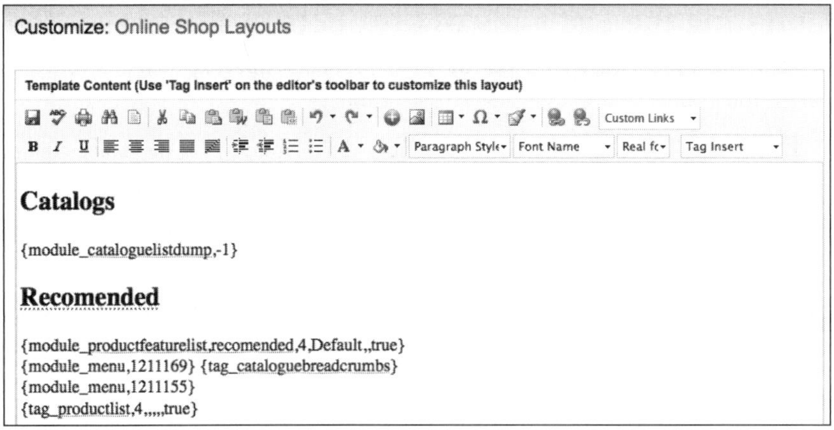

FIGURE 6.16
Module tags define the overall
layout of the store.

4. In the sidebar, click View Customization Options (or click the Back button) to return to the list of store layouts.

The next group of layouts defines how individual catalogs and product views are displayed. The Individual Catalog layout is basic and just includes the tags to display the catalog's name and its image (if one is provided). There's no need to edit that file, but you can open it to review its contents.

The other three layouts in the Customize Online Shop Elements section are the three views used to display individual products:

- Individual Product - Small
- Individual Product - Small (Backup)
- Individual Product - Large

Individual Product - Small and the Individual Product - Large are the two you'll use most often. They define how the product is displayed in its List view (Small) and its Detail view (Large) within the context of the Overall Layout file. The naming convention is a bit confusing, but it helps to remember that the name corresponds with the images you created earlier for the product's details; the small image of the product is displayed when viewing a list of products in the catalog. The large image of the product is shown in the Detail view when a customer clicks on a product to see the product's details.

Updating the List view of products in store layouts

In this section, you'll update the way the list of products appears within the store pages. You'll add a new feature: a Buy Now button.

1. Click the layout named Individual Product - Small to open it in the online editor.

   Take a moment to review the existing tags. The List view displays the smaller image of the product, a custom tag, the product's name, and the sale price of the item.

   ➕ **TIP:** In addition to the predefined tag attributes you can insert in layout files, Business Catalyst includes four custom tags in the store layout files that you can set up to display whatever data you'd prefer. For example, you can set a custom tag to display a message or image alongside the product in List or Detail view.

   First, edit the layout files to insert one of the four custom tags with the Tag Insert menu (using either Dreamweaver or the Admin Console).

   Then, access the product details by choosing eCommerce > Products and selecting the desired product from the list. In the Products Details page, click Show More Options and scroll down to the Miscellaneous section. Enter the information that will display for the custom tag in the layout by editing the corresponding field. For example, you can add a URL to an image in the site or enter a line of text. The content you enter will appear in the location on the layout where you inserted the custom tag (for each product that contains that option in its product details). This is handy if you'd like to display a NEW or ON SALE message next to specific products in the store.

2. Click after the Sales Price tag and press Enter (Windows) or Return (Mac) twice to move the cursor down to its own line with a line of space between the other tags. After placing the cursor at this location, use the Tag Insert menu to insert the tag for the Buy Now button (FIGURE 6.17).

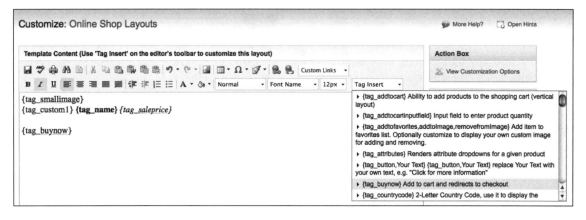

FIGURE 6.17
Add the Buy Now tag to the Individual Product - Small Layout.

3. Scroll down and click Save to save the changes to the layout.

If you'd like to see the results of editing the Individual Product - Small layout file, switch to the other browser window displaying the live site. Refresh the home page of the store and notice that the catalogs display each product in List view with a Buy

Now button. This button facilitates sales because it enables customers to immediately add an item to their cart without viewing the product's details.

The data displayed on the store's pages is controlled with the layout file named Overall Layout. The top-left sidebar displays the same list of catalogs that are displayed in the Admin Console when you choose eCommerce > Catalogs. The lower part of the left sidebar contains the recommended products.

The breadcrumb-style store navigation links at the top of the page make it easy for customers to access the products in each catalog and then return to the store's home page (named Webshop in this site). The home icon in the navigation bar is linked to the home page of the site.

The center region of the store's home page displays two sections: In The Spotlight and Special Offers. When configuring stores, you can set up these featured areas so that businesses can prominently display their most popular merchandise. Click the new Clearance Items catalog link in the left sidebar to see the list of products display. This List view also displays the Buy Now buttons (FIGURE 6.18).

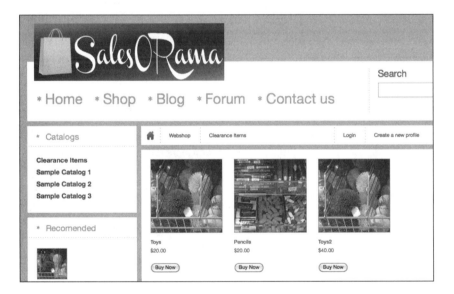

FIGURE 6.18
The Home page of the online store reflects the recent changes.

If you click the links to view Sample Catalog 2 or Sample Catalog 3, a message appears indicating that the catalog has no products. This occurs because you deleted the sample products that were included with the trial site. In the next section, you'll learn how you can manage products to group them and subdivide them. This trial site is preconfigured to use tags to display products, so you'll see how to work with tags to specify how products are displayed in the various sections of the store.

USING THE INDIVIDUAL PRODUCT - SMALL (BACKUP) LAYOUT FILE

This layout file also displays a List view of products. However, it's different from the other two product layouts, because you can insert its module tag and display this list on web pages only—it cannot be inserted in the layout files.

Use this layout when you want to display a list of featured products outside the store pages. For example, you could configure the home page of the site to display a small list of products with tiny thumbnails to drive traffic to the online store. This third layout offers you the option to design a separate list of products that displays differently than it does when viewed in the store.

To work with this layout file, follow these steps:

1. In eCommerce > Products, click the item in the Action Box sidebar to Tag this item to tag the selected product with specific keywords. For example, you could create a keyword called homepage and tag the products that you want to feature on the site's home page. Later in this chapter you'll learn more about tagging products.

2. Choose Websites > Web Pages and create or edit an existing page. Edit the file in the online editor in the Web Page Details page. Click the page in the location where you want to insert the list of tagged products.

3. Launch the Module Manager so that it appears in the right sidebar. Expand the catalog section and select the option Display List Of Products By Tag.

4. The Module Manager updates to display a Tags field. Enter the name of the tag you used to tag the products that will be featured on the home page: homepage. Click the Customize link.

5. Edit the Row Length, Sort Type, and Target Frame fields, if desired. Select the Use Backup Template checkbox to enable it.

6. Click Insert. The module tag is inserted on the page at the cursor's location:

   {module_productfeaturelist,homepage,4,Default,,true}

7. Save and publish the page. If you refresh the trial site in a browser and look at the page, you'll see the list of tagged products displayed.

This strategy is helpful because you can teach your clients how to tag products so that they can rotate the products displayed on their site's home page (or any other high-traffic area of the site).

To insert this module tag to display the product list outside the store's pages, you must use the Module Manager and insert it in a web page. You cannot insert this tag using the 1-Click Insert menu in the Admin Console or Dreamweaver.

Tagging products

Follow these steps to group products and assign tags to them:

1. In the Admin Console, choose eCommerce > Products. The list of products in the store is displayed. Click the Pencils product in the list to access the product's details.

2. The page updates to display the information about the selected product. In the Action Box sidebar, click the option Tag This Item (**FIGURE 6.19**).

3. The Tags window appears. The existing tags that were included with the trial site are listed in the left side. If you want to tag the current product (so that it appears in the Spotlight, Recommended, or Special Offers section of the store), select the name of the item and then click the top single, right-pointing arrow button to move the tag to the right side. Any tags that are added to the right side will add the product to those site areas.

   For example, select the Special Offers tag in the left side and move it to the right side. This operation sets the Pencils product to display in the Special Offers section of the store.

   If you want to create new tags, click the Manage Tags button and enter the new tag names. When you've finished adding tags, simply click Close to dismiss the window and then navigate to another page. There's no need to click Save because the tags added to the right side are saved automatically.

   If you switch to the browser that displays the live site, you can click the Shop menu item to refresh the shop's home page. Notice that the Pencils product that you tagged with the Special Offers tag is now displayed in the Special Offers section.

   Take a moment to test how tags work.

4. Experiment with adding tags to other products. For example, choose eCommerce > Products and select one of the products you created earlier when you copied products and renamed them.

   In the Product Details page, click the option Tag This Item. Use the Tags window to add the In the Spotlight and Special Offers tags and then close the Tags window (**FIGURE 6.20**).

FIGURE 6.19
Click Tag This Item in the Action Box sidebar to add tags to products.

 NOTE: In addition to tagging products, you can click the Create Upsell / Crosssell option in the Action Box sidebar. This feature enables you to choose related products from the entire list of products (to specify items that are similar to the selected product you're editing). Use this feature to suggest related products to customers as they shop for items in the store.

FIGURE 6.20
Move tags from left to right to
tag a product.

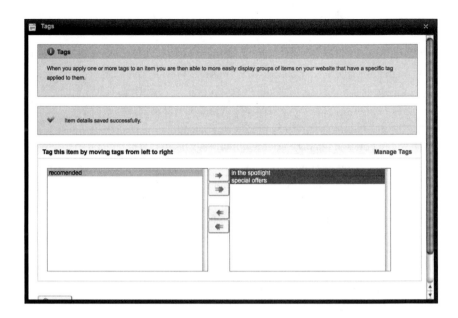

Refresh the browser page that displays the live site and visit the store again. By add-ing tags to products, you can make them appear in the various sections of the store.

When you create your own store, you can set up similar sections of the store and name them however you'd like. And you can click the Manage Tags button in the Tags window to create tags that correspond to each of the store sections.

If your clients would like to run their own store, you can train them how to use the Admin Console to add tags to the products they want to feature. This system offers a business complete control over the items displayed in the store and the ability to promote specific merchandise to increase sales.

Displaying multiple product images in the Detail view

Depending on the products sold in a store, it may be helpful to display more than one large image when a customer clicks on a product in a catalog to view the prod-uct's details. Customers may be more likely to purchase items if they can view both the back and front sides of an item. Providing close-up images can help customers decide which products to add to their cart.

If you want to use this feature, you'll need to prepare multiple image files for the product and upload them to the site using the File Manager, Dreamweaver, or a third-party FTP client. While you're editing the product details for a specific product, you can choose the option Add Poplet Images in the Action Box sidebar.

GROUPING PRODUCTS

Create groups of products to manage them as sets and make it easy for the business to sell related products. For example, imagine that the online store sells T-shirts. Each T-shirt is available in small, medium, and large sizes.

The system includes two ways you can handle product groups:

OPTION 1: GROUP PRODUCTS TOGETHER

This approach involves adding multiple products to the store and then grouping them together so that the set displays on the store page as one item. In this scenario, if the same T-shirt design is available in three sizes, the Admin Console contains three products so that each T-shirt (T-shirt - small, T-shirt - medium, T-shirt - large) represents a separate product in the store inventory.

The three different grouped products are displayed as one single item in the store, which is desirable because the product images look identical. When customers add a T-shirt to their cart and check out, they select the shirt size using a menu provided in the shopping cart.

Although this option is more labor intensive (more products are created in the database), the business can track the inventory of each size and use a different product SKU or item number to identify each shirt (small, medium, and large) because they are separate product records in the system.

To access this option, choose Group Products Together in the Action Box sidebar.

OPTION 2: CREATE ATTRIBUTE GROUPS

This approach can make it easier for businesses to work with products because they have fewer records to manage in the Admin Console.

In this scenario, the same T-shirt is available in three sizes (small, medium, and large) but the T-shirt product is only added to the products area of the Admin Console once. A single product record represents all three different sizes.

The business might find it easier to set up attributes (such as size) and then edit the list of their products to set the available size attributes to each shirt design.

Although this option is easier and faster to set up, the small, medium, and large T-shirts all reference the same record in the database. That way, all sizes use the same SKU or item number.

To access this option, choose Create Attribute Groups in the Action Box sidebar.

Familiarize yourself with these two methods of managing grouped products and assigning attributes. Use the option that works best for each client's inventory and store configuration. You can use both options in the same store, if desired, to manage different sets of products.

Use the resulting interface to browse and select the images that you want to present to customers in the Detail view of the product in the store. You can add up to 10 images for each product. Click Save to save the changes and click the X in the top-right corner to close the window.

When you switch to the other browser window and view the live site, you can click the product to see the product details. Notice that the system created thumbnail images below the Add To Cart area in the product's Detail view. Click any of the thumbnail images to see a lightbox image gallery dim the page temporarily and display the series of product images when you click the Next and Previous buttons. This functionality appears because the Poplets feature was added to the online store's layout file by inserting the tag {tag_poplets}.

Editing store layouts in Dreamweaver

In Chapter 4, you learned how to edit the module layout files to control the data that was displayed in both the List and Detail views of the FAQ module. You can use a similar workflow to make changes to the layout files for the online store. And just like the module layout files, you can edit the online store layout files in both the Admin Console and Dreamweaver.

1. In Dreamweaver, sync the entire site to get the newer remote files. This ensures that you are working with the latest version of the site files after editing them in the Admin Console.

2. Open the Business Catalyst panel. Make sure that the trial site is selected and that you're logged in.

3. Open the Files panel and click the Layouts folder to expand it. The layout files for the online store are located in the OnlineShop folder (FIGURE 6.21).

FIGURE 6.21
The layout files for the store are in the OnlineShop subfolder of the Layouts folder.

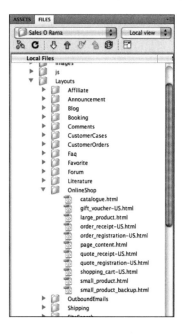

As mentioned previously, it's a best practice to create a local backup copy of the entire Layouts folder. That way, you can always swap out an edited layout file with the original version that matches the trial site—if you want the layout file to revert to the way it was originally and then start over.

To edit a layout file for the online store, double-click the layout file in the Online-Shop folder to open it in the Document window. Use the HTML editing tools to make design changes and add CSS styles. While a layout file is open, you can use the Tag Insert menu in the Business Catalyst panel to insert module tags into layout files to define the elements that you want to appear, the same way you added the Buy Now button to the List view of products.

The trial site layout files are already working well for this sample project, so there's no need to make any revisions. If you'd like to explore them later, you can open the layout files in Dreamweaver and make changes as desired. Remember to always upload (put) the files you change to the remote server in order to update the live site with your changes.

Adding a Product Search Form to the Store's Home Page

Although online stores created with the Business Catalyst Platform include a complex system of interconnected functionality, you'll work with the online store modules the same way you work with other modules. You can insert module functionality for online stores using both the Admin Console (the Module Manager and the 1-Click Insert menu) and Dreamweaver.

In this section, you'll update the online store's home page to add new store features within the Dreamweaver workspace.

1. In Dreamweaver, if you've made any changes in the Admin Console, synchronize the entire site to get the newer files from the remote server.

2. Open the Files panel and double-click the file named shop.htm to open it in the Document window.

   In Design view, locate the second section in the center column with the header named Special Offers. This area currently displays products tagged with the Special Offers keyword, but it essentially replicates the functionality of the In the Spotlight section above it.

   You'll replace the Special Offers section with a product search feature instead to make it easy for customers to enter keywords and find specific products in the store.

3. In Design view, select the existing module tag immediately below the Special Offers header:

   {module_productfeaturelist,special offers}

   Press the Delete key to remove the module tag.

   Leave your cursor in the location on the page where the Special Offers module tag was. This is the location where you'll insert the product search feature.

NOTE: The 11 layout files listed in the OnlineShop folder are the same 11 layout files that you access in the Admin Console when you choose Admin > More Customization Options and choose the Online Shop layouts. However, in some cases the files are named differently. For example, the file in the Admin Console named Overall Layout is named page_content.html in the OnlineShop folder.

4. In the Business Catalyst panel, click the Catalogs folder to expand it and see the list of online store modules (FIGURE 6.22).

FIGURE 6.22
Expand the Catalogs section of the Business Catalyst panel to add store modules to pages.

NOTE: The second module in the list, **Display List Of Products By Tag,** is the module used by the trial site to insert a list of products that are tagged with a specific keyword on the page. This is the functionality used by the trial site to display the In The Spotlight and Recommended sections of the store you worked with previously.

Double-click the module named Product Search. The Module Configure wizard appears. Click Insert to add the product search form to the page.

The form code for the product search is inserted on the page. The product search form includes its own header, but it doesn't fit the page design so you'll delete it.

5. In Design view, click the H3 header named PRODUCT SEARCH. In the Tag Selector at the bottom of the Document window, click the <h3> tag to select the entire header. Press the Delete key to delete the header that came with the product search form.

6. Also in Design view, select the H2 header above the form that currently says Special Offers.

Edit the Special Offers H2 header by typing **Product Search** (FIGURE 6.23).

The product search form includes several menus and a Keywords text field to help customers find the products they want to purchase. The Product Search header is now consistent with the other headers on the page. After a user submits the search form, the {module_productresults} tag displays the matching search results below the form. When configuring search functionality, remember that the tags that display search results should always be added to web pages or templates; the search results tag cannot be added to the layout files.

7. Choose File > Save and then File > Put to upload the changes you made to shop.htm to the remote server. In the Dependent Files dialog box that appears, click No.

FIGURE 6.23
Edit the shop.htm file to
change the Special Offers
header to Product Search.

If you switch to the browser window that displays the live site, you can refresh the online store home page by clicking the Shop menu item. When the store's home page reloads, you'll see that the Special Offers section is replaced with a product search form. Test the form by entering a search term in the field, such as **pencils**, and clicking the Search button. Products that match the search criteria are listed in the search results below.

Click around the pages of the store and notice that the product search form you added is only displayed on the store's home page rather than on every page of the store. It's an important distinction that when you want to add a feature to a single page of the store, you'll add it to a web page. When you want to add a feature to every page in a store, you'll add it to the module's layout file.

Setting Up Shipping Options

The configuration of the online store is nearly finished. There are just a couple of remaining items to set up before it's ready for customers. The remaining two tasks, creating shipping options and setting up payment gateways, can only be accomplished in the Admin Console.

In this section, you'll take a look at setting up the shipping options for the store.

1. In the Admin Console, choose eCommerce > Shipping Options to access the area where you can set up the shipping options that are available to customers in the shopping cart when they check out.

    Before you configure this area, meet with your client to get a better understanding of their business and the type of shipping services they will provide. There are two main ways you can set up shipping:

- User Defined: This option is good for small businesses that sell a single type of product that has a consistent weight and box dimension. For example, a site that sells earrings or T-shirts can predict the shipping costs associated with shipping these boxes and can charge a flat-fee rate, such as $5, for each shipment. Or you could set up several flat-fee rates—named standard, expedited, and rush—that allow the customer to choose the shipping option that corresponds to the price and delivery speed they prefer.

- Shipping Vendor Defined: This option works best for medium-sized businesses that sell a wide variety of items of different weights and sizes. In this scenario, the business creates an account with a third-party shipping vendor, such as FedEx, UPS, or USPS. The business enters their shipping account information into the site, and the details for each product include the item's weight and box dimensions. When customers choose the shipping option in the shopping cart during checkout, they are presented with all the available options and prices offered by the third-party vendor. This strategy has many benefits, because the pricing and shipping calculations are handled automatically; any future shipping rate increases are automatically applied. However, this method does require a bit more setup initially to ensure that every product includes the correct weight and dimensions (added to the fields in the Show More Options section of the Product Details page).

2. To set up a user-defined shipping flat fee, leave the Type menu set to User Defined. In the Description field, enter a name for the shipping method, such as Standard. In the Shipping Price field, enter a numeric value in the format 5.00 and click Save.

   The new a user-defined shipping fee, US - Standard ($5), is displayed in the Shipping Options list on the left side (FIGURE 6.24).

FIGURE 6.24
Enter the shipping details in the Shipping Options page.

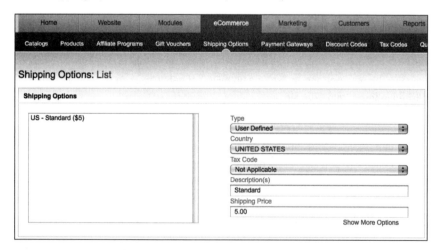

3. To set up a shipping vendor–defined method, use the Type menu to select the name of the shipping vendor, such as UPS. The form fields update to display the applicable codes, depending on the shipping vendor you select. (The information required varies based on the shipping vendor your client uses.)

   Use the provided fields to enter the shipping account information, including the account number, password, origin zip code, and any other required details (FIGURE 6.25).

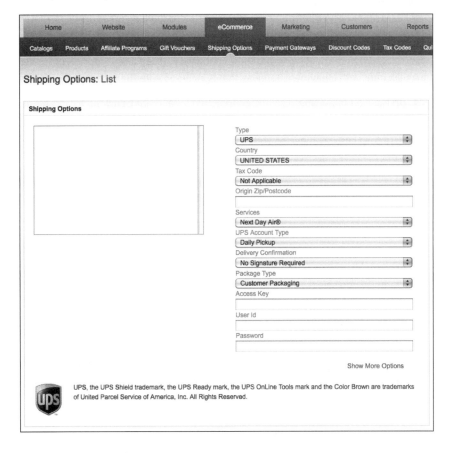

FIGURE 6.25
Enter your shipping vendor account information in the Shipping Options fields.

Click the Show More Options link to expand the fields. The new fields that appear include the fields to specify the item's maximum weight and box dimensions. These settings are used to compare the data in the Show More Options fields of the product being purchased during the checkout process. The shipping vendor populates the available shipping fees that will be charged in the shopping cart as a drop-down menu. Customers can choose from the available shipping options as they complete their transaction.

4. After entering the shipping information, scroll down and click Save.

Configuring Payment Gateways

Payment gateways are vendors that handle the processing of payment transactions whenever a customer completes a purchase in the online store. Payment gateways perform the critical job of receiving the payment based on the customer's credit card or PayPal information and transferring the funds to your client's account. Although you can also set up stores that process the transactions offline, this is a much more labor-intensive option for your clients because they have to manually process the credit cards themselves before shipping the items and fulfilling the order.

It's important to familiarize yourself with the supported payment gateways in Business Catalyst before meeting with clients. That way, you can direct your clients to set up an account with a payment gateway that is included with the system.

1. In the Admin Console, choose eCommerce > Payment Gateways to access the Payment Gateways List page.

2. Use the Gateway menu to view the list of available payment gateways you can set up. Make a note of this area and refer to it when your client asks if a particular payment gateway is supported.

3. Once your client creates an account with a payment gateway, they'll forward you the account details so that you can enter their account information into the system.

4. Use the Gateway menu to select the corresponding payment gateway. The form fields update to display the applicable fields, depending on the payment gateway you select. (The information required varies based on the payment gateway vendor.)

5. After entering the account information, scroll down and click Save.

Once a site's pages have been designed and the final version is approved, the site is almost ready for the general public. At that time, you'll upgrade the site and begin the monthly hosting fees. After upgrading a site, obtain your client's payment gateway account information and enter it into the Payment Gateway List page. At that time, before redelegating the domain name, you can perform tests on the live site to check that the store is processing transactions as expected.

After testing, update the domain name for the site and officially launch it. Be sure to also test the final configuration of the site by purchasing an item in the live online store to ensure that the checkout operation goes smoothly and the payments are transferred into your client's account.

SETTING UP PAYMENT GATEWAYS

There are a few important things to consider when configuring payment gateways:

- Make sure your client creates an account with a supported payment gateway.

- You cannot set up a test gateway or process transactions on the trial site. You must upgrade the site as a paid site (by entering a credit card account to pay the monthly hosting fees) before this option is enabled. To upgrade a site, view the site's details in the Clients tab of the Partner Portal and click Upgrade.

- Do not attempt to add a payment gateway to the trial site before upgrading it. The first attempt causes an error message to appear at the top of the Payment Gateways List page (FIGURE 6.26).

Subsequent visits to the Payment Gateway page do not display the error message, but if you ignore the message and attempt to add a payment gateway to the trial site, issues may occur that are difficult to resolve.

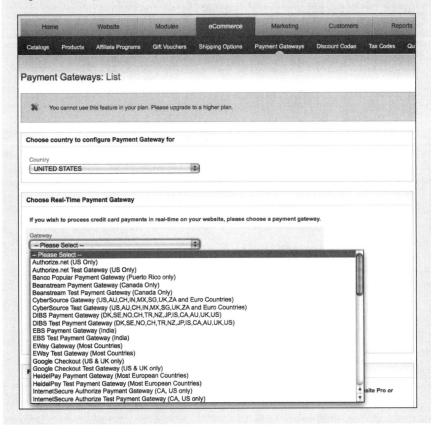

FIGURE 6.26
Set up the payment gateways for the site after upgrading it.

Working with the eCommerce Tools to Build Online Stores

It's a good idea to do some preplanning before creating catalogs and adding products to a store. You may find it helpful to map out the catalogs on paper and create lists of the products that you'll include in each department. You can group, tag, subdivide, or slice and dice the merchandise any way you like, but creating a game plan is helpful to ensure that the products are organized intuitively and the catalogs in the store are easy to navigate.

You may also find it useful to prepare the image files for the store and upload them in advance. That way, you can add images as you set up the catalogs and manage the products—although you can also update them at any time if you'd prefer to add images to the store later, once you've finalized the functionality.

Follow this workflow to set up a store in the Admin Console:

1. Build the catalogs to define the various sections of a store.
2. Import or manually add products to populate the catalogs with inventory.
3. Tag or group related items, or set up product attribute groups.
4. Design the appearance of the store by editing the layout files.
5. Set up the shipping options (unless the store only sells e-products).
6. Configure the currency and tax codes for the store's target markets.
7. Add discount codes and gift vouchers to facilitate online sales promotions.
8. Integrate the sales data with QuickBooks (if applicable).
9. Enable Affiliate Programs to cross-link with other sites and drive traffic.
10. Upgrade the site from a trial site to a paid site.
11. Gather your client's account information for their payment gateways and configure it in the system.
12. Test the live site to ensure that transactions are processed successfully.

Before configuring the online store, it's important to spend some time with your clients and interview them to understand the products or services that they're selling. Learn their preferred shipping methods and the currency they want to support. Work with them to set up accounts for one or more payment gateways, and discuss the shipping options involved when working with third-party shipping vendors. As you've seen in this chapter, the structure of the catalogs is completely flexible and there are many configuration options. Using your knowledge of the business, you can customize the appearance and behavior of the online store to maximize revenue and increase sales.

Related Links

 Setting Up the Online Store:
http://www.adobe.com/go/bc_setting_up_online_stores

 Build Amazing Online Stores:
http://www.adobe.com/go/bc_powerful_online_stores

 Importing eCommerce Data:
http://www.adobe.com/go/bc_import_products

 Setting Up Recurring Billing:
http://www.adobe.com/go/bc_recurring_billing

 Setting Up Shipping Options:
http://www.adobe.com/go/bc_shipping_options

 Setting Up Tax Codes:
http://www.adobe.com/go/bc_tax_codes

 Customizing Your Online Store Layouts:
http://www.adobe.com/go/bc_customize_layouts

 Managing Your Online Store via the Admin Console:
http://www.adobe.com/go/bc_manage_online_stores

CHAPTER 7

Understanding Customer Management and the Site's Database

Contents

Configuring Web Forms to Generate Cases	135
Updating the Steps in a Workflow	138
Working with Cases	139
Adding Notes and Tasks	142
Searching for Cases	144
Managing Approvals in Workflow Steps	146
Using Workflows to Facilitate Business Goals	148
Examining How Secure Zones Gather Data	148
Setting the Landing Page of a Secure Zone	152
Updating the Header to Add a Logout Link	154
Testing the Changes to the Site	155

Throughout this book you've explored the site as both the site developer (in the Admin Console) and the visitor (on the live site), but you haven't spent much time exploring how the site is managed by the business owner—your client—after you grant them access and train them how to work with the Admin Console.

At this point you've seen how to configure the main areas of the site. You know how to add and set up the site features using modules and how to build the online store and control the products that are displayed in catalogs.

In this chapter, you'll see how the features included in the Business Catalyst Platform support your client's business. You'll work with the data stored in the site's database to get a better understanding of how the business owners can access it to manage their customers. By interacting with the site as a business owner, you'll be able to convey these opportunities to your clients when you describe the site you are building for them.

You'll learn how to set up the features in the Admin Console as you build sites to leverage the data-gathering capabilities. In addition, you'll see how the site can be scaled as the business grows.

The data collected in the database after a site launch is critical to helping you and your clients understand the target audience for the site. By analyzing the data, you can learn their preferences and respond to them by fine-tuning the site.

In a typical non–Business Catalyst site, you (the developer) and your client (the business owner) use multiple systems to manage the site, update content, and run the business.

To manage a typical online store, a web developer might:

- Use an HTML editor to log in to the site and maintain it (using the hosting password)
- Use a third-party shopping cart service to manage products (using a separate password)
- Use a third-party blog system, such as WordPress, to post to the blog (using another password)

NOTE: In Chapter 11, "Upgrading Sites and Managing Domain Names," which is available for download from peachpit.com, we'll show you how to set up a user account to enable your clients to log in. You'll learn how to enable the features that you want clients to use—and more importantly, how to hide the features in the Admin Console that you don't want them to see or accidentally edit.

In this scenario, your client would send you e-mail messages or call you to:

- Request text changes to the site
- Send e-mail messages to newsletter recipients
- Update the products in the online store
- Add new pictures to photo galleries
- Run site analytic and shopping cart reports to identify traffic and sales statistics

In Business Catalyst, your clients can manage their own site and run their business from one centralized interface: the same Admin Console you're using to develop the site and add new features.

In this chapter, you'll learn how to work with cases to respond to customer inquiries. The case system enables online businesses to handle customer questions and set up customer support incidents in the system. Every form added to a site can be set up to create a case number, which displays a specific status until the case is resolved. Managers can see all the correspondence related to each customer inquiry. Team members can log in and set up tasks with reminders to ensure that customers are answered in a timely manner.

Configuring Web Forms to Generate Cases

In previous chapters, you learned how web forms gather and store customer data and then generate a customer case with a unique ID number. Every time a form is submitted, a new case is created (unless you disable the case option when building the form).

It's important to note that the same tracking system is in place for the online store. Every time a customer submits a purchase, an order is automatically generated with its own unique ID number. As with cases, you can track orders that are processed by the eCommerce system.

Because you can't test the order functionality until after you upgrade a site and set up a payment gateway, you'll explore how to work with customer cases instead. As you follow along with this chapter, remember that the system tracks and manages order data the same way it handles cases.

Understanding how case data is stored, accessed, and edited

In the trial site, visitors can use two web forms to contact the business directly:

- Contact Us Form
- Suggestion Box form

To better understand how cases work, you'll review how the forms are configured to collect data, trigger workflows, and generate cases.

1. In the Admin Console, choose Modules > Web Forms.
2. The list of existing web forms in the trial site is displayed. Click the Suggestion Box form link to access the Web Form creation page.
3. Directly below the form's header, use the Click To Edit link to access the Web Form details window.

These options include settings that control which workflow the form will use when the visitors submit data (FIGURE 7.1).

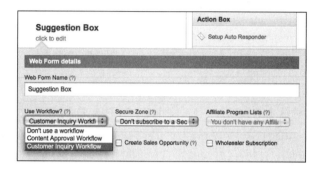

Now that you see how the form is connected to use a specific workflow, you'll identify where to control the steps that are included in the workflows attached to web forms.

1. In the upper-right corner of the window, choose Admin > Manage Workflows.

2. The list of existing workflows is displayed. Click the link to access the details for the Customer Inquiry workflow. On the Workflow Details page, click Next to see the list of workflow steps. Select the first workflow step: Notify via SMS.

This workflow currently includes two steps to notify the users in a specific role by sending both text messages and e-mail notifications (FIGURE 7.2).

Workflows: Customer Inquiry Workflow (Workflow ID: 10044)

Workflow Steps

Notify via SMS
Notify via Email

Task Name	Task Duration
Notify via SMS	N/A Minute(s)

Role Responsible	Remind Before Expiry
Administrators	N/A Minute(s)

Escalate To Role	Escalate After Expiry
-- Choose Role --	N/A Minute(s)

Notification Method	Must Approve?
SMS	

Also Send Workflow Notification To (separate by semi-colons)

Send Workflow Message to Customer

UNDERSTANDING USERS AND ROLES

At this time, the site only has a single user (you) and your user account is added to two roles: Administrators and Users. But imagine that after the site launches, there may be five or ten users who can log in to the Admin Console. These other users are the team members (your client and their employees) who run the business. You can set up any number of additional roles, and then add specific team members to roles so that they can be notified by the system at various times during a workflow's steps.

Using this functionality, various team members in each department can be assigned responsibilities. As the site gathers input from visitors, these "assignments" are doled out to the appropriate team member(s) and they are notified that they need to complete the current task.

The Customer Inquiry workflow is currently a simple notification mechanism that is triggered whenever visitors submit the form. At the moment, you are the only "team member" receiving these notifications, but you could easily create more user accounts (based on the site's hosting plan) after upgrading the site and add these team members to the roles that will also receive the notifications. Once everything is working as expected, you can remove the Administrator role from the existing workflow steps so that you no longer continue to receive the notifications.

Click each one of the workflow steps (Notify via SMS and Notify via Email) to see the step details. Take a few moments to review the other options that are available when configuring workflows:

- Duration specifies the length of time to complete a workflow step. Each step in a workflow can have its own duration setting.
- Reminders notify a team member to perform an activity before the specified duration has been reached.
- Escalations notify another role (the manager) if a workflow's step duration has elapsed and an activity has not been completed.
- Approvals are an optional setting that causes the workflow steps to pause until proceeding to the next step. If a workflow contains a series of steps and the option Must Approve is not enabled, all steps are processed simultaneously.

As you can see, the workflow system becomes very powerful when you use it to communicate with an entire team. Each department receives notifications, clicks the links in an e-mail, or logs in to the system after receiving a text message to see the newest data. After completing their tasks, they can update statuses and move the workflow to the next activity or mark it as closed so that everyone knows that the item has been completed.

You can create dependencies and set up a foolproof customer response system. If cases are not handled in a timely manner, they are automatically escalated to other team members.

Rather than a customer contacting a single employee by sending a message to their e-mail address, several members of the team are notified. This approach is helpful in situations where a team member is out of the office or unavailable. Workflow notifications ensure that a business can efficiently follow up on customer inquiries.

NOTE: If you haven't already done so, you may want to choose Home > My Details and enter your cell phone number now so that you can test the SMS text message features later. As of this writing, SMS notifications for trial sites are limited to 10 per month.

To further research how the system ties the workflows to roles, notice that the workflow steps currently list the role of the users who will be notified (Administrator) and the method of notification. In this section, you'll review how specific users in the system are added to roles.

1. Use the Admin menu again to choose Admin > Manage Users.

2. The list of users for the site is displayed. At this time, you are the only user in the system. Click the link to access the details for your user account.

3. Click Next to access the next page where you can see how the roles are assigned to the current user (FIGURE 7.3).

FIGURE 7.3
When you create a site, your account is automatically added to the Administrators and Users roles.

As you can see, the trial site comes preconfigured with two basic roles: Users and Administrators. Use this area to assign each user to additional roles (after you have created the roles in the Admin > Manage Roles area). Your user account is assigned to both of the roles so that as you test the site, workflow notifications sent to the Administrators role are sent to the contact information you entered for your user account.

NOTE: Do not remove either of these roles from your own user account! If you do, you'll be locked out of accessing your own site. The only way to regain access is to contact the Business Catalyst Support Team to have them resolve the issue for you.

Updating the Steps in a Workflow

Before testing the case system by submitting another form entry, you'll update the steps in the Customer Inquiry workflow to get a better understanding of how they work.

1. In the Admin Console, choose Admin > Manage Workflows.

2. The list of current workflows is displayed. Click the link to access the details for the Customer Inquiry workflow.

3. The first details page is displayed. Click Next.

The two steps currently added to the Customer Inquiry workflow are listed on the left side.

4. Select the first step: Notify Via SMS.

Enable the Must Approve option by selecting the checkbox.

5. Scroll down and click the Save Step button.

Working with Cases

In this section, you'll access the live site to submit a form with a workflow and see how the system creates cases and stores the data you enter in the fields.

1. Switch to a browser that displays the live trial site.

2. In the Our Company section of the footer, click the link to visit the Suggestion Box.

3. The Suggestion Box page loads. Complete the form's fields and click Submit (FIGURE 7.4).

4. Check your cell phone to see the SMS notification appear.

TIP: If you haven't added a valid cell phone number to your user account and you'd prefer to not test the SMS text message system, you can update this step to send an e-mail notification instead. The workflow will function the same way but will send you an e-mail message instead of a text message when the form is first submitted.

FIGURE 7.4
Enter placeholder text in the fields and submit the Suggestion Box form.

The text message you receive includes the name of the person (James Smith) who submitted the form and posted a suggestion to the suggestion box.

Notice that if you check your Inbox, you did not also receive an e-mail notification (as described in the second step of the workflow). That happens later, after the first workflow step's dependencies have been completed and the task has been approved.

Accessing cases in the Admin Console

To continue following the case in the system, you'll take a look at how the business team can use the Admin Console to track new inquiries as they're submitted.

At this point, a visitor has submitted a form (with a workflow applied) that triggered an SMS notification that the message was received. This SMS notification informs a team member that they need to take action by reviewing the case details and resolving the case that was created by the form.

1. Log in to the Admin Console.
2. The Dashboard is displayed. The Inquiries statistic indicates that new inquiries have been received. The Live Feed section includes links of the site's recent activity (FIGURE 7.5).

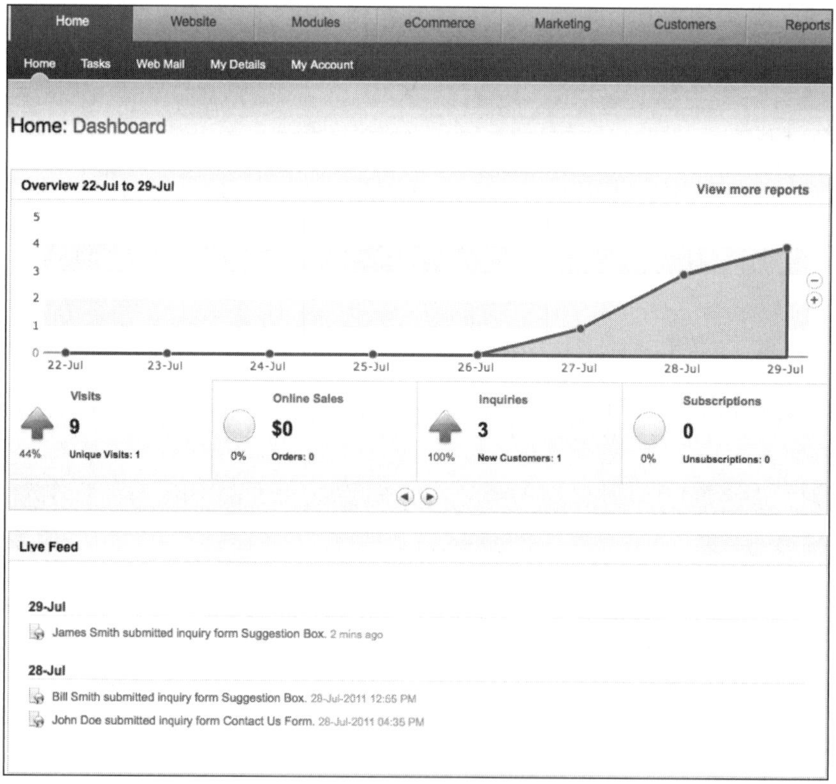

FIGURE 7.5
The Live Feed displays links with all the recent site activity.

3. Click the link that describes the recent submission to the Suggestion Box form. The Customer Summary page appears so that the team member can immediately see the details about the person who submitted the form.

   At the bottom of each customer record is a list of links (a mini–Live Feed) that display the activities performed by the current customer. Use this list of links to review the history of their interactions with the site. This list includes every form submission and purchase. When a site is active, you'll also see links that reference their comments, forum posts, bookings, and times they've logged in to a secure zone (password-protected area) of the site. This history archive enables you to better understand the visitors that frequent your site.

4. In the Action Box sidebar, click Customer Cases (FIGURE 7.6).

   The new case that was created when the Suggestion Box form was submitted is displayed. The case includes all the details that were entered in the Suggestion Box form. At the time the form was submitted, a notification (triggered by a workflow) was also sent to any team members (user accounts) who were added to the specified role. The team member can start tracking the customer interaction on this page.

5. Scroll down to the bottom of the Case page and click the Edit link at the bottom. The fields on the page become editable, making it easy to update the data stored in the case.

   For example, the team member can change the status to Open, which indicates to the other team members that the customer inquiry has not been resolved yet. Or they can set the status to Closed so that every team member who logs in (or runs a report) can see that no further action is needed to help this customer. The customer's question has been answered and the case is completed.

6. Use the Status menu to set the status to Open.

   Team members can use the Details field to enter details about the case so that the next person who accesses this record knows how this support incident was handled. If desired, they can also specify the team member who is responsible for finalizing the case so that the team can log in to the Admin Console to check the status of cases, rather than sending e-mail messages back and forth.

7. Type some placeholder text in the Details field (FIGURE 7.7).

8. Click Save & Finish. Scroll down to see that a thread summary has been created. If the bottom of the page doesn't update, refresh the page to see the updated thread summary.

FIGURE 7.6
Select the Customer Cases option in the Action Box sidebar.

 NOTE: Each time a form is submitted, the system evaluates the e-mail address field to look for matching records. If the visitor who submits the form has not previously interacted with the site, the system generates a brand-new customer record and uses their e-mail address as the unique identifier. If the visitor already has a matching record in the system, the data they entered in the form is added to their existing customer record.

FIGURE 7.7
Enter information about the
current case in the Details
field.

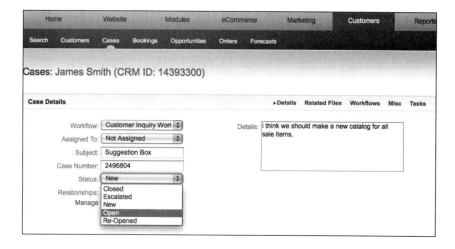

FIGURE 7.7
Enter information about the
current case in the Details
field.

The summary lists the entire history of the customer's interactions and the team's correspondence. The support activities are documented, making it easy for a team to work together as they respond to questions and provide customer support (**FIGURE 7.8**).

FIGURE 7.8
The Thread Summary displays
a log of all activity related to
the case.

Team members can also track important details about the customer in the Cases section of the Admin Console. In the next section, you'll see how to work with notes and tasks to organize the information related to each support incident and schedule reminders to ensure that customers are answered and issues are resolved in a timely manner.

Adding Notes and Tasks

To access the interface to add tasks and notes, hover over the Tasks link (**FIGURE 7.9**).

The pop-up window includes two options: Add A Note and Add A Task. The Notes feature enables you to add more information about a case. You can access the notes that are attached to a case whenever the Notes pane is open. You can insert information about your recent communication with the customer and include preferences, like documenting the best time or method to reach them. If you track details a customer mentions while on the phone, you can enter this information as a note alongside their case record. Doing so enables the business team to easily retrieve

FIGURE 7.9
Access Notes and Tasks by
clicking the Tasks link.

personal details—making customers feel as if they belong to an elite set of VIPs and that their feedback is valued (**FIGURE 7.10**).

Tasks are even more useful because they include additional features. For example, a team member can add a task to a case to make sure they follow up with the inquiry or support request.

You can see how this works by setting a task for the entry that was just submitted into the Suggestion Box form. Because the customer mentioned they would like a catalog, it is a good idea to set up a task to remind the team member to send an e-mail message to the customer who requested it (once the catalog is available).

Set up a task and enter a due date that is a few days from today's date. Then schedule a reminder a day prior to the due date so that the team member can prepare the catalog and begin composing the e-mail message to the customer (**FIGURE 7.11**).

Tasks are helpful because they alert team members when a deadline is approaching. In addition to sending an e-mail reminder, upcoming tasks are displayed in the Dashboard of the Admin Console (**FIGURE 7.12**).

Whenever a team member logs in to the Admin Console, they'll immediately see the list of tasks. They can click the link to jump right to the task details and complete the goal. This is a great way to ensure that nothing slips through the cracks.

FIGURE 7.10
Enter data you want to store with the case in the Notes field.

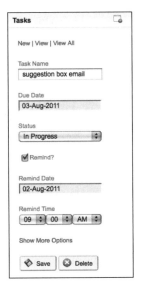

FIGURE 7.11
Use the Tasks window to schedule task deadlines and set reminders.

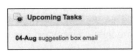

FIGURE 7.12
A list of upcoming tasks is displayed in the Dashboard.

ADDING NOTES AND TASKS TO CONTACT RECORDS AND ORDERS

You can also add notes and tasks to customer records. Choose Customers > Search to locate a customer's record. Click the View link to access the Contact Details. Alternatively, click a link in the Live Feed to visit the Customer Summary page and then click the option Work With Customer Details in the Action Box sidebar to access their Contact Details and set them up.

On the Contact Details page, hover over the Tasks link and you'll see the same interface appear in the top-right area of the page.

By adding notes and tasks here, team members can track general details that are related to the customer, rather than to a specific case. Notes added to the Customer Details page are summarized on the page along with each customer's record, and tasks are displayed just like the case tasks: with links in the sidebar of the Dashboard.

You can also add notes and tasks to orders while editing an Order Details page.

Searching for Cases

As you've been following along with the instructions in this chapter, you created a customer case by submitting a form. Then, you logged in to the Admin Console immediately afterward and clicked the link in the Live Feed to access the case information and see the message that the visitor submitted on the site.

But consider that most business teams are not logged in to the Admin Console all day and a site can receive a great deal of traffic. The Live Feed links are displayed chronologically with the most recent activities listed at the top of the list. Over time, the list of items in the Live Feed is rotated and the older activities are no longer displayed.

Next, you'll explore other methods your clients can use to find cases stored in the site's database.

1. In the Admin Console, choose Customers > Cases.
2. The Customers Search page is displayed. Use the filter menus to search for cases by selecting the name of the team member the case is assigned to, the date range when the case was submitted, the case's status, and the web form used to generate the case.

Team members will find this strategy helpful for obtaining a list of all cases submitted within a specific time duration, to find all cases submitted last week, last month, or last year. Once you display a list of cases, you can sort the list by status or assignments (FIGURE 7.13).

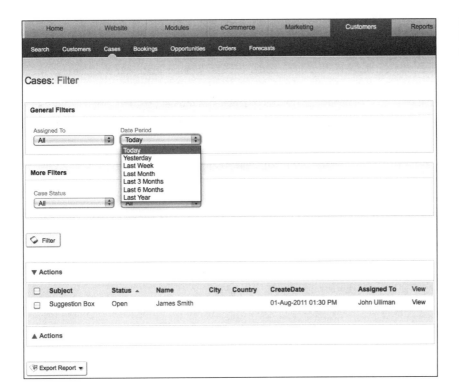

FIGURE 7.13
Use the Filter menus to locate a specific case in the database.

Managers can filter cases to review recent site activity and read the feedback posted by visitors to track business trends. They can also use this data to verify that team members are doing a good job of responding to customer inquiries and fulfilling orders.

Your clients can use the following ways to locate cases and orders in the system:

- Using the Live Feed
- Choosing Customers > Cases and filtering the list of cases
- Choosing Customers > Search and searching for cases
- While on the Contacts page, clicking Customer Cases in the Action Box sidebar
- Clicking a link in an e-mail of a workflow notification

NOTE: The same features described here also apply to orders generated after a customer purchases an item in the online store. After upgrading a site and setting up a payment gateway, you can process some test transactions to create orders and see that they work the same way in the system.

Managing Approvals in Workflow Steps

When you pitch the Business Catalyst Platform to potential clients, you can show them the database features they can use to run their business with the Admin Console. The data-gathering forms, notification messages, and easy-to-access customer data all facilitate business processes. In the next section, you'll explore another benefit of using customized workflows: using the approval mechanism to create dependencies in workflow steps.

You'll learn how to take customer management a step further by setting up a chain of events that ensure each task is completed from inception until the customer interaction is complete. This technique involves using the Needs Approval feature that you enabled in the Customer Inquiry workflow when you edited the workflow steps earlier in this chapter.

1. In the Admin Console, click the link in the Live Feed on the Dashboard to view the Summary page for the Suggestion Box form submission. In the Action Box sidebar, click the Customer Cases option.

2. The list of cases triggered by that customer is displayed. Click the top link to visit the most recent case that was created when the customer submitted the Suggestion Box form.

3. The Case Details page appears. Click the Workflows link to view the workflow details associated with this case.

   The Customer Inquiry workflow that you set up previously to send the SMS text message is displayed. When you edited the workflow steps earlier in this chapter, you enabled the Must Approve option. Consequently, the Case Details page displays the Approve Task button (FIGURE 7.14).

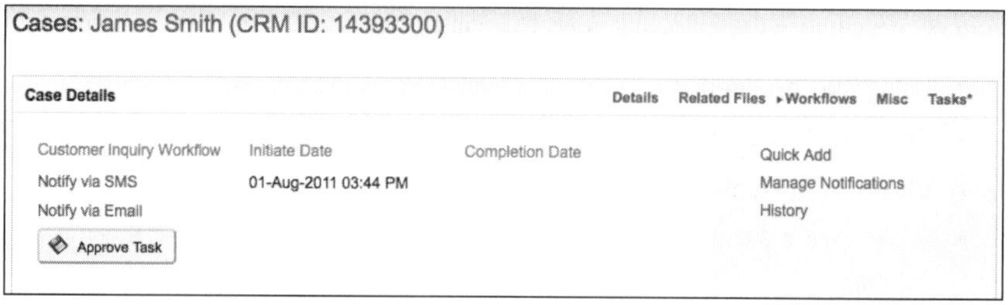

FIGURE 7.14
The workflow applied to the case is displayed in the Case Details page.

The workflow is working as expected because previously it sent an SMS notification as you configured it. In the Case Details page, the Approve Task button enables team members to approve the task after they've completed it.

It's important to note that the Approve Task button will only be displayed to the logged-in users who have been added to the role specified in the workflow. In this example, your user account is added to the Administrators role specified in the workflow steps, which is why you see the Approve Task button appear.

In a real-world site, you can set up roles for any number of team departments, such as customer service, order processing, shipping, and managers. That way, the workflow steps you configure can specifically notify team members who fulfill various activities in the system. The users who correspond to approving a task in a workflow are the only users who see the Approve Task button.

4. Because your user account has the necessary permissions to confirm that this case has been handled and the task is complete, click the Approve Task button. Then, click the next button that is displayed: Initiate Workflow. By clicking the second button, you are allowing the workflow to proceed to the next step.

5. Check your Inbox. Once the task was approved for the first step, the workflow continued to the second step in the series and sent you an e-mail notification.

Although SMS text messages are great for contacting team members immediately, e-mail notifications are especially useful because they contain a link in the message. By clicking the link in the notification message, you can jump directly to the case in the Admin Console and manage it (FIGURE 7.15).

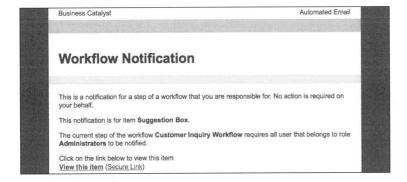

FIGURE 7.15
Your clients can use workflow notification messages to manage cases.

Workflows are extremely powerful when you configure a series of dependent steps and set up roles for various departments in a business. Each team member receives notifications, completes their assignments, and then approves the task to move the workflow to the next step. As a workflow proceeds from the initial creation of a case or order all the way to completion, the Admin Console tracks its progress and displays the current status. Teams work more efficiently because each team member receives and processes their task. By clicking the Approve Task and Initiate Workflow buttons, they trigger the subsequent workflow step, which contacts the next team member in the series. Reminders and escalations ensure tasks are completed on time and in the right order.

By customizing workflows and connecting user roles to assignments, you can create a robust system that streamlines the way your clients run their businesses.

Using Workflows to Facilitate Business Goals

Now that you have a better understanding of how you can set up complex workflows with multiple steps, take a moment to envision the ways you could configure them to meet the business needs of your clients. The workflow steps you set up are followed in the order they are listed from top to bottom.

For example, if the business offers customer service and guarantees an answer within 24 hours of receiving an inquiry, you could create a workflow that helps achieve that goal.

Create a workflow called customer support and set the 24-hour time limit first. Then add earlier, periodic reminders to help team members respond to the inquiry quickly. Set up an escalation step that sends a notification to a manager role if the deadline is approaching and the status of the case if not yet closed. You could also choose to send a workflow message to the customer during the tech support process to notify them that a team member will be contacting them soon.

> **NOTE:** You can attach workflows to orders, cases, bookings, and content changes. You can use the included Content Approval workflow in situations when the content of the live site changes due to a visitor submitting a forum post or comment. Using this approach, you can assign a team member the responsibility of reviewing and approving each change before allowing the post to appear on the live site. This is a helpful strategy to eliminate spam.

In a different scenario, you could create a workflow for a larger business to process orders. The workflow could be named order processing and can be applied to the checkout form so that it's triggered every time a customer makes a purchase in the online store. The first workflow step would notify the inventory department to gather the merchandise from the warehouse and box it up. After someone in the inventory department clicks the Approve Task and Initiate Workflow buttons, the workflow continues to the next step, which sends a notification to the shipping department to let them know the box is packaged and waiting for shipment. After the shipping department approves the task as completed, the workflow notifies the accounting department so that they can update their records. Simultaneously, the workflow sends an e-mail message to the customer letting them know that their order has shipped.

Examining How Secure Zones Gather Data

The Business Catalyst Platform is built on a central database that connects to the site to track all the data entered in forms, purchases, and other site activities. To gain a clearer understanding of what the target audience wants, it is helpful to gather as much data as possible. The more data, the easier it is to implement successful marketing strategies and add features to the site that generate the most revenue and impact.

It's important to consider the goal of gathering more data as you design new features for your clients' sites. Use the existing statistics to learn which areas of the site get the most traffic and discover which products are best sellers in the store. Everything you can do to maximize a business's understanding of their customers (especially focusing on the customers who make repeat purchases) helps that business grow.

To facilitate more data collection, you can set up secure zones. Secure zones are password-protected areas of the site that require a visitor to register and then enter their username and password to log in. Once visitors sign in, the system is able to capture much more data about their activities on a site because they've identified themselves during the login process.

The trial site already contains a secure zone, so take a moment to explore how to register and log in from the visitor's point of view.

Understanding secure zones

There are several components on a website that make up a secure zone:

- A registration form (to enable visitors to create a profile online)
- A login form (to enable registered visitors to log in to the site)
- A secure zone landing page (a page that loads after logging in)

The trial site contains all three of these pieces, so you can test how it works:

1. Switch to the browser that displays the trial site.

   In the top-left corner of the header, there's a menu that contains the following options:

   - Log In
   - Create A New Profile
   - View Orders

   These links are inserted using the Dynamic Menu module.

   Notice that the links are duplicated in the footer of the site. You can click the link to view orders in the Orders & Payments section. Or you can log in and create a new profile in the Profile section of the footer (FIGURE 7.16).

2. Click the Login link to visit the site's Login page.

   This page contains a form on the left for existing registered visitors to sign in by entering their username and password. On the right side, they can retrieve a lost password by entering their username or e-mail address in the provided field.

   Although this Login page does not include one, it's a good idea to add a link on the Login page to the Registration page. Make it as easy as possible for new visitors to create a profile and log in.

   At the moment, the secure zone on the trial site currently only contains one page: Orders. This page displays the order history to the registered visitors once they log in. It is the landing page for the secure zone.

3. Click the View Your Orders link in the footer to visit the Orders page.

   The page loads, but it displays a message stating that you are not currently logged in. Only registered visitors can log in to see the list of their previous orders in the system.

FIGURE 7.16
Click the Login link in the footer to visit the Login page.

Creating a new profile

In this section, you use the Register page to submit the form and register to access the secure zone.

1. In the footer, click the link in the Profile section to create a new profile.

   The Register page loads. Review the current registration form. The sample trial site template's form highlights mistakes you should avoid when building your own sites. Avoid requiring too much information—especially home addresses. Also, clearly indicate which fields are required. (Every field in the registration form is required, although some asterisk indicators have been hidden using styles, making the form more difficult for visitors to fill out.) Even if you check the Use Home Address For Shipping option in the form, it is still necessary to fill out the form fields for both the Home and Shipping addresses in order to successfully submit the form.

   If you'd like, you can practice the steps outlined in Chapter 5, "Building Web Forms to Gather Visitor Data," to create a brand-new form. In the Web Form Details section of the new form, set the Secure Zone menu to Members Only Area to connect the new form to the existing trial site's secure zone. Then, edit the Register page to delete the old form and replace it with the new registration form.

   Follow these steps to create a new profile and register a new account so that you can log in to the secure zone.

2. Enter placeholder data in every field of the form and submit the form. Make a note of the username and password you enter so that you can log in to the site again later.

   Notice that form validation causes errors to display if you do not enter data in every required field.

3. After creating a new profile, the page redirects to the Orders page. As you'll recall, the Orders page is the landing page of the secure zone. When you see this page load, it means that you have successfully logged in to the secure zone.

   The Orders page states that you have not placed any orders, which is correct. The online store can't process orders until it has been upgraded and a payment gateway has been set up.

   But the Orders page is a bit underwhelming. When you create your own sites, you can create a home page for the secure zone that welcomes registered visitors to the secure area with links to premium content.

The trial site also doesn't include a logout button yet—so in the next section, you'll set up a few things in the Admin Console to provide a better experience for registered visitors.

BEST PRACTICES WHEN CREATING REGISTRATION FORMS

As mentioned earlier, one of the site's primary goals is to encourage visitors to register so that more site data can be collected in the database. The registration process should be as seamless as possible so that visitors can sign up quickly and easily.

Registration forms only need the following required fields:

- E-mail address
- Username
- Password

When you create registration forms for your site, you can add extra fields if you'd like to invite visitors to provide additional information (such as their birth date, astrological sign, or favorite hobby). Keep the form short, or it will seem too difficult to fill out. And always set these extra fields as Optional.

If you ask for too much information and set all the fields in the form as required, visitors may decide not to register or enter placeholder data because they may not want to submit all their personal data (such as their home address) when registering for the first time.

Later, when customers make a purchase, you can gather information such as their home address and phone numbers, which is added to their existing contact record. Customers understand why you are requiring their home address at the time of a purchase and they'll be happy to provide it then.

Experiment with offering incentives to register, such as access to free download files, a private forum, premium articles by guest authors, or other online promotions. List the incentives on both the Home and Registration pages. These promotions encourage more visitors to sign in to the site.

Setting the Landing Page of a Secure Zone

In this section, you'll learn how to access the secure zone in the Admin Console and specify which page loads after visitors have successfully logged in.

1. Switch to the browser window that contains the Admin Console and log in.

   The Dashboard loads and the Live Feed section displays links to the recent site activity (FIGURE 7.17).

FIGURE 7.17
The Live Feed displays the recent secure zone and registration activity.

After interacting with the site, the database has gathered data about a Registration form submission and recorded the activity when the visitor logged in to the secure zone (named Members Only Area). By creating a single profile, you can already see more information appearing in the site's Live Feed links.

2. Choose Website > Secure Zones to access the list of existing secure zones.

   At the moment, the site only contains one secure zone named Members Only Area. However, you can set up as many secure zones as you'd like for a site.

3. Click the link to see the details for the Members Only Area secure zone.

   The Secure Zone Details page appears. The Landing Page menu is set to display the Orders page. This menu enables you to choose any page in the site as the first page presented to registered visitors when they log in (FIGURE 7.18).

FIGURE 7.18
The Secure Zone Details page includes a menu to set the landing page.

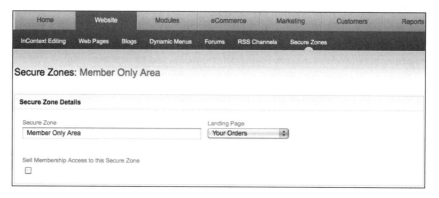

4. Click the Next button to visit the next page of the Secure Zones section.

   This interface enables you to specify the site content included in the password-protected area. The left side lists every page in the trial site. Any pages you move to the right side are automatically added to the secure zone.

   Currently, only the Orders page is included in the secure zone.

5. Use the menu above the list of pages to choose Forums. There's only one forum created for the Trial site, and it's named Forum.

Select the Forum page in the left pane and click the top right-pointing arrow to move it to the right pane. This operation moves it inside the secure zone (FIGURE 7.19).

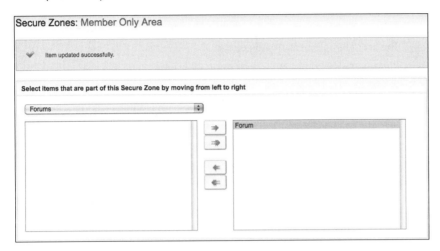

FIGURE 7.19
Add the forum to the secure zone by moving it to the list on the right side.

Next, you'll update the site to add a feature to enable registered visitors to log out of the site.

CUSTOMIZING A LANDING PAGE FOR A SECURE ZONE

When you build your own sites, you can make a special landing page for each secure zone.

For example, you could create a new page for the Members Only Area secure zone. The page could include a welcome message and links to VIP member benefits like file downloads (using Literature modules) or private forums. You could also display a promo code that offers customers discounts when they shop in the online store.

If desired, you can use the Dynamic Menu system to create a navigation bar specifically for navigating the secure zone pages. You could also design a special version of the template to apply to pages that are included in the secure zone to highlight that it is different from the main site.

By conveying a sense of exclusivity, you are thanking visitors for taking the time to register to the site. It's easy and inexpensive to create incentives that encourage registered visitors to log back in. Consider offering rewards, contests, and promotions, as well as personalization features (such as enabling visitors to upload a unique image as their avatar or referring to them by their username).

Updating the Header to Add a Logout Link

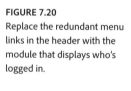

NOTE: You could update the header to add the module using either Dreamweaver or the Admin Console. Because you're already working in the Admin Console, you'll continue to update the site here.

In this section, you'll add a new functionality to the header of the trial site. Currently the top-left corner of the header contains links that are duplicated in the footer area of the site. You'll replace that duplicate navigation with a module that displays the name of the currently logged-in user and a link to log out.

1. In the Admin Console, choose Admin > Manage Site Wide Templates.

   The list of templates is displayed.

2. Click the link to access the details for the main template.

   The Templates Details page appears. The module tag that displays the Dynamic menu in the header is displayed at the top of the template. It looks like this:

   {module_menu,1199503}

3. In the online editor, select the module tag and press Delete to remove it. Leave your cursor in that location so that you can insert a new module tag to replace it.

4. Click the blue plus icon in the toolbar of the online editor to open the Module Manager. Click the Secure Zones category to expand it and see the available suboptions. Select Display Who Is Logged In.

5. The Module Manager updates. Click the Insert button to insert the new module tag (FIGURE 7.20).

   The new module looks like this:

   {module_whosloggedin}

6. Scroll down and click Save And Publish to push the changes to the live site.

FIGURE 7.20
Replace the redundant menu links in the header with the module that displays who's logged in.

Testing the Changes to the Site

After updating the site, you'll view it in a browser to see how the changes you made in the Admin Console affect the visitor's experience.

1. Switch back to the browser that displays the trial site and refresh the Home page.

   Because you logged in before (and there was no way to log out), the user profile you created should still be logged in.

   When you reload the page, you'll see that the Who's Logged In module displays the current username in the top-left header area, and it includes a logout button as well.

   Next, explore how the changes have affected the live site.

2. Click the Log Out button to log out of the site.

3. Click the Forums menu item to access the Forum page. Since you moved the Forum Home page to the secure zone, it now presents an error message that you have to be logged in to see the page, if you are not already logged in.

4. Enter the username and password that you used before you log in to the site.

   Once you have successfully logged in, the Who's Logged In module in the header updates again to indicate that you are logged in.

5. Click the Forums menu item again to access the forums. This time, the forum page is displayed because you are logged in to the secure zone.

Secure zones offer online businesses new opportunities to reward their best customers. By setting up exclusive password-protected areas, you can foster online communities and greatly improve the site's ability to gather data in the database. Using this information, you can communicate with visitors more effectively and improve customer relationships.

Related Links

 Setting Up Workflows:
http://www.adobe.com/go/bc_workflows

 Setting Up a Secure Customer Service Zone:
http://www.adobe.com/go/bc_customer_service_zones

 Importing Customer Data:
http://www.adobe.com/go/bc_import_customers

 Tracking Customer Data:
http://www.adobe.com/go/bc_track_data

CHAPTER 8

Marketing with E-mail Campaigns

Contents

Examining the Newsletter Signup Form on the Trial Site	159
Working with Subscribers and Recipient Lists	160
Creating and Inserting Subscription Forms	165
Editing Web Forms to Add an Option to Subscribe to a Newsletter	166
Creating and Sending E-mail Campaigns	168
Tracking E-mail Campaign Statistics	175
Creating a Recipient List to Target a Segment of the Customer Database	177

In this chapter, you'll learn how to use the integrated marketing tools to send newsletters and e-mail messages to subscribers and customers. Your clients can use e-mail campaigns to promote their business and offer discounts in the online store.

Once a site has been upgraded and the payment gateway has been configured, the online store can begin selling products and processing transactions. At that point, you can help your clients evaluate the data collected by the site and send e-mail messages to customers by using the contact records stored in the database.

Begin by meeting with your client to learn about their marketing strategies and define the types of promotions and messaging they want to send to their existing and potential customers. When you're first setting up a site, you can help guide them through the process of sending e-mail campaigns. Once business owners are more familiar with how it works, clients may optionally choose to begin managing e-mail campaigns themselves (if you grant them access to the e-mail campaign features in the Admin Console).

Once the site is upgraded, they can send campaigns to large lists of recipients. For example, as of this writing, your clients can send 10,000 e-mails a month with a standard Pro account.

E-mail campaigns work like other areas of the Business Catalyst system. Your clients can access the central database to find customer records, cases, orders, and site statistics to learn how to best segment sets of customers and send them targeted promotions and marketing messages.

Using the e-mail campaign functionality provided by the Business Catalyst Platform, you can choose to design custom newsletter templates or use the included e-mail templates and add trackable links to the messages.

The publishing tool makes it possible to schedule e-mail campaigns to send the messages on a specific date or send them as soon as they are ready. You can set up e-mail campaigns in advance to promote upcoming events or product launches. The system handles the management of recipient lists so that visitors can sign up to receive newsletters online. You can also enter subscribers manually or import a batch of contact data using a spreadsheet.

After sending a campaign, the system tracks all the interaction information in the site's database. View the overall performance statistics in the summary of each e-mail campaign, or drill down to see precisely which recipients opened and clicked the links in the newsletters. This information is extremely helpful because the business can learn which messages are most successful and fine-tune the content of future e-mail campaigns to improve their performance.

Examining the Newsletter Signup Form on the Trial Site

In this section, you'll explore the site as a visitor to see how new subscribers can sign up to receive a newsletter online.

1. Open a browser window and visit the trial site.

   The Home page of the trial site includes a Newsletter Signup form that invites visitors to enter their contact details and subscribe to a newsletter (FIGURE 8.1).

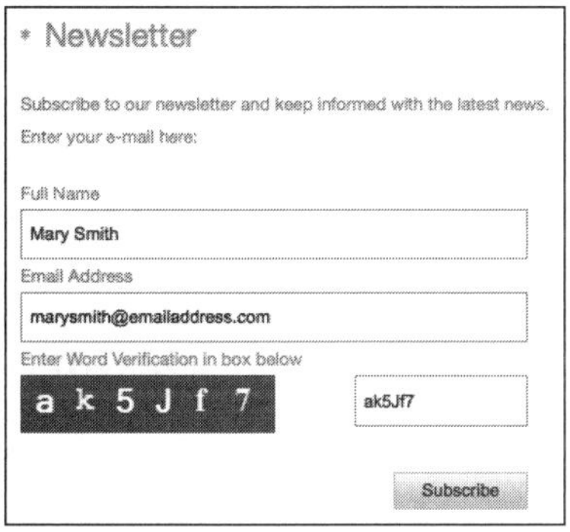

FIGURE 8.1
Visitors can sign up online to receive newsletters.

   If desired, you can add messaging on the Home page that describes the newsletter and its contents, such as promoting upcoming events or news about a specific product.

   Like secure zones, newsletter subscriptions are a great way to gather new contacts in the site's database—so it's important to encourage visitors to sign up. Once you've populated a recipient list with a set of subscribers, you can evaluate the activity of potential customers to learn more about them. By analyzing the visitors who show interest, you can determine how to best market to them. For example, you can offer them special discounts in the online store and send them promo codes they can enter during the checkout process. You can also send product announcements when new merchandise becomes available.

2. Enter placeholder data in the fields of the subscription form and submit it. To test the e-mail publishing system later, be sure to use a valid e-mail address.

   By submitting the Newsletter Signup form, you've automatically added a new subscriber to the monthly newsletter's recipient list. The system displays a confirmation message indicating your request to subscribe was successful. If desired, you can customize the system messages displayed by choosing Admin > Customize System Messages in the Admin Console.

3. Check your Inbox to see an e-mail message verifying your subscription. Click the link in the message to opt-in to receive future e-mail campaigns.

FIGURE 8.2
The Dashboard statistics panel displays the new subscription activity.

FIGURE 8.3
The subscription is listed in the Live Feed.

Working with Subscribers and Recipient Lists

Now that you've reviewed the Newsletter Signup form used to gather new subscribers online, you'll log in to the Admin Console to learn how the system captures the visitor's subscription data and makes it easy to access.

1. Switch to another browser window and log in to the Admin Console.

2. The Dashboard is displayed. Notice that the statistics for Subscriptions updates to reflect the recent subscription (FIGURE 8.2).

   Scroll down to see that the Live Feed displays a link describing the subscription (FIGURE 8.3).

When you create newsletters and prepare them for publication, you'll use the Marketing area of the interface.

3. Choose Marketing > E-mail Campaigns to see the list of existing e-mail campaigns.

Use the e-mail marketing tools to create new e-mail campaigns in the system. You can design the newsletters using the online editor or use Dreamweaver to design the HTML files. When campaigns are ready to be sent (after testing e-mail messages), use this area to publish campaigns and send the messages to subscribers.

You'll explore the steps of creating and publishing an e-mail campaign later in this chapter.

Manually adding new recipients to lists with the Quick Subscribe form

Next, you'll learn how to manually add new contact data to an existing recipient list. In addition to configuring the site to enable visitors to subscribe to newsletters online, you and your clients can use the Admin Console to manually add recipient contact data to a list.

For example, perhaps your client attended a trade show and encouraged attendees to write their name on a clipboard or leave their business card in a jar to receive future e-mail notifications about upcoming products, events, or services. In this scenario, they could log in to the Admin Console and manually enter the contact information to populate the list by typing the data into the List Subscribers window.

It's important to tell your clients to only add the contact information of customers who indicated that they want to receive messages from the business. If they add unknown people's contact information, the recipients may perceive the messages as spam, which can hurt the business rather than helping it.

1. In the Admin Console, choose Marketing > Lists.

   The existing recipient lists are displayed. These lists contain the contact information for subscribers who have signed up to receive the e-mail campaigns sent by the business. Use this area to manage the lists of recipients who will receive the newsletters by adding and deleting new contacts.

   The trial site currently includes one recipient list: Monthly Newsletter. The Monthly Newsletter list is connected to the Newsletter Signup form displayed on the trial site's Home page.

2. Click the Monthly Newsletter link to view the List Details page. The name of the recipient list is displayed.

3. Click Subscribers in the Action Box sidebar.

   The List Subscribers window appears, displaying the test subscriber that you created when you submitted the Newsletter Signup form on the trial site. Once a visitor submits the form on the site, they're automatically added to the list of subscribers (FIGURE 8.4).

NOTE: As you follow along with these steps, populate the list with a few additional recipients (using valid e-mail addresses, if possible) so that you can test the e-mail marketing publishing and reporting features described later in this chapter.

List Subscribers

This is the list of customers currently subscribed to this item. You can easily add or remove subscribers to this item. Alternatively you can view any customer's record and centrally manage their subscriptions to the various aspects of your website.

Full Name	Email Address	Opt-In Status	Subscribe Date	View	Remove
Mary Smith	marysmith@emailaddress.com	☐	04-Aug-2011	View	Remove

|◁ ◁ 1 ▷ ▷| Page size: 20 ▼   Displaying page 1 of 1, items 1 to 1 of 1

FIGURE 8.4
The list of subscribers is displayed.

If the recipient hasn't verified their subscription by clicking the link in the verification e-mail message, the Opt-in Status checkbox is not enabled.

4. Scroll down to the Quick Subscribe section and enter a placeholder name in the Full Name field and enter a valid e-mail address in the Email Address Field. Click Subscribe (FIGURE 8.5).

   When you manually add subscribers using the Quick Subscribe feature, the system evaluates each address added in the Email Address field. If a matching e-mail address exists in the database, the customer record is updated to add the existing customer to the list (rather than creating a duplicate). If the system doesn't find a matching e-mail address, it will generate a new customer record in the database automatically.

FIGURE 8.5
Use the Quick Subscribe form to add new recipients to a list.

IMPORTING NEW RECIPIENTS WITH A SPREADSHEET

If you need to enter a significant amount of contact data into the system at once, you can import a spreadsheet of contact data.

1. In the Admin Console, choose Marketing > Lists. The Lists page appears.

2. In the Action Box sidebar, click the option Create A New List.

3. The New List page appears. Enter the list name in the Name field and click Save.

4. In the sidebar, click Step 3: Import Recipient's List.

5. Click the Download Import Template File link and save the XLS file to your machine.

6. Use Microsoft Excel to prepare the import file and add the new contact data.

7. Export the spreadsheet from Excel as either a comma- or a tab-delimited file.

8. Click the Browse button and select the exported file. Choose the matching file type.

9. Click Import (FIGURE 8.6).

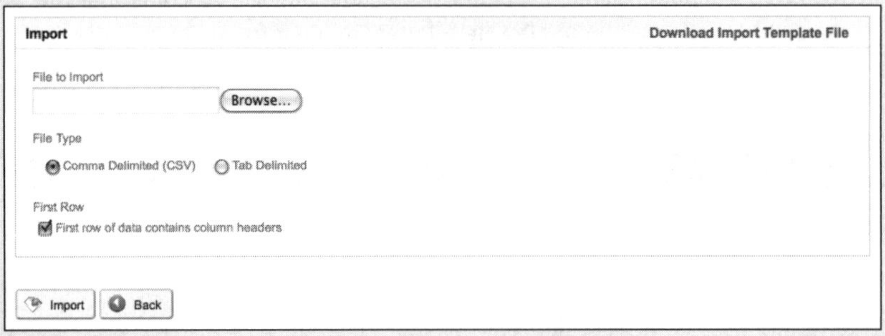

FIGURE 8.6
Select the import file on your hard drive and import the contact data.

This strategy is helpful when a business collects contact data in person or if the business has a set of existing contact data they exported from another system. Use batch importing to add a large quantity of new subscribers to the customer database quickly.

Subscribing existing customers to a recipient list

In the previous section, you used the Quick Subscribe form to manually enter the name and e-mail addresses to add several more new subscribers to a recipient list. Now you'll learn how to access a specific customer's record in the database and sign them up to receive e-mail messages from the business.

This is helpful in the situation where you're interacting with a customer offline (in a brick-and-mortar store) or outside the site (e-mail or phone conversation) and the existing customer mentions verbally that they'd like to be added to the site's newsletter mailing list.

Rather than telling the customer to visit the site and subscribe using the newsletter subscription form, you can manage the subscription process for them by accessing their contact data in the site's database. You can also use this strategy to remove existing subscribers from a recipient list.

1. In the Admin Console, choose from one of these four options:

   - Choose Customers > Search. Enter the customer's name and search for the record in the Customers database.

   - Choose Customers > Customers. Use the filter menus to find a specific customer record.

   - Choose Customers > Cases. Use the filter menus to find a specific case record. In the Case Details page, click the option Work With Customer Details in the Action Box sidebar.

   - Click a link in the Live Feed to access a customer's record.

2. Once you access the Customer Summary page, click the Manage Customer Subscriptions option in the Action Box sidebar.

   The Customer Details page for the selected customer is displayed. You can use the options on this page to manually subscribe or unsubscribe a customer to any of the site's campaign lists or grant them access to log in to secure zones. You can also manage other customer programs, such as enabling the customer to purchase products in the online store as a wholesaler, providing them with discounts to catalogs, or enrolling them in affiliate programs.

3. In the Campaign List Subscriptions section, click the Edit button. The list of e-mail campaigns is displayed.

4. Click the checkbox next to the Monthly Newsletter campaign and click the Save & Finish button.

NOTE: To follow along, click one of the form submission links listed in the Live Feed to view the Customer Summary page for an existing customer in the database. For example, you can click the link to view the name of the visitor that submitted an inquiry in the Suggestion Box form.

WORKING WITH AUTO RESPONDERS

Each web form you create in the system automatically includes an auto-responder (auto-reply) e-mail message. Every time a visitor submits a form on the site, an e-mail message is sent to the e-mail address entered in the form. To update the content of the auto-responder message, choose Modules > Web Forms and select the name of the desired web form from the List page. While you are on the Web Form Builder page, click the Setup Auto Responder option in the Action Box sidebar. The Auto Responder page is displayed in the online editor (FIGURE 8.7).

You can update the text to customize the e-mail message as desired. You can also use the Tag Insert menu to enter tag attributes to personalize the message; the tags are dynamically generated to use the data that matches each recipient's contact record. The auto responder also contains a link the subscriber can click to verify their subscription to the newsletter.

If you fill out the newsletter subscription form using a valid e-mail address, you'll receive the default auto-responder e-mail message when you check your Inbox. Test the subscription verification process to see how it works.

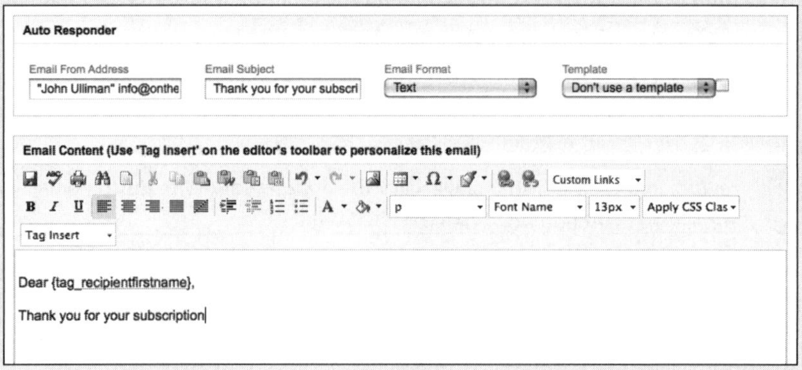

FIGURE 8.7
Edit the content of the Auto Responder in the Email Content field.

The Business Catalyst publishing system follows the industry-standard practice of requiring subscribers to "opt-in" after subscribing to a recipient list. This verification process requires subscribers (who signed up online or were manually subscribed using the Admin Console) to click a link in the e-mail message they receive to confirm that they want to receive e-mail correspondence.

The Opt-In Status box is enabled next to the names of subscribers who have verified their subscription in the List Subscribers window.

If necessary, you can manually opt-in a customer by clicking the Force Opt-In button in the Manage Customer Subscriptions page.

Creating and Inserting Subscription Forms

You can create as many e-mail campaigns as desired for a site. Each e-mail campaign you create is sent to at least one recipient list. You can optionally generate a Newsletter Signup form for each list to gather new subscribers on the live site. The Newsletter Signup forms you create in the system are linked to a specific recipient list.

Inserting a newsletter signup form on a web page

To create a subscription form and insert it on a page, you can choose between two options.

Option 1: Use the 1-Click Insert menu to insert the subscription form

Use this option to quickly add a subscription form to a page as you're managing recipient lists.

1. In the Admin Console, choose Marketing > Lists.
2. Click the option Add Subscribe Box To A Web Page in the Action Box sidebar.
3. The 1-Click Insert window appears. Choose the name of the page where you want to insert the form. The window updates with the page displayed in the online editor.
4. Place your cursor at the location on the page where you want to insert the form. Use the 1-Click Insert menu to choose Insert: Subscription Box For This Campaign.

This process is identical to the process of adding modules and web forms to pages.

Option 2: Copy the source code of the subscription form and add it to pages

Use this option when you want to customize the subscription form and update its appearance with CSS styles.

1. In the Admin Console, choose Marketing > Lists.
2. Click the option Get Subscribe Box HTML Code in the Action Box sidebar.
3. The HTML CodeList window appears. If you want to configure the Newsletter Signup form to redirect the subscriber to a confirmation or thank-you page after submitting the form, click the option Redirect To Different Web Page After User Submits Form. Enter the absolute path to the page in the field that appears. You can also click the Customize Subscription Form link in the upper-right corner to add custom fields to the form (FIGURE 8.8).

FIGURE 8.8
Customize the Newsletter Signup form and then copy the source code.

TIP: You can also add Newsletter Signup forms to pages with the Module Manager > Campaigns option (while editing web pages in the online editor) and the Business Catalyst panel (while editing web pages in Dreamweaver).

4. After configuring the Newsletter Signup form, click the field that contains the source code, select all by pressing Ctrl+A (Windows) or Command+A (Mac) and then copy the selection to the clipboard by pressing Ctrl+C (Windows) or Command+C (Mac).

5. Open a web page in the online editor (or open a page in the Document window in Dreamweaver) and paste the code in the desired location.

Editing Web Forms to Add an Option to Subscribe to a Newsletter

In addition to creating Newsletter Signup forms, you can add an option to any other web form on the site that lets visitors sign up to the newsletter. This is an interesting method of gathering new subscribers; as they're completing a form for a different purpose (such as contacting the business, registering to a secure zone, or purchasing a product), they can simultaneously request to be added to the mailing list and receive future e-mail campaigns.

In this example, you'll update the existing Contact Us page to add the option to subscribe to the Monthly Newsletter.

1. In the Admin Console, choose Modules > Web Forms.

2. The list of existing web forms is displayed. Click the link to access the details of the Contact Us Form.

3. The Web Form Builder appears and displays a preview of the Contact Us Form. Click the List tab in the Add New Items panel on the left side of the page and select the Monthly Newsletter option (**FIGURE 8.9**).

4. The preview of the Contact Us Form updates to display the new form element: an optional checkbox that enables visitors to subscribe to the Monthly Newsletter.

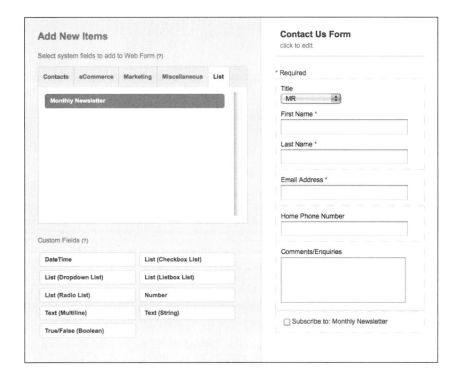

FIGURE 8.9
Add an option to sign up for
the newsletter in the Contact
Us Form.

When visitors submit the Contact Us Form (or other forms that you add to the site),
you can encourage them to sign up for future e-mail campaigns by clicking a single
checkbox. If desired, the business can create custom e-mail campaigns that reflect
different products or relate to different sections of the site, and then use forms to
gather subscribers who are interested in receiving information about a specific product or topic. It's a best practice to add multiple methods on the site that a visitor can
use to sign up.

Now that you've updated the Contact Us Form, you'll need to delete and reinsert the
form on the Contact page in order to update the live site.

Updating the Contact Us Form with Dreamweaver

In this section, you'll update the Contact page to delete the older instance of the
Contact Us Form and replace it with the newer version. Remember that this is necessary whenever you update forms that are already live on a site (unless you insert
the forms as module tags). You could update the page using either the online editor
in the Admin Console or Dreamweaver. In this section, you'll use the HTML editing
tools to edit the page in the Dreamweaver workspace.

1. Launch Dreamweaver. In the Files panel, click the Sync button to synchronize the entire site and get the newer remote files. This ensures that you are working with the latest version of the site files after editing them in the Admin Console.

2. Open the Business Catalyst panel. Make sure that the trial site is selected and that you're logged in.

3. Open the Files panel and double-click the contact.htm page to open it in the Document window.

4. In Design view, click anywhere inside the contact form.

5. Click <form> in Tag Selector to select the entire Contact Us Form code.

6. Press Delete to delete the existing source code of the older form.

7. Leave your cursor at its current location. You'll insert the new form code in the same spot to replace the form you just deleted. Open the Business Catalyst panel. Click the WebForms category to expand it. The list of suboptions appears. Double-click the Web Form suboption.

8. In the Module Configure wizard that appears, select the Contact Us Form. Click Next. Leave the URL field blank and click Next. On the final screen of the wizard, click Insert. The new form code is submitted on the Contact page.

9. Save the contact.htm page. While it is selected, choose Site > Put to upload it to the live site. In the Dependent Files dialog box that appears, click No.

After uploading the Contact page, you can switch to the other browser window that displays the live site. Click Contact to visit the Contact page and notice that the Contact Us Form now displays the new option to subscribe to the Monthly Newsletter. To see how this works, enter placeholder data with a different e-mail address and enable the checkbox to subscribe to the newsletter. Submit the Contact Us Form.

Return to the Admin Console and choose Marketing > Lists. Select the Monthly Newsletter List to see the List Details page and notice that the test visitor who just submitted the Contact Us Form has now subscribed to the Monthly Newsletter.

Creating and Sending E-mail Campaigns

In the previous sections of this chapter you learned several methods for adding subscribers to recipient lists. The site's database must collect contact data and add the subscribers to a recipient list before the business can begin sending e-mail campaigns. In this section, you'll see how the e-mail campaign tools guide you through the process of creating and publishing e-mail messages to send them to a list of subscribers.

1. In the Admin Console, choose Marketing > Email Campaigns.

2. In the Action Box sidebar, click the option Create A New Campaign.

The e-mail campaign creation and publication wizard contains seven steps to guide you through setting up the campaign details and completing the publication process. The numbered steps are listed in the sidebar. As you work through the steps, you can click the links to jump to each section if you need to move back and forth.

3. The New Campaign page is displayed.

   This is Step 1: Choose Type Of Campaign.

   As you create an e-mail campaign, you have two choices:

   • Send A One-off Email Broadcast To Recipients You Choose

   • Create A Customer Loyalty Program For Recipients You Choose

   For this example, select the one-off option. This selection sends e-mail campaign messages to all the recipients on a single date (FIGURE 8.10).

FIGURE 8.10
Use the one-off e-mail broadcast option to send a single e-mail message to a list.

   When you send one-off e-mail messages, you specify the date and time of day the message will be sent.

4. Click Next to proceed to Step 2: Campaign Details. The Campaign Details page is displayed.

   Enter the campaign details:

   • In the Campaign Name field, enter **August Newsletter**.

   • In the Email From fields, enter the desired name and e-mail address.

   • Change the subject of the e-mail by updating the Email Subject field.

   • Update the Delivery Date and Delivery Time settings to change the delivery date and time to any time in the future. If you set the date to occur in the past, the e-mail campaign is sent immediately when you click the Save And Send button.

   • Leave the Template menu set to Don't Use A Template.

   • In the Email Format menu, leave the option set to HTML.

   NOTE: Do not click the Save And Send button until you're ready to send the campaign. When you click the button, the system sends the message to the list of recipients, even if the e-mail message content is blank.

   By default, the system enters the same e-mail address you entered for your user account as the From (return) address for the e-mail campaign. You can enter a different e-mail address if you'd like. And later, when you launch the site for clients, you'll update this field and enter your client's e-mail address. But for testing purposes, leave the From address set to use your e-mail address for now.

UNDERSTANDING THE DIFFERENCE BETWEEN HTML AND TEXT E-MAIL FORMATS

When you and your clients prepare e-mail campaigns, you should use the HTML e-mail format unless there's a specific reason why you need to target a set of recipients who can only receive text-formatted messages. Use the Email Format menu to select the HTML option (FIGURE 8.11).

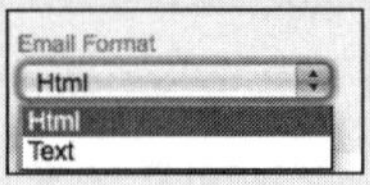

FIGURE 8.11
Choose the HTML option in the Email Format menu.

Generally speaking, most visitors can receive HTML e-mail messages using standard e-mail clients. When you choose the HTML e-mail format, the e-mail message can include images, embedded links, and formatting to make the e-mail content look similar to web-page content.

Additionally, you must choose the HTML e-mail format to take advantage of the reporting features provided in Business Catalyst to track the success of e-mail campaigns. When e-mail campaigns are sent using text formatting, all of the tracking code is stripped from the message and statistics about the campaign's performance are not recorded.

FIGURE 8.12
A red x icon indicates that your e-mail address has not been verified.

You'll notice that a red x icon is displayed next to your e-mail address (FIGURE 8.12). This x indicates that your e-mail address has not been verified in the system. The x corresponds to the warning message you'll see on the next page.

It's necessary to verify your e-mail address before you can send e-mail campaigns with the trial site. Verification is a simple, onetime process that confirms that the From address of the e-mail campaign uses a valid e-mail address. Later in these steps you'll verify your address by accessing the verification message in your Inbox and clicking the link in the message and clicking the link in the message to confirm that you are the owner of the e-mail address used to send messages through the system.

5. Click Next to proceed to Step 3: Choose The Campaign Recipients. The warning message about the unverified e-mail address is displayed at the top of the page (FIGURE 8.13).

FIGURE 8.13
A warning message reminds you to verify your e-mail address before attempting to send the campaign.

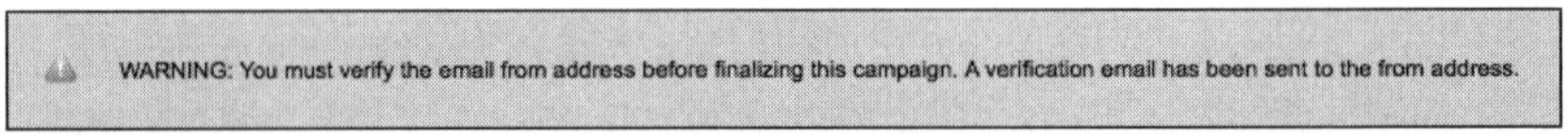

⚠ WARNING: You must verify the email from address before finalizing this campaign. A verification email has been sent to the from address.

UNDERSTANDING LOYALTY PROGRAMS

If you select the loyalty program option, the form updates to list the various types of anniversaries (dates stored in the database) to trigger the system to send e-mail messages. Loyalty programs enable businesses to use a variable date (the date a visitor submitted an inquiry, registered for the site, purchased an item, or any date provided by visitors in a form). Rather than one-off campaigns, where all recipients receive the message at once, the Loyalty Campaign feature checks the database every day to identify matching criteria and sends messages to individual subscribers when their specified date occurs.

For example, you could create a list of customers who have opted-in to receive promotions and then send each customer an e-mail message one week after the date they made a purchase in the online store. You can also configure the publishing system to automatically send messages on the birth date of visitors, based on the personal information they provided when they filled out a web form (FIGURE 8.14).

After selecting the anniversary type, specify a delivery date. The delivery date sets the number of days from the event that you want the e-mail message to be delivered.

For example, if the subscriber entered their birth date as May 1 and you want to send them a birthday greeting on the same day, set the delivery day to 0. The 0 setting causes the system to generate the message on the date of their birthday.

If you want to send subscribers a message to wish them happy birthday a day before the date they entered in the system, set the delivery day to -1. The -1 setting causes the system to generate the message and send a day earlier than the date in the database.

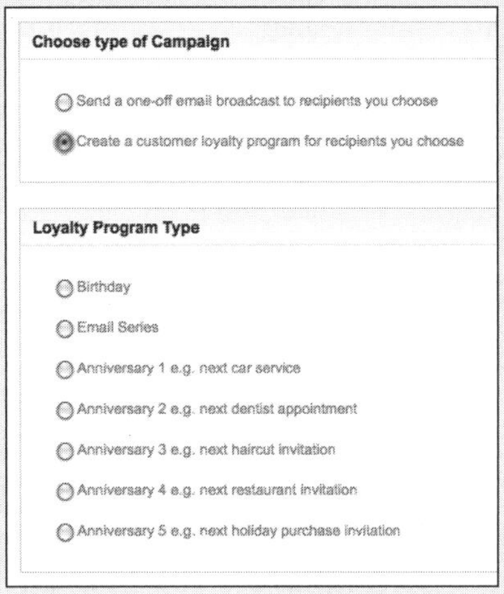

FIGURE 8.14
Choose the type of loyalty program from the list of options.

In another example, you could use an anniversary of the date of a customer's first purchase in the online store. Configure the loyalty program to send subscribed customers a follow-up e-mail message a week after their purchase by setting the delivery date to 7.

If you want to send a series of e-mails, select the Email Series option. This is the same feature used by the Adobe Business Catalyst team to send you a series of weekly e-mail messages, based on the date you create your first trial site.

Loyalty programs are easy to set up and they make customers feel appreciated. Once you set up a recurring campaign in the e-mail campaign system, it will automatically check for matching customer data in the database and send the messages each day without any additional work from you or your clients.

6. The Choose Recipients page is displayed. Click the Monthly Newsletter option to set the recipient list (FIGURE 8.15).

FIGURE 8.15
The recipient list displays the number of recipients who have opted-in.

Campaigns: August Newsletter (Draft)

✔ Campaign saved in draft mode successfully.

Choose Recipients   Next Step: Choose Layout

○ New List

○ Entire Customer Database (3 opted-in recipients)

● Monthly Newsletter (3 opted-in recipients)

Add to Your List

○ Upload and import a list of recipients

○ Add a recipient manually

TIP: You can use the Add A Recipient Manually option to add a few more subscribers. Be sure to use valid e-mail addresses for testing purposes. Later in these instructions, it is easier to see how the system tracks the performance of e-mail campaigns if you create three or four recipients and opt-in to receive the newsletter. After sending the campaign, access the subscriber's messages. Replicate a real-world campaign experience by opening some (but not all) of the messages, and click on links when viewing a couple of the newsletters to see how the activity is tracked. If you have only one recipient, the statistics will reflect the single subscriber's interaction with the e-mail campaign.

After selecting a recipient list, the page updates to display the Add To Your List section.

If desired, you can use the Add To Your List section to make last-minute changes to the list. Choose between importing a list of recipients and manually adding new recipients.

7. Click Next to proceed to Step 4: Choose Design Template.

You can select one of the prebuilt templates or leave the option set to Blank. It is a best practice to use Dreamweaver to create a custom HTML page using the business's logo and branding. For example, you can leave this option set to Blank and be sure to save the draft. Once a draft is saved, you can launch Dreamweaver and synchronize the site to get the newer files. Edit the HTML file for the campaign and then upload it to the remote server. You can edit existing HTML files with Dreamweaver to design the campaign content, but remember that you cannot create new e-mail campaigns or publish them using Dreamweaver. If you use Dreamweaver to edit the newsletter file, return to the Admin Console to publish the campaign.

Take a moment to explore the prebuilt e-mail campaign templates by choosing various industry and style options to see the combinations that are available.

8. To follow along with this example, choose the Retail option from the Choose Industry pull-down menu and the Fun option from the Choose Style pull-down menu (FIGURE 8.16).

If you leave the default Blank option in the Choose Industry menu, the online editor will display a blank field in the Email Content field in the next step.

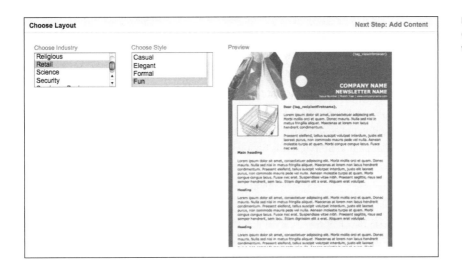

FIGURE 8.16
Choose a template to use for
the sample e-mail campaign.

9. Click Next to proceed to Step 5: Provide Campaign Content.

   The online editor displays the template you selected in Step 4.

10. In the Email Content field, enter some placeholder text for testing purposes.
    For example, you can add the following text: **Test Link to the Shop Page**.

    Select the text you just typed and then use the Custom Links menu to select
    Catalogs > Sample Catalog 1 to add a text link (FIGURE 8.17).

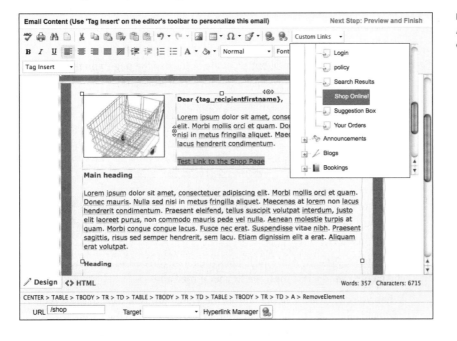

FIGURE 8.17
Add a link to the text content
of the e-mail message.

Links in e-mail campaigns are automatically tracked. You don't have to add any special code to track them in the system. You can add additional links to the content if you'd like to extend the tests and see how the e-mail campaign tracking system reflects click activity in the reports later.

11. If desired, use the online editor to format the text content.

12. Be sure to click the Save Draft button on this page before continuing to Step 6. If you don't click the Save Draft button and click Next, you'll see a blank preview appear in Step 6. If this happens, simply click the Back button, click Save Draft, and then click Next again. The Email Content page doesn't automatically save, so be sure to click Save Draft every time you make a change to the field's contents.

13. Click Next to proceed to Step 6: Preview And Finish.

The Preview window displays the message so that you can review how it will appear to recipients. If you need to make changes to the message before sending it, click the Back button and update the message. Click Save Draft in Step 5, and then click Next to return to the Preview page again.

Remember, you can't send any e-mail campaigns until you verify the e-mail address in the Email From field first. In the next step, you'll verify your e-mail address.

14. Check the Inbox of the e-mail address you used to create your user account. Locate the e-mail verification message. Click the link in the message to verify your user account's e-mail address to send e-mail campaigns through the system.

If you checked your Inbox and you didn't receive the verification e-mail, click the Send Verification Email button at the bottom of the page, and then check your Inbox again to verify your e-mail address (**FIGURE 8.18**).

Click the Send Verification Email button.

TIP: If you want to design the newsletter in Dreamweaver, first create the e-mail campaign and save the draft as described. Then, launch Dreamweaver and synchronize the site, to get the new files. In the Files panel, locate the _System folder and expand it. Inside the Campaigns folder, you'll find a copy of your saved newsletter draft in the Draft folder. Double-click the HTML file to open it in the Document window and make changes. When you are finished, upload the file to the remote server and return to the Admin Console to finish publishing the newsletter.

FIGURE 8.18
When you click the Send Verification Email button, the system generates a new verification e-mail message.

FIGURE 8.19
The green checkmark indicates your e-mail address has been verified.

15. Return to the Admin Console. If you click Step 2: Campaign Details in the sidebar, you'll see that the e-mail address in the Email From Address field is verified (**FIGURE 8.19**).

16. Click Step 6: Preview And Finish. Click the Email Me button at the bottom of the page to send a test message to your e-mail address.

When you click the Email Me button, the system sends a copy of the e-mail campaign message to the e-mail address associated with the current campaign. It doesn't send a copy to every subscriber in the recipient list.

17. Check your Inbox to see how the e-mail message displays in your e-mail client. Always test messages by sending the e-mail campaign to a single address before sending it to a large set of subscribers. Some e-mail clients do not support CSS styles or specific HTML code, so check that the message displays as expected in the e-mail clients you are targeting before publishing it to an entire recipient list.

    Return to the Admin Console and make changes to the content of the e-mail message if desired. Click the Email Me button to retest the message. Continue following this process until you're pleased with the display of the e-mail message delivered to your Inbox.

18. When you're ready to publish the message to the entire list, click the Save And Send button to send the e-mail campaign to the entire list of recipients.

19. In the window that appears, confirm that you want to send the message.

To test the capabilities of the e-mail campaign tracking system, make sure the recipient list includes several subscribers with valid e-mail addresses who have opted-in. When the campaign is sent, access the Inboxes to open some, but not all, of the messages. Of the messages you open, only click the link in some instances to create a varied set of campaign statistics.

Tracking E-mail Campaign Statistics

At this point, you have sent an e-mail campaign using the publishing system, and you've opened some of the newsletters and clicked the link in a few of the messages. Next, you'll use the Admin Console to check on the status of the published e-mail campaign to see how many messages were opened and to identify which subscribers interacted with the links.

1. In the Admin Console, choose Marketing > Email Campaigns. Click the name of the e-mail campaign you want to track: August Newsletter.

2. The campaign statistics are displayed. If you don't immediately see them, click Step 7: Reports And Performance in the sidebar (FIGURE 8.20).

If you accessed the messages sent to subscriber's e-mail addresses and opened some of the e-mail messages, you can see how the system tracked which recipients opened the messages and clicked on the links. The system tracks all the e-mail campaign data in the site's database.

The system continues tracking an e-mail campaign for the lifetime of the site, so you and your clients can return to this area as often as you'd like to see how a campaign performed.

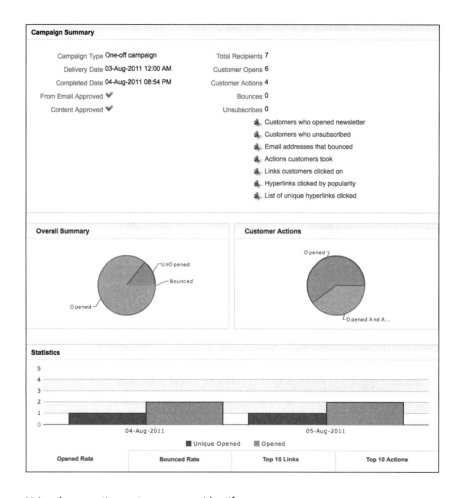

Using the reporting system, you can identify:

- The number of e-mail messages that were opened
- The number of e-mail messages that bounced (could not be delivered)
- The number of links that were clicked in the e-mail campaign
- The actions that subscribers took after interacting with the campaign

This is valuable information that can help you and your clients determine the content and recipients to target in the next e-mail campaign. By tracking the performance of e-mail campaigns, you can adjust the messaging you send to subscribers and learn how to improve communications with a specific customer base.

Creating a Recipient List to Target a Segment of the Customer Database

When you first launch a client's site, you can add a Newsletter Signup form to invite visitors to subscribe to the mailing list. Once the site gathers some recipients, you can help your clients send out their first newsletter as a starting point for e-mail marketing. As the business grows, you can create and send special campaigns to target various sections of a customer base. As you evaluate reports and the Live Feed links to learn more about different sets of customers, you can respond to the interactions they make on the site.

For example, you can identify the customers who share a specific attribute:

- Customers who spend the most money in the online store
- New customers who have recently purchased their first item
- Customers who have purchased repeatedly within a specific time range

Reports are helpful for identifying a group of customers who match the type of promotions the business wants to send. They allow you to send VIP customers marketing information and discount codes to encourage them to visit the online store or sign up for an upcoming event.

Previously, you created a Suggestion Box form and added it to the trial site. Imagine that some time has passed and many visitors have submitted great suggestions in the form. The business wants to send a personal e-mail message to thank these visitors for their feedback. To do this, you'll create a new recipient list and populate it with existing customer data in the system (instead of gathering recipients online with a Newsletter Signup form).

1. In the Admin Console, choose Marketing > Lists. In the Action Box sidebar, choose the option Create A New List.
2. In the List Details, enter the name of the new list in the Name field: Subscription Box Thank You. Click Save (FIGURE 8.21).
3. Click Next. The Auto Responder page is displayed.

Because the list will be populated with existing customer data in the system, rather than having subscribers sign up online, this auto-responder e-mail message will never be sent (even though it is still attached to the list). You'll run a report to identify visitors who previously interacted with the Suggestion Box form, and then add them to this thank-you list.

> **NOTE:** Encourage your clients to practice good e-mail etiquette by only sending e-mail messages to people who have indicated they are interested in receiving correspondence from the business. Generate recipient lists with customers who have opted-in to receive newsletters or promotions. One way to encourage visitors to opt-in on the site involves creating a recipient list for general correspondence from a business and including a checkbox option on the site's registration form that says "Please send me sales notifications, promotions, and special discounts via e-mail."

FIGURE 8.21
In the Name field, enter the
name of the new recipient list.

Creating custom reports using the customer database

Follow along with these steps to create a new recipient list with a segment of the existing contact records in the database (that share an attribute, such as customers who have made a purchase in the last month). This task involves running a report to create a collection of existing customers and adding them to a recipient list.

1. In the Admin Console, choose Marketing > Segment Customer Database (which loads the Reports > Create A Customer Report page).

2. In the Action Box sidebar, click the option Create A New Customer Report.

   The New Customer Report page is displayed. Use the interface to sift through all the customers in the site's database based on a specific set of criteria.

3. In the Choose Report Type section, click the radio button to choose the data you want to search. In this example, the goal is to identify the list of visitors who submitted the Suggestion Box form. The Suggestion Box form generates cases, so click the option to search for customers and cases (**FIGURE 8.22**).

4. Click Next. The Data Fields page appears. Use this page to specify the matching data you want to find.

   Because you are gathering contact data to add to a recipient list, you only need to include the following information in the report:

   - Customer Name
   - Email 1 (Primary)
   - Case Subject

   Select the checkboxes next to these options (**FIGURE 8.23**).

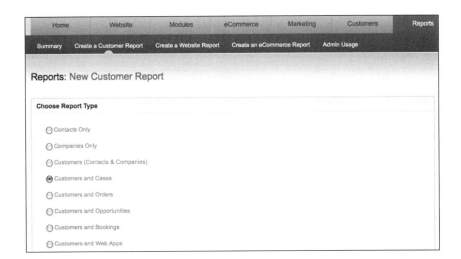

FIGURE 8.22
Select the report type in the New Customer Report page.

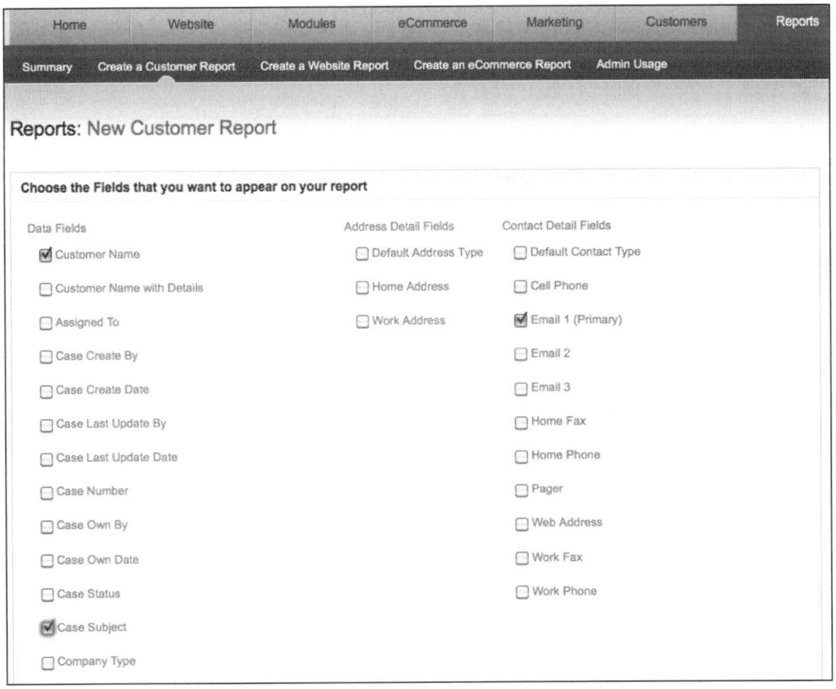

FIGURE 8.23
Select the data fields to specify the data in the custom report.

5. Click Next. The Filters page appears.

   Use the filter menus to locate case records in the system for this set of customers. Take a moment to explore the types of criteria you can use to filter
   the report results. For example, you can find matching records to locate cases
   assigned to a specific team member, the date a case was created, or its current
   status (**FIGURE 8.24**).

FIGURE 8.24
Use the menus in the Filter
By Fields section to select
the criteria used to filter the
report results.

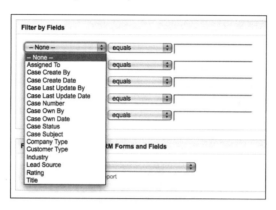

LOCATING RELATED CUSTOMERS IN THE DATABASE

Use the filter menu options to sort and locate customer data records. After
identifying a set of customers who match specific attributes, you can use their
contact data to engage them with promotions and targeted messages.

For example, you can search for customers who have purchased items in the
online store or locate the subset of specific types of orders.

You could run reports to locate the following:

• Customers who bought merchandise in the last week or the last month

• Customers who purchased a specific product

• Customers who spent more than $100

By slicing the customer records this way, you can identify a business's most
loyal customer base and send them marketing campaigns that correspond to
their recent site activities (**FIGURE 8.25**).

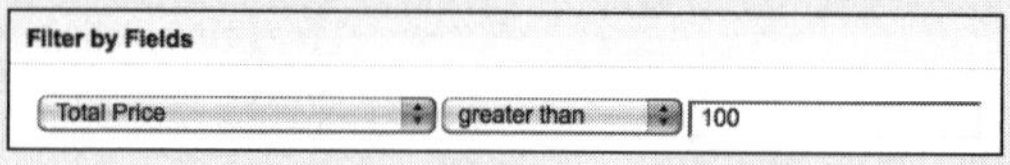

FIGURE 8.25
You can use the filter
menus to create a list of
customers who spent over
a hundred dollars in the
online store.

6. For now, see what happens when you don't apply any filters. Click the Generate Report button.

   The list of visitors who submitted any inquiries into any of the forms on the site is displayed.

7. Return to the previous page by clicking the Back button. This time, you'll add a filter in the section titled Filter By Your Own Custom CRM Forms And Fields. Use the menu to choose the Suggestion Box form (FIGURE 8.26).

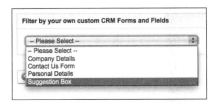

FIGURE 8.26
Use the CRM Forms And Fields menu to select Suggestion Box.

8. Click the Generate Report button again.

   This time when you create the report, it only includes the visitors who submitted the Suggestion Box form. This is the set of contact data that you'll use to add to the recipient list so that you can send them a thank-you message.

9. Click the Add Customers To button.

   In the Add Customers To section that appears, select the Campaign List option and use the menu to select the name of the recipient list: Suggestion Box Thank You (FIGURE 8.27).

NOTE: If desired, you can click the Export Report button to export the report as a spreadsheet and open it in Microsoft Excel to view it offline.

FIGURE 8.27
Choose the name of the recipient list: Suggestion Box Thank You.

   Notice that you can also use this search technique to locate sets of customers to add to secure zones or affiliate programs.

10. Click Submit.

By clicking Submit, you've achieved the goal of running a custom report to add to a new recipient list the contact data of visitors who have submitted a suggestion in the Suggestion Box form.

Now that you've generated the new recipient list, you could use the process to create and send a customized e-mail campaign message to thank this group for submitting feedback in the Suggestion Box form.

In the next section, you'll learn how to save this report in the system.

Saving a custom report

If you plan on reusing the customer report you've created so that you can run the same report in the future, follow these steps to save it:

1. After creating the custom report as described earlier, click the Back button.

2. In the sidebar, click Step 5: Save Report.

3. The page updates to enable you to save the report. Enter a descriptive report name in the Report Name field, such as Suggestion Box Customers.

4. Click the Save Report button.

The report is saved in the site's database. Whenever you or your clients want to access it in the future, either click View All Customer Reports in the Related sidebar, or choose Reports > Create A Customer Report and view the list of existing saved reports.

Customer reports are very powerful. You can experiment with using filters to search through the customer database to locate specific subsets of contact records. Brainstorm with your client to develop marketing strategies to identify the customer base most likely to purchase products and services from the business in the future.

Related Links

 Setting Up Email Marketing:
http://www.adobe.com/go/bc_email_marketing

 Sending an Email Newsletter:
http://www.adobe.com/go/bc_newsletters

CHAPTER 9

Creating Custom Content Types with Web Apps

Contents

Building a Sample Web App	185
Populating Web App Items	191
Inserting Web Apps on a Page	193
Adding Search Functionality to a Web App	196
Creating Web Apps Populated with Visitor Data	198
Inserting the Web App Item Submission Form on a Page	200
Testing the Web App Item Submission Form	203
Workflow for Building Web Apps	207

Business Catalyst comes with many different modules you can use to add new features to the trial site. As you learned in Chapter 4, "Configuring, Inserting, and Customizing Modules," the system includes prebuilt features you can set up and add to pages. Each module has its own set of data fields. For example, the FAQs module uses two fields to display the question and the answer for each FAQ item.

Before meeting with clients, you should become familiar with the modules included with the Business Catalyst Platform. Learn how each one works and understand the data fields it manages and tracks. When you consult with clients, you can describe the features that are available right out of the box. Whenever possible, leverage the existing modules to display different types of content on the site.

In the Admin Console, click the Modules tab to see the list of modules displayed (FIGURE 9.1).

FIGURE 9.1
The modules included
with Business Catalyst are
displayed on the Modules
List page.

You aren't limited to working with these modules to create new site features. Although the modules include many common functionalities that clients often request (such as photo galleries and trackable download files), there are situations when clients request a special type of content that isn't handled by the default configurations in Business Catalyst. Clients may specify that they want to display a custom set of data on the site that cannot be created using the existing modules.

For example, when you develop sites for clients, the requirements may include the ability to submit and display a particular type of content on the site.

Here are some examples of features built with Web Apps:

- Part specifications (displayed in a list with search functionality)
- Business team member profiles and contact information
- Career pages that lists job opportunities
- Real estate property listings
- Retail store locations and hours

Web Apps are completely configurable, enabling you to define the content and make it as simple or as complex as needed for each project.

Imagine that the business has a network of product distributors. Your client has asked you to create a site feature that enables visitors to quickly locate the closest distributor. By creating a mini-database of the distributor names, addresses, phone numbers, and links to a Google map, you can create a Web App that enables visitors to enter their zip code and obtain a list of the nearest distributors.

In another example, you could build a Web App that enables visitors to submit data to share it with an online community. You can set up a Web App and a web form that allows visitors to submit data, such as the following:

- Classified ads
- Favorite recipes
- Artwork images (for a contest)
- Screenplays and short stories
- Product ratings and product reviews

Use Web Apps whenever you want to manage sets of data that don't fit into the existing module functionality. Although the features you create with modules are the most common examples of data on business sites, you can create any type of custom content you can imagine.

Building a Sample Web App

In this chapter, you'll learn how to make a basic Web App and then expand it. The clients who requested the Web App run a brick-and-mortar store as well as an online business. They want to drive traffic to their retail store by promoting nearby local businesses on their website. The client feels strongly that shopping locally is an important consideration for their customer base. They requested a site feature, called Local Favorites, to encourage shoppers to visit their neighborhood and support the other stores in the area.

When you first begin building a Web App, it's important to map it out to determine the types of data that will be presented on the page. You'll find it helpful to create a list of the items that will be included in the Web App first so that you can refer to the list as you're setting up the custom data fields.

In this local business example, the following data is required:

- Store name
- Store address
- Description of the retail store
- Photo of the retail store

In the first iteration of the Web App, the client agrees that they can populate the local business information themselves. But in the future, they see the Web App as an interactive site feature. They want registered visitors to log in and share their favorite local businesses, which enables the online community to participate in recommending retail stores in the neighborhood.

Creating a new Web App

When you develop client sites, remember that you can only create and populate Web Apps in the Admin Console. To get started, follow these steps:

1. In the Admin Console, choose Modules > Web Apps.

2. The Web App List page is displayed. In the Action Box sidebar, click the option Build A New Web App (FIGURE 9.2).

   The Web App Details page is displayed. Notice that this is Step 1 in the four-step process to build Web Apps. If you need to access other steps at any time during the Web App creation process, click the links in the sidebar to jump to a specific step.

3. Enter the name of the Web App in the Web App Name field. For this example, enter Local Favorites (FIGURE 9.3).

FIGURE 9.2
Choose the option to build a new Web App.

FIGURE 9.3
Enter the name of the Web App in the Web App Name field.

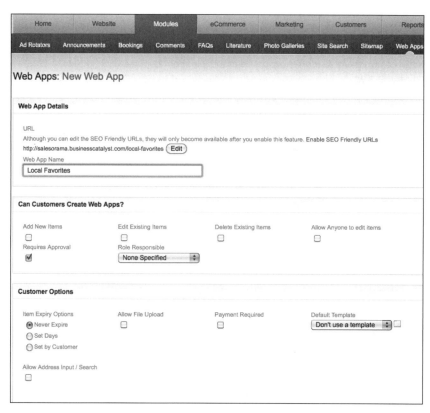

4. Later, you'll return to this page to set up the customer options. For now, just click Next. The Custom Fields page is displayed. This is Step 2.

Use this interface to add the data fields that you want to include in the Web App. By default, every Web App includes a name and description, so it isn't necessary to add fields for those two data items. However, the requirements for this Web App include two other fields: one to display the store's location and the other to display a photo of each store.

Begin by adding the field for displaying the store location. For the first data type, it's important to be able to add an entire mailing address in the field.

Explore the options in the Field Type menu to see the wide variety of field types. Each of these form elements can be used to submit, store, and display the data that corresponds to the content type.

5. In the Field Name, enter the name **location**.

In the Field Type menu, choose the Text (Multiline) option to create a field that contains multiple lines for displaying the store's street address (**FIGURE 9.4**).

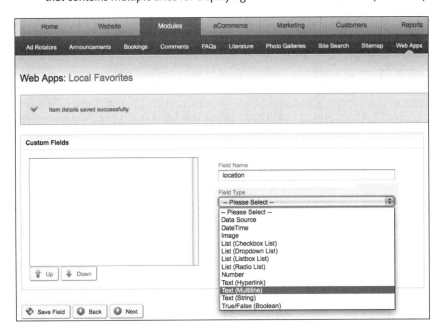

FIGURE 9.4
Use the Field Type menu to choose Text (Multiline).

As you define each custom field, choose the field type that's appropriate for the data you want to submit and display in the Web App.

When configuring each field, you specify whether or not it will be a mandatory field. If the field is set to mandatory, then it must include data as each new Web App item is submitted.

6. Enable the Mandatory checkbox. Click the Save Field button to save the field you created.

   Now there's just one more field to create. This field will be used to upload a photo of the store to entice other visitors to visit the store and shop there.

7. In the Field Name, enter **photo**.

   Use the Field Type menu to select the Image option. This field type enables you to display image files.

8. In some cases, a photo of the store may not be available. This time, as you are configuring the Image field, leave the Mandatory checkbox unselected (**FIGURE 9.5**).

FIGURE 9.5
The mandatory fields are marked with an asterisk in the list.

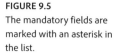

TIP: When editing layouts for Web Apps, you can access them the same way you access other module layouts by choosing Admin > More Customization Options and selecting the desired layout in the list of options. You can also use Dreamweaver or a third-party FTP client to open the Layouts folder at the root level of the site and update the layout files.

At this point, you've added two custom data fields to the Web App in addition to the default Name and Description fields that are included automatically. Although not needed for this project, notice that if you need to rearrange the order of the custom fields, you can select the desired field name in the list and click the Up or Down button to reposition it.

9. Click Next to access Step 3: Customize Web App Layout. When you visit this page, the interface displays the layout files for the Web App.

   The menu at the top of the page includes the available layout files. Web Apps include several layout files you can edit to control how different views of the Web App display.

   You'll access the List layout and Detail layout files first. As you'll recall, the List layout file controls how the List view appears when a list of Web App items are displayed on the page. The Detail layout file controls how the Detail view appears once a visitor has clicked a link in the list of Web App items to get more information about a selected item.

10. Use the menu to select the List layout file and review the contents in the on-line editor.

    The List layout file currently contains two tags:

    {tag_counter}

    {tag_name}

    The first tag is a counter feature that adds a number to itemize the numbered list of Web App items. The second tag displays the data in the Name field for each Web App item (**FIGURE 9.6**).

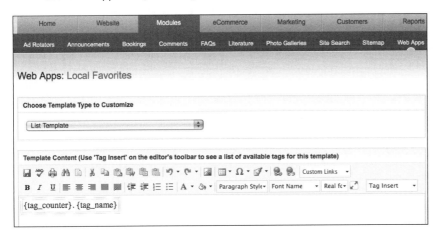

FIGURE 9.6
Review the tags in the List layout file.

    For now, the List layout file already contains the tags needed for the Local Favorites Web App.

11. Use the menu at the top of the page to select the Detail option.

    The Detail layout file currently only contains tags to display the Name and Description fields. (These are the default options that match the fields that are included automatically.) In this section, you'll update the Detail layout to add the tags that correspond to the other two custom data fields you added previously.

    Notice that this layout uses an HTML table to align the data of the two tags. Keep in mind that when you build your own Web Apps, you can click the HTML tab and replace the table cells with <div> tags or any other code you'd like to use. For now, you'll just add more rows to the existing table in the Detail layout file.

12. Click the description tag. Click the Table Wizard icon in the top of the online editor toolbar. Hover over the icons in the Table Wizard that appears to see their tooltips. Click the option Insert Row Above (**FIGURE 9.7**).

NOTE: You can also right-click (or Control-click) on the table in the Design tab to access a context menu to format the table. Select the Insert Row Above option from the menu.

FIGURE 9.7
Use the Table Wizard to create a row above the bottom row that contains the description tag.

After clicking the Table Wizard icon, select the Insert Row Above option.

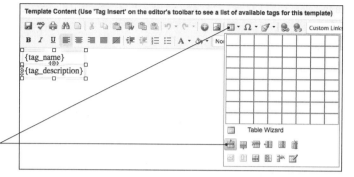

Just as when editing other module layout files, you can add more tags using the Tag Insert menu. If you click the Tag Insert menu and scroll down through the list of available options, you'll see the system tags included with the Web App feature displayed first. If you scroll to the very bottom, you'll see the tags that correspond to the custom data fields you added to the Web App.

13. Click inside the middle (empty) row and select the {tag_photo} option to insert the photo tag inside the second table cell from the top (FIGURE 9.8).

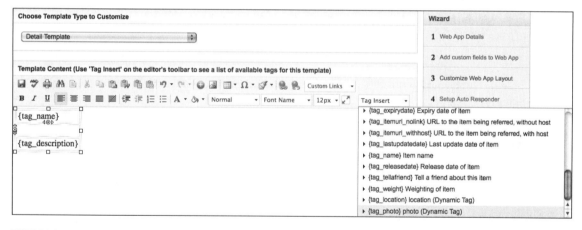

FIGURE 9.8
Use the Tag Insert menu to select the {tag_photo} tag.

14. Use the Table Wizard (or the context menu) to insert another row into the table. This time, click the bottom row and then insert a row below so that it appears at the bottom of the table. While the bottom empty row is selected, use the Tag Insert menu to insert the location tag.

15. Click Save to save your changes.

Populating Web App Items

In the previous section, you created a new Web App named Local Favorites that high-lights recommended local businesses in a specific neighborhood. Next, you'll learn how to add some items to the Web App to populate the four data fields with content.

1. In the Admin Console, choose Modules > Web Apps.

2. The list of Web Apps is displayed. Click the Local Favorites item to view the Web App Item List page. At the moment, the page indicates that there aren't any Web App items.

3. In the Action Box sidebar, click the option Create A New Web App Item. The New Item page is displayed.

4. In the Item Details section, enter the following information:

   In the Item Name field, enter **Fred's Flower Shop**.

   In the Location field, enter the address of the business:

   1387 Hayes St.
   San Francisco, CA 94117

   In the Photo field, click the square icon to the right of the field and select the filename of the image that you want to display.

5. The Item Content field (in the online editor) is the description field for the Web App item. Enter a placeholder description of the business, like this:

   Fred's Flower Shop always has a fantastic variety of flowers for sale. The staff is extremely helpful and they will create custom bouquets for you. I enjoy visiting their shop to check out the flower arrangements.

6. Be sure to leave the Enabled checkbox selected. Scroll down and click Save (FIGURE 9.9).

7. Repeat step 4 by clicking the Create Another Web App Item option in the Related sidebar. In the Item Details section of the New Item page, enter the name of the second Web App item: **Robin's Clothing Boutique**.

   Enter placeholder data to populate the store's location and description.

   Click the square icon next to the Photo field and browse to select the image file you want to associate with the Web App item (FIGURE 9.10).

NOTE: If you'd like to follow along with these instructions, use an image-editing program to create three image files depicting retail stores. Crop them to 300 × 225 pixels. Use the File Manager, Dreamweaver, or a third-party FTP client to upload the files to the images folder of the site. Later, you'll browse to select these images to populate the image field and display a picture of each business.

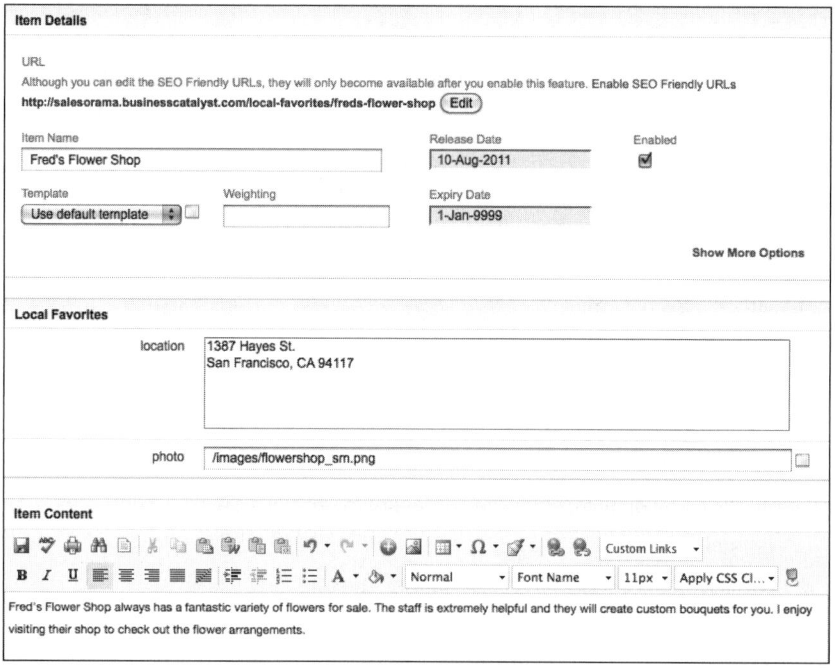

FIGURE 9.9
Enter data in the fields in the Item Details and Item Content areas.

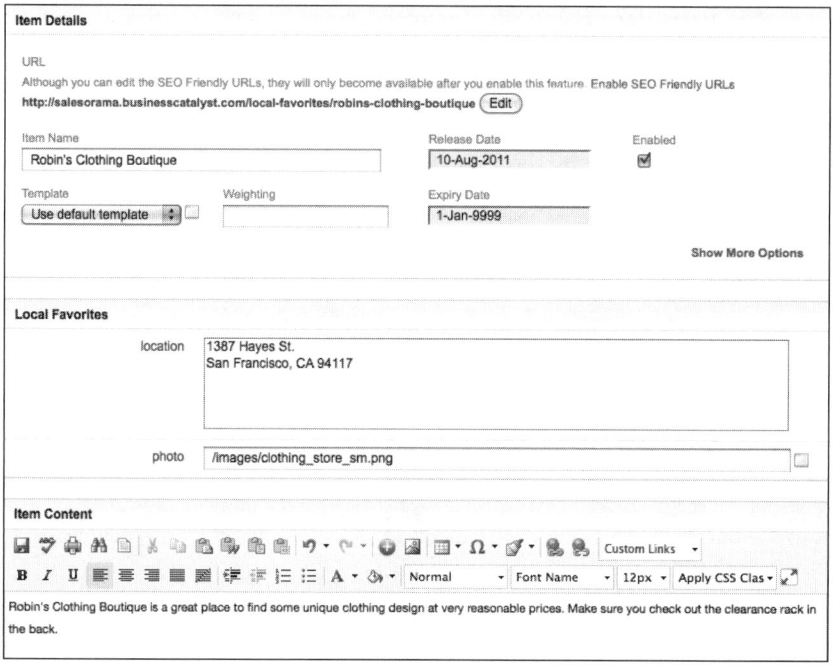

Item Details

URL
Although you can edit the SEO Friendly URLs, they will only become available after you enable this feature. Enable SEO Friendly URLs
http://salesorama.businesscatalyst.com/local-favorites/freds-flower-shop (Edit)

Item Name
Fred's Flower Shop

Release Date
10-Aug-2011

Enabled
☑

Template
Use default template

Weighting

Expiry Date
1-Jan-9999

Show More Options

Local Favorites

location
1387 Hayes St.
San Francisco, CA 94117

photo
/images/flowershop_sm.png

Item Content

Fred's Flower Shop always has a fantastic variety of flowers for sale. The staff is extremely helpful and they will create custom bouquets for you. I enjoy visiting their shop to check out the flower arrangements.

FIGURE 9.10
Create another Web App Item by entering data about the fictitious business.

Item Details

URL
Although you can edit the SEO Friendly URLs, they will only become available after you enable this feature. Enable SEO Friendly URLs
http://salesorama.businesscatalyst.com/local-favorites/robins-clothing-boutique (Edit)

Item Name
Robin's Clothing Boutique

Release Date
10-Aug-2011

Enabled
☑

Template
Use default template

Weighting

Expiry Date
1-Jan-9999

Show More Options

Local Favorites

location
1387 Hayes St.
San Francisco, CA 94117

photo
/images/clothing_store_sm.png

Item Content

Robin's Clothing Boutique is a great place to find some unique clothing design at very reasonable prices. Make sure you check out the clearance rack in the back.

You can create more Web App items if you'd like to practice adding them. Be sure to create at least two items so that you can test how the List view and search functionality work later in this chapter.

Inserting Web Apps on a Page

At this point, you've created a Web App and populated it with at least two Web App items. You've also updated the Web App layout files to control the data that is displayed in the List and Detail views. In this section, you'll learn how to add the Web App to a page and display it on the live site.

1. Launch Dreamweaver. Click the Synchronize button at the top of the Files panel to sync the entire site to get the newer remote files. This ensures that you're working with the latest version of the site files after editing them in the Admin Console.

2. Open the Business Catalyst panel (Window > Business Catalyst). Make sure that the trial site is currently selected and that you're logged in.

3. In the Files panel, double-click the about.htm page to open it in the Document window.

4. In Design view, locate the bottom paragraph that begins with the header Drive Repeat Sales With Email Marketing. Select the header text and replace it with this header text: **Favorite Local Shops**.

5. Move down to the paragraph below the header you just updated; the paragraph begins with "Email marketing is a powerful tool..."

6. In Design view, click anywhere in that paragraph, and then click the <p> tag in the Tag Selector at the bottom of the Document window to select the entire paragraph. Press Delete to delete the existing paragraph. Press Enter (Windows) or Return (Mac) once to create a new paragraph. Type some placeholder text, like this:

    We know you won't buy everything on the Internet. That's why we would like to share with you some of our favorite local places to shop.

7. At the end of the paragraph (while still in Design view), press Enter (Windows) or Return (Mac) once again to create another new paragraph. This is the location where you'll insert the Web App module.

8. In the Business Catalyst panel, scroll down and click the WebApps category to expand it and see its suboptions. Double-click the Web Apps option (FIGURE 9.11).

9. The Module Configure wizard appears. Choose the Local Favorites Web App and click Next (FIGURE 9.12).

NOTE: You can add Web Apps to pages using the same process you used to insert modules and web forms on pages. You can accomplish this using either the Admin Console or Dreamweaver. In this example, you'll use Dreamweaver to take advantage of the HTML editing tools in the Document window.

FIGURE 9.11
Double-click the Web Apps suboption in the Business Catalyst panel.

FIGURE 9.12
Select the name of the Web App in the Module Configure wizard.

10. In the next screen of the Module Configure wizard, choose All Items and click Next (**FIGURE 9.13**).

FIGURE 9.13
Select All Items to set the display criteria.

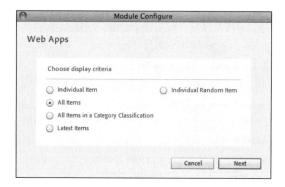

11. On the final screen of the Module Configure wizard, click Insert to insert the list of Web App items at the location of the cursor. In Design view, the new tag is inserted on the page (**FIGURE 9.14**).

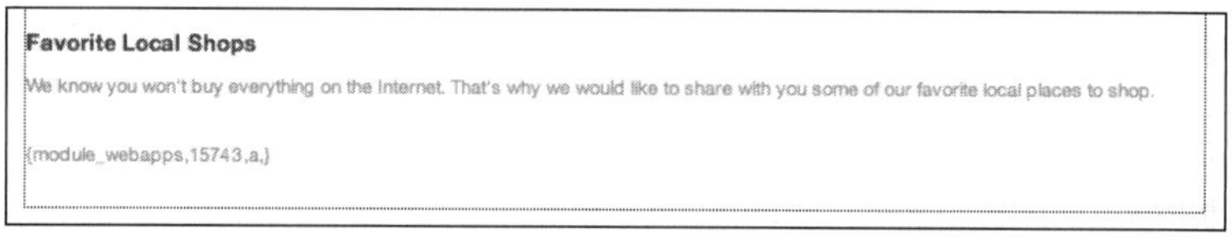

FIGURE 9.14
The Web App module tag includes an a at the end, signifying that it will display a list of all Web App items.

Favorite Local Shops

We know you won't buy everything on the Internet. That's why we would like to share with you some of our favorite local places to shop.

{module_webapps,15743,a,}

12. Save the page. Choose Site > Put to upload it to the host server. In the Dependent Files dialog box that appears, click No.

    If you switch to another browser window and visit the About page in the trial site, the Web App module tag appears to be working. However, the Web App Detail layout file doesn't contain the <div> tag with the style necessary to display the white background (used by the trial site template to format the other site pages).

13. Return to Dreamweaver. In the Files panel, click the Layouts folder to expand it and then open the WebApps subfolder. Notice that there's a subfolder named Local Favorites that corresponds to the Web App name. Open the Local Favorites folder and then double-click on the detail.html page to open it in the Document window (FIGURE 9.15).

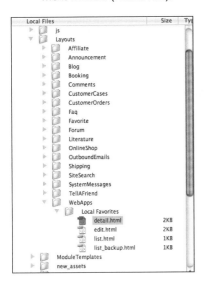

FIGURE 9.15
Each Web App uses its own set of layout files; they're stored in a folder with the corresponding name.

14. In Design view, click the table. In the Tag Selector at the bottom of the Document window, click the <table> tag to select the entire table. In Code view, type the following tag immediately above the table code:

`<div class="main-holder">`

Add the closing `</div>` tag immediately after the table code to surround the table inside the div container with a CSS style that displays a white background (FIGURE 9.16).

```
10   </head>
11   <body>
12 ▼ <div class="main-holder">
13   <table>
14     <tbody>
15       <tr>
16         <td>{tag_name}</td>
17       </tr>
18       <tr>
19         <td>{tag_photo}</td>
20       </tr>
21       <tr>
22         <td>{tag_description}</td>
23       </tr>
24       <tr>
25         <td>{tag_location}</td>
26       </tr>
27     </tbody>
28   </table>
29   </div>
30   </body>
31
```

FIGURE 9.16
Wrap the table in a div container to set a white background on the page.

15. Finally, to make the Detail view look a bit better, select the {tag_name} tag and use the Format menu in the HTML section of the Property inspector to set the text to the Heading 2 format. The H2 style will make the name of the local business stand out in the Detail view of the Web App.

16. Save and put the details.html layout file to upload it to the host server. Because it doesn't have any dependent files, click No in the Dependent Files dialog box.

If you return to the other browser window that displays the trial site and refresh the About page, you'll see the effects of the recent updates. The list of Web Apps is displayed. When you click one of the items to see the Details view, the Web App item details have a white background with a formatted header that matches the other web pages in the trial site.

Adding Search Functionality to a Web App

In the previous section, you added the module tag to display all items in the Local Favorites Web App on the About page. When you viewed the live site, you saw that the list of Web App items is displayed below the header. You also learned how to adjust the display of the Web App by editing and publishing the Web App's specific layout files.

For the moment, everything is functioning as expected. The business team could continue to add more Web App items using the Admin Console, and the new items will automatically display in the List view on the About page. It's not necessary to reinsert the module tag or republish the About page to see the new items appear on the live site.

In some cases, such as a store locator, a Web App may contain only a finite number of Web App items that do not change often. Depending on the content and desired functionality, the Web App in its current state might work well for the client.

But consider that this Web App is designed to feature retail stores in the neighborhood. At the moment, the Web App contains only two Web App items, but this Local Favorites list will grow over time. Each time a new store is added, the list gets longer. Eventually, the list will become difficult to navigate and will cause the About page to expand vertically.

Instead of displaying a simple list of all existing Web App items on the About page, you can replace that list with a search feature that enables visitors to choose the type of business they want to find.

In this section, you'll replace the Web App module tag that displays a list of all the items. The new tag will instead display a search interface.

1. Return to Dreamweaver. If you've made any changes to the site using the Admin Console since you last worked in Dreamweaver, be sure to synchronize the site to get the newer files from the remote server.

2. If about.htm is not already open in the Document window, use the Files panel to locate and open that page.

3. Select the existing Web App module tag that you inserted below the Local Favorites header. It looks something like this:

   ```
   {module_webapps,15743,a,}
   ```

   With the entire tag selected, press Delete. Leave your cursor in the location where the deleted tag once was.

4. Open the Business Catalyst panel. Scroll down and click the WebApps category to expand it. Double-click the Web Apps Search Box suboption.

   The Module Configure wizard appears. Select the Web App named Local Favorites and click Next. In the next screen of the Module Configure wizard, click Insert.

5. The Web App search form source code is inserted on the About page. The search interface automatically includes search fields for each custom text field added to the Web App. In addition to a keyword search, the form includes input items to search for the store's location and category.

   In this example, the Web App named Local Favorites doesn't use the categories feature. It's easy to delete unwanted fields by editing the source code of the inserted form using Dreamweaver.

6. In Design view, click inside the Category field. Click the `<div.item>` tag in the Tag Selector at the bottom of the Document window. With the Category field selected, press Delete to delete it. After you make this change, the Design view shows the two remaining fields that enable visitors to search by keywords or location (**FIGURE 9.17**).

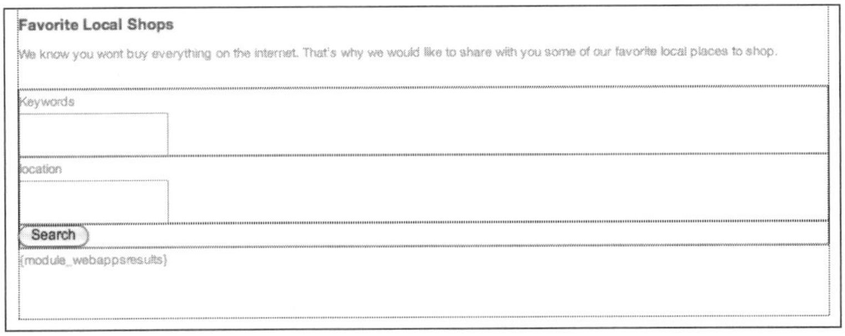

FIGURE 9.17
Delete the Category field from the search form.

7. Save the page and choose Site > Put to upload it to the host server. In the Dependent Files dialog box that appears, click No.

If you return to the browser window that displays the trial site and refresh the About page, you'll see that the search interface replaces the list of Web App items. If desired, you can test the form to see how the search works. For example, if you enter **flower** as a keyword search term, you'll find Fred's Flower Shop. Or if you enter **San Francisco** in the location field and click Search, both local businesses are listed in the search results. (Your search results will vary if you entered different placeholder text when creating the Web App items).

Creating Web Apps Populated with Visitor Data

Earlier in the project development, the client requested a Web App that featured nearby neighborhood businesses to encourage visitors to shop locally. At this point, the Web App achieves that goal because the business team can periodically log in to the Admin Console and add more featured local businesses by creating new Web App items. Visitors can search for businesses on the About page and see the matching Web App items.

However, the client also specified that down the road, they wanted to open up the recommendations to the online community. The goal is to enable site visitors to add their own favorite local stores and suggest them to other visitors.

Because visitors cannot access the Admin Console, this next phase of the project involves creating a new form for the site that is tied to the Web App so that visitors can submit their own Web App items and post them on the site. The Web App requires some new configurations to enable this functionality, so you'll complete the next section using the Admin Console.

FIGURE 9.18
Select the Manage Web Apps suboption in the Web Apps menu.

1. In the Admin Console, choose Modules > Web Apps > Manage Web Apps (**FIGURE 9.18**).

2. The Web Apps List page appears. In the list, click the name of the Web App: Local Favorites.

3. The Web App Details section is displayed. Scroll down to the section titled Can Customers Create Web Apps? and set the following options:
   - Select the checkbox next to Add New Items.
   - Use the menu to set the Role Responsible to Users.
   - Keep the Requires Approval checkbox enabled.

NOTE: The Requires Approval option (which is selected by default) enables content moderation for the Web App Item submission form and sends e-mail notifications to the role specified in the Role Responsible menu.

4. Scroll down to the section titled Customer Options. Enable the Allow File Uploads checkbox and use the Default Upload Folder menu that appears to set the folder to images.

   These two settings will enable visitors to upload a photo of the local business, and the system will save the uploaded files to the /images/ folder (**FIGURE 9.19**).

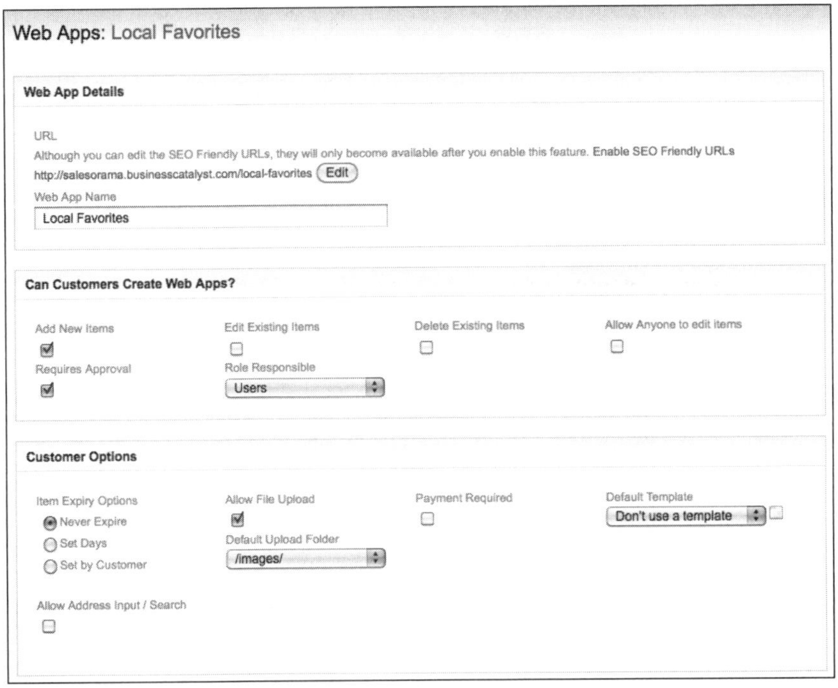

FIGURE 9.19
Use the Default Upload Folder menu to specify the folder where the uploaded images will be stored.

The content moderation feature is activated for the Web App Item submission form. This means that any user accounts included in the Users role will receive an e-mail notification every time a visitor submits a new Web App item using the online submission form.

When the team members included in the Users role receive the e-mail notification, they'll need to click the link in the e-mail (or log in to the Admin Console), review the Web App item submission, and then approve it before the content is displayed on the site. This approval process ensures that only Web App–related content is published to the site—eliminating the possibility that visitors can post spam or inappropriate content.

5. Scroll down and click Save.

Customizing the Web App Edit layout file

In this section, you'll update another Web App layout file. Previously, you edited the List layout file (to control how the list of module items appears) and the Detail layout file (to control how the Detail view is displayed after a visitor clicks on a specific item to learn more about it). Next, you'll update the Web App Edit layout to control the form that visitors will use on the site to enter their own favorite local businesses.

1. In the Admin Console, choose Modules > Web Apps > Manage Web Apps.

2. In the list of Web Apps, select the name of the Web App: Local Favorites. The Web App Details section is displayed.

3. In the sidebar, click the option Customize Web App Layouts. The page reloads to display the List layout file in the online editor. Use the menu at the top of the page to choose the Edit layout file.

4. The page updates to display the default contents of the Edit layout file. Currently it includes only two fields: Item Name and Item Description.

   Scroll to the bottom of the page and click the Reset To Original button. This operation causes the form to update, using the custom data fields that you added to the Web App when you created it. The updated form includes all the fields so that visitors can enter data into each of the four form input areas to provide the store's name, description, and location. They can also upload a photo, if desired. Click Save.

NOTE: In the Customer Options section of the Web App Details, you previously enabled the Allow File Uploads option. That Web App configuration is reflected in the Edit layout file's form, which includes the Browse button to allow visitors to browse and select a file to upload from their local machine.

Inserting the Web App Item Submission Form on a Page

After resetting the Edit layout file to display the necessary data fields, you can insert the Web App item submission form on a page. You can do so using either Dreamweaver or the Admin Console. This time, you'll use the Admin Console.

1. In the Admin Console, choose Website > Web Pages > Create A New Web Page.

2. The Web Page Details page is displayed.

   Enter the following information:

   • In the Page URL field, enter **addFavorite.htm**

   • In the Page Name field, enter **Add a Favorite Place**.

   Leave the Template menu set to Use Default Template.

3. Scroll down to the Web Page Content field in the online editor. Type the following line of text:

   Send us your favorite local places to shop!

To add a line space, press Enter/Return after typing the end of the line. Leave your cursor at its current location so that you can enter the Web App Item Submission form.

4. Either click the blue cross icon or click the option Add Modules To Web Page in the Action Box sidebar. The Module Manager appears in the right sidebar.

5. Click the Web Apps category to expand it. In the list of Web App suboptions, click the option Web Apps Input Form For Customers. Although this option may wrap over two lines in the Module Manager list, you only have to click the first line to select it.

6. The Module Manager updates to display the Select Web App menu. Use the menu to choose the desired Web App: Local Favorites.

The preview area updates to display the Web App Item submission form. Click Insert to insert the form at the current location of the cursor (FIGURE 9.20).

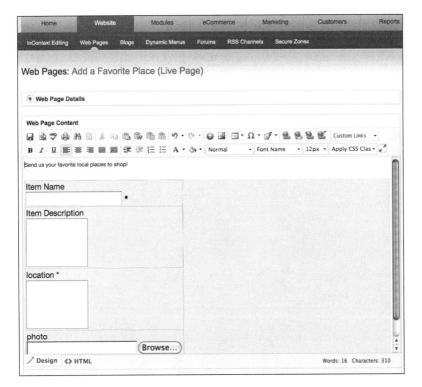

FIGURE 9.20
The submission form is inserted on the page.

7. The trial site template file requires a div container with the style class main-holder in order to display the white background. To add the white background to this new page, click the HTML tab to view the HTML source code. Add the following tags to create a div container that displays the white background for the new form.

At the very top of the page, type:

`<div class="main-holder">`

Scroll to the bottom of the source code, press Enter/Return once to create a new line below the `</form>` tag, and type the closing `<div>` tag:

`</div>`

8. Click Save And Publish to upload the new addFavorite.htm to the live site.

   There's one more thing to do before testing the Web App Item submission form on the live site. To minimize the number of spam submissions posted by the general public, you'll move the new page inside the secure zone so that only registered visitors can access it.

9. Still in the Admin Console, choose Websites > Secure Zones. The list of existing secure zones is displayed.

10. Select the Members Only Area secure zone to edit it. The Secure Zone Details are displayed. Click Next.

11. Use the interface to select the Add A Favorite Place page in the left pane. Click the top, right-pointing arrow to move the page into the right pane so that it is listed along with the Your Orders page (FIGURE 9.21).

FIGURE 9.21
Move the selected web page from the left pane to the right pane.

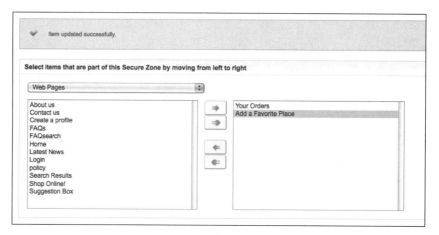

This step ensures that only registered visitors can access the form and submit their favorite local businesses. Because the registered visitors are logged in to the trial site, they are less likely to enter placeholder data or inappropriate content in the form. This strategy has the additional benefit of offering a new feature that is available only to registered visitors, which is another way to entice new visitors to sign up.

Testing the Web App Item Submission Form

To test the recent updates to the Web App and see how it works from a visitor's perspective, follow these steps:

1. Switch to the browser window that displays the trial site. The new page doesn't currently have a link to access it, so type the filename of the page at the end of the home page URL. The address will look something like this:

   http://www.trial-site.businesscatalyst.com/addFavorite.htm

   The Add A Favorite Place page loads. If you're not already logged in to the secure zone, the page displays a form requesting that you log in.

2. Enter the same username and password you used before, when you registered to access the secure zone in Chapter 7, "Understanding Customer Management and the Site's Database." Or if you prefer, create a new profile and log in as a new registered visitor (**FIGURE 9.22**).

FIGURE 9.22
Use the form to log in to the trial site and access the secure zone.

After you log in, the addFavorite.htm page displays the Web App Item Submission form.

3. Enter placeholder data to submit a new fictitious local business in the form. If you'd like, you can click the Browse button and upload an image file from your computer (**FIGURE 9.23**).

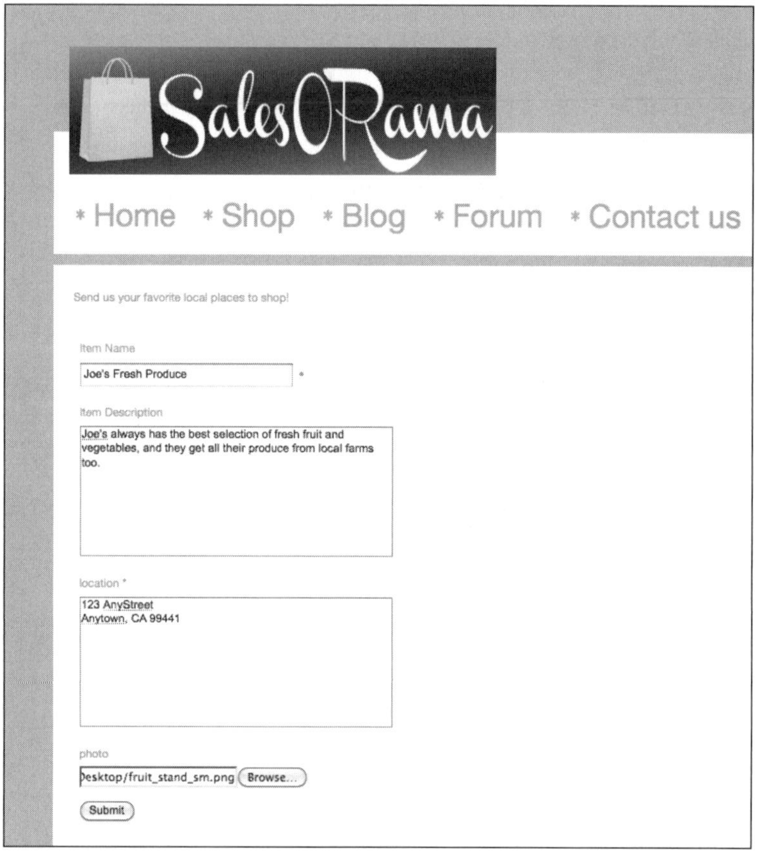

FIGURE 9.23
Enter placeholder data into the submission form fields.

4. Click Submit to submit the new form data. A confirmation message appears to thank the visitor for their suggestion (**FIGURE 9.24**).

FIGURE 9.24
The confirmation message states that the form submission will be reviewed by the business team prior to publishing the item.

Thank you for your submission

Thank you for submitting a new item. One of our representatives will review this item shortly.

Since the submission form is enabled for content moderation, this confirmation message is helpful to ensure that visitors understand the site is not broken. Their suggestion is not immediately displayed on the site because it has been added to the moderation queue.

Your user account for the site is added to both the Administrators and Users roles (and the Role Responsible menu in the Web App configuration is set to notify any user that's added to the Users role). You'll receive an e-mail notification that new content has been submitted and is awaiting approval. In this next step, you'll test the moderation process used by team members to review and publish new Web App items to the live site.

5. Check your Inbox to access the notification e-mail message. Click the link in the e-mail message or log in to the Admin Console to visit the list of pending Web App items. You can use the navigation to choose Modules > Web Apps > Local Favorites and jump directly to the list of Web App items.

   Previously, there were only two Web App items, but now a third (disabled) item appears in the list (FIGURE 9.25).

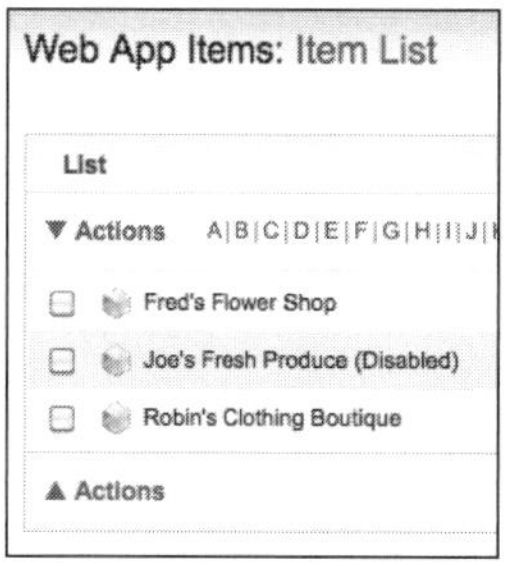

6. Click the name of the new item in the list to access the submitted data.

   The team members responsible for approving content can moderate several new items at a time by opening each one and reading the form data that was submitted. For this example, assume that the team member has reviewed the data and agrees that the item should be added to the live site.

7. Select the Enabled checkbox to approve the new Web App item (FIGURE 9.26).

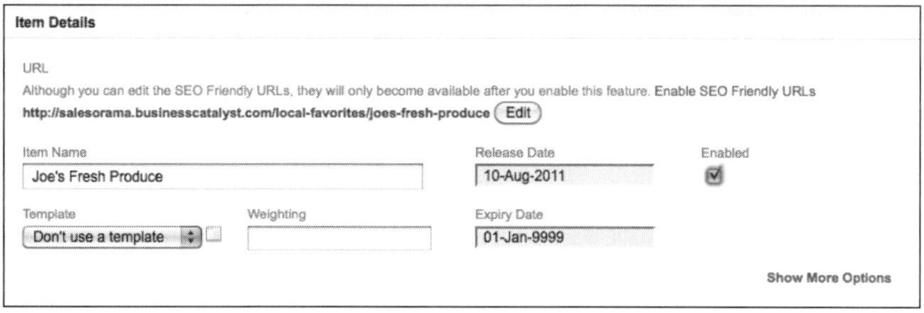

FIGURE 9.25
The new Web App item is listed and marked as disabled.

FIGURE 9.26
Select the Enabled checkbox to approve disabled items.

8. Scroll down and click Save to publish the new item to the live site.

Before checking the trial site to see the new item appear, you'll add a link to the new page using Dreamweaver.

Updating the About page to add a link to the submission form

In this section, you'll return to Dreamweaver to make one final change to the About page. You'll update the text and add a link so that visitors who are searching to find favorite local shops can easily navigate to the page where they can submit their own suggestions.

1. Launch Dreamweaver. Click the Synchronize button at the top of the Files panel to sync the entire site to get the newer remote files. This ensures that you're working with the latest version of the site files after editing them in the Admin Console.

2. Open the Business Catalyst panel (Window > Business Catalyst). Make sure that the trial site is currently selected and that you're logged in.

3. In the Files panel, double-click the about.htm page to open it in the Document window.

4. In Design view, click after the end of the sentence: "... places to shop." Press Enter/Return to create a new line. Type the following text:

   If you are one of our members, you can add your own favorite places.

5. Select the text "favorite places." While it is selected, click the folder icon next to the Link field in the HTML section of the Property inspector. Browse to select the addFavorite.htm file. Click Choose to add the link to the selected text (FIGURE 9.27).

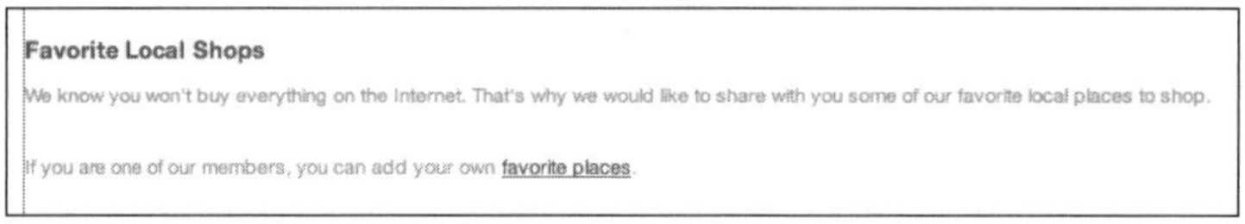

FIGURE 9.27
Create a link on the About page to make it easy for visitors to submit new Web App items.

> **Favorite Local Shops**
> We know you won't buy everything on the Internet. That's why we would like to share with you some of our favorite local places to shop.
>
> If you are one of our members, you can add your own **favorite places**.

6. Save and put the about.htm page. In the Dependent Files dialog box that appears, click No.

Switch to the browser window that displays the trial site. In the footer, click the About Us link in the Our Company section to visit the About page. The page loads and displays the search interface for Local Favorites Web App. Click the new link you just added to visit the addFavorite.htm page.

If you're still logged in to the secure zone, you'll see the Web App Item Submission form displayed. If not, enter your username and password and click Login to access the page to submit new local businesses.

As you can see, Web Apps are completely customizable. They enable you to display custom content as sets of data fields in a List or Details view. By default, they can be populated by users with access to the Admin Console. Or you can expand them to enable registered visitors to log in and post suggestions online. Using the moderation settings available when configuring Web Apps, you can create a notification and approval system that ensures only valid and applicable content is approved and published to the site.

Experiment with making some small Web Apps first, to practice defining custom fields and specifying the types of data that are displayed. Also investigate the tags available in the Tag Insert menu when you're editing the Web App layout files (in Dreamweaver or the Admin Console) to discover other ways you can display the Web App items and related functionality on web pages.

Workflow for Building Web Apps

When you work with Web Apps to add custom site features for clients, you'll generally follow these steps:

1. In the Admin Console, create a new Web App and define its custom data fields.
2. Update the Web App layout files to adjust how the data is displayed. Insert tag attributes to display additional data (as desired) in the List and Details views. You can use either the Admin Console or Dreamweaver to edit the layout files.
3. In the Admin Console, add Web App items to populate the Web App with data. Fill in the custom fields to enter the content you want to appear for each item.
4. Using either Dreamweaver or the Admin Console, insert the Web App module on a page. Edit the other content on the page as desired.
5. Using either Dreamweaver or the Admin Console, insert a search field for the Web App.
6. If desired, return to the Admin Console and configure the Web App to enable customer submissions.
7. Create a secure zone for the site (if one doesn't already exist). Insert a registration form and a login form on the live site. Also specify the secure zone's landing page.
8. Insert a Web App submission form on a web page and publish it. Move the web page inside the secure zone.
9. Log in to the live site and test the Web App as the visitor by submitting new Web App items. Access the Admin Console as a team member to make sure everything works as expected.

Now that you understand how to set up Web Apps and how valuable they can be to generate traffic and participation on a client site, also consider that you could charge visitors to access a secure zone. An online business could offer access to secure zone based on receiving payment for a monthly subscription or a flat fee. This is an alternate method that the online business can use to increase revenue.

NOTE: To process transactions on the site, you must first upgrade the site and set up at least one payment gateway.

To require payment in the registration form used by visitors to sign up to access a secure zone, choose Website > Secure Zones. Click the name of the secure zone in the list that is displayed. In the Secure Zone Details section, enable the Sell Membership Access To This Secure Zone checkbox.

Related Links

 Awesome Web Apps Without Coding:
http://www.adobe.com/go/bc_without_coding

 Customizing The Look and Feel of Web Apps:
http://www.adobe.com/go/bc_customize_web_apps

 Inserting Web App Listings on a Page:
http://www.adobe.com/go/bc_insert_web_app

CHAPTER 10

Analyzing Performance and Revenue with Reports

Contents

Accessing Report Summary Information   212

Generating and Saving Custom Reports   216

In this chapter, you'll analyze the Business Catalyst reporting section and learn how statistics and charts will appear after a site has launched and begun gathering customer data.

Your clients are more likely to log in and access the features in the Reports tab than any other area of the Admin Console. They can view the charts on the Summary page to see the overall site performance, and then use the report interface to drill down into the site's database to check specific statistics. The report information is updated throughout the day, so they can check the direct influence of their marketing efforts.

Business Catalyst lets you generate and save custom reports to obtain statistics for a particular type of data. To ensure that the reports are not skewed by the activity generated by the web team and business members, you can configure the reports to ignore specific IP addresses.

Because you're working with a trial site that hasn't been upgraded or launched yet, the report pages of your trial won't contain a lot of traffic analytics or statistics yet. As you follow along with this chapter, you can log in to the Admin Console to identify the report areas in this interface, but you'll find it most helpful to review the screenshots taken from a live Business Catalyst site. Use these instructions to learn how to access critical site information and track trends using the site's reporting features. Later, after you've launched your first client site, you can return to this chapter and compare the live site's reports to analyze the site's activity.

Once you are familiar with the reports and have experience measuring statistics, you can train your clients to log in to the Admin Console so that they can view the reports and track trends to learn how their business is growing.

You'll begin by exploring the data provided on the Home page of the Admin Console by viewing the charts in the Dashboard.

1. Log in to the Admin Console to visit the Dashboard.

   This area offers a summary of the overall site performance. Your clients can access the Dashboard to quickly identify key statistics and get a better understanding of their online business.

2. To measure the overall health of the site, review the information provided in the Overview section at the top of the page (FIGURE 10.1).

FIGURE 10.1
The Overview section of the Dashboard displays a chart with key statistics.

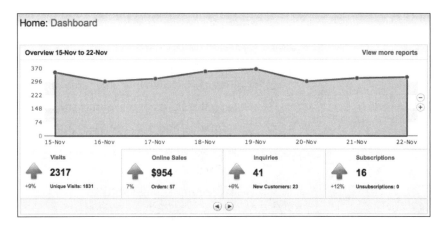

As you click on each item, the corresponding chart for the top-level area is displayed:

- Visits
- Online Sales
- Inquiries
- Subscriptions

By default, the Overview chart displays a week's worth of data. You can click the minus (–) button to zoom out; each click adds an additional week to the report's date range (FIGURE 10.2).

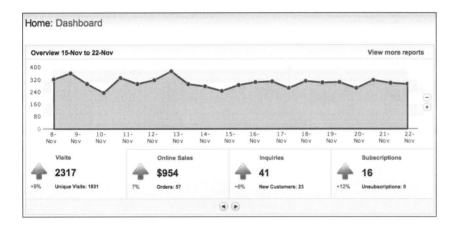

FIGURE 10.2
Increase the date range by clicking the minus (–) button to add additional weeks to the reporting period.

Click the plus (+) button to reduce the number of weeks analyzed in the chart and return to the week view. If you click the left and right arrow buttons below the set of statistics, the panel rotates to show another set of quick reports and charts that display the number of Forum Posts, Bookings, Secure Zone Logins, and Affiliate Referrals (FIGURE 10.3).

FIGURE 10.3
Click the left- and right-pointing buttons to rotate the statistics and see other categories.

The Dashboard is a great way to access the high-level site information. Report summaries make it easy for you and your clients to review the statistics and identify the top-performing areas of the site and the areas that need improvement. With minimal effort, your clients can log in to their online business every day to better understand their customer base and learn how the site's features are generating traffic and revenue.

Accessing Report Summary Information

Whenever your clients want to dive into data and learn more details about specific areas of the business, they can visit the Reports section of the Admin Console.

1. In the Admin Console, choose Reports > Summary. Use the Date Period menu to choose the time span of the report data (FIGURE 10.4).

FIGURE 10.4
The Reports Summary page includes more helpful data to track site activity and traffic.

The resulting page includes the following charts:

- Geo Location, a map that visually indicates the physical location of site visitors

- Visits and Page Views, an itemized day-to-day list detailing the number of site visits and web pages accessed

- New and Returning Visits, a pie chart outlining how the site attracts new visitors

- Top Sources, a list of the five most effective external links that are driving traffic to the site

FIGURE 10.5
In addition to the Overview, the Summary category includes Marketing and Content Summary pages.

2. Use the accordion panel on the right side to navigate the reports. The home page of the Reports summary is the Overview level; this page contains the charts you are currently viewing. The Summary section includes two more sections: Marketing and Content (FIGURE 10.5).

3. Click the Marketing option and take a moment to review the Marketing Summary page (FIGURE 10.6).

FIGURE 10.6
The Marketing Summary page displays charts you can use to learn how visitors are discovering the site.

This page includes charts that let you see at a glance how visitors are being routed to the site. This area highlights the search engines, keyword phrases, and top referrers that drive traffic to the site.

4. Click the Content option to access the Content Summary page (**FIGURE 10.7**).

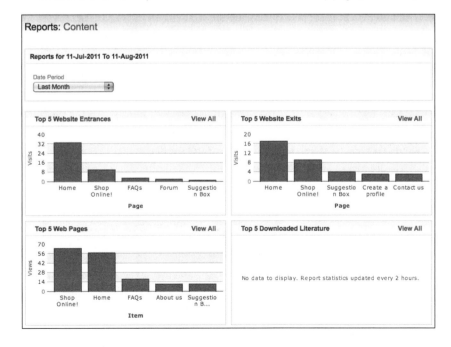

FIGURE 10.7
The Content Summary page makes it easy to tell which areas of the site are receiving the most attention and interaction.

FIGURE 10.8
Use the categories in the right sidebar to access the detailed reports.

Use these reports to identify and track the most popular entrance and exit pages. You and your clients can use the information displayed here to help you fine-tune the content and rearrange the site flow to optimize its performance. In addition to listing the top five most highly trafficked web pages, the system tracks the Literature items that have been downloaded most often from the site.

5. Return to the right sidebar and review the contents below the Summary section. Each of these categories contains even more detailed reports highlighting every aspect of the site (FIGURE 10.8).

A description of each section follows:

Traffic: Click the Total Traffic option to see total traffic and bandwidth statistics for the site. The daily graph includes in and out data statistics. *In* refers to files and data uploaded to your site by visitors and *out* reflects the files and data provided on the site that visitors have downloaded.

Path: Click the Entry Page option to learn the page of the site where visitors enter. Click the Exit Page option to analyze the pages where they leave the site. This area is an expanded view of the visits and page views chart on the Reports Summary page.

Visitors: Use this series of reports to review visitor data in granular detail. The Visitors category includes the following options:

- **Visits by IP address:** Identify unique visitors, the number of times each computer visited the site and the visitor's country of origin.

- **Visitor Details:** Learn the date, number of page views, visitors' location, and duration of time spent accessing the site.

- **Visits And Page Views:** See the consolidated number of visits and page views per day.

- **Total Visits:** Track the number of unique (new) visitors and returning visitors within a specific date range.

- **Visits By Source:** Examine the methods used by visitors to access the site directly: via a link from a referring website or using a search engine.

- **Visitor Loyalty:** Compare the number of visitors with the number of visits to the site to research traffic patterns.

- **Spy Lens:** Access visitor's personal information, including name, IP address, location, page views, and visit dates.

Browsers: Choose the Browser option to learn the browsers used to visit the site. Click the Platform option to see a breakdown of visitors' operating systems. By researching the browsers and computer platforms used by the customer base, you can make informed design and code decisions to tailor content to work for the site's audience.

Search Engine: Use the Search Engine Referrals data to discover how search engines are directing traffic to the site. The Search Phrase option displays the keyword search terms used by visitors to locate the site. Select the Spider option to determine which search-engine spiders have indexed the site.

Geographic: Select the Geographic Location option to understand the traffic originating from various countries around the world. Countries are ranked by popularity to help businesses track the location details about visitors. These statistics elaborate on the Geo Location chart provided on the Report Summary page.

Website Content: Choose the applicable type of content such as web pages, announcements, FAQ lists, Literature items, Web App items, catalogs, products, forum posts, blog entries, and bookings to track site content. This area includes metrics about all of the module features as well. Use Website Content to learn which areas of the site are most popular with visitors. Create strategies to increase traffic to areas of the site that are not receiving as much attention.

Marketing: This section includes Overview, Campaign, Subscriber Geographic Location, Subscriptions vs. Unsubscriptions, and Newsletters Sent. Analyze these statistics to learn more about e-mail campaign subscribers and their habits.

Leads: Choose Overview, Inquirer Geographic Location, Inquiries, and Top Web Form Usage to track specific customer inquiries and other data submitted in forms. Find out where potential customers live and which forms are generating the most submissions.

eCommerce: Select the Overview, Shopper Geographic Location, Sales, Top Products, and Abandon Rate options in this section to get helpful information about product sales. Evaluate the top products in the online store and determine where the customers are located. You can track the shopping cart abandon rate and then use the statistics to develop sales strategies to keep customers engaged and encourage them to make more purchases.

Miscellaneous: Click the Ignored IP Address List option to manage the list of IP addresses that the system will ignore so that the traffic reports are not skewed by the visits of the business team and the web developers working on the site. Gather your IP addresses (as well as the team members who run the online business) so that you can add them to this list and ensure they are not counted in the site analytics.

Generating and Saving Custom Reports

The Business Catalyst Platform includes a wealth of report information. The Report section of the Admin Console includes many detailed report sections that let you see how the site is operating and determine the activity of site visitors. After launching a site, make it a habit to frequently check the report data to see how visitors are navigating to the site, which products they are purchasing, and which features they use most often.

The report functionality is standardized so that they are easy to use. The detailed reports are designed to display the specific data you and your clients need to make informed business decisions. The interfaces are all similar, so use these steps to see how they work:

1. In the Admin Console, choose Reports > Summary. In the right sidebar, click the Browsers category to expand it. Select the Browser suboption to visit the Browser Reports page.

    All of the detailed reports include a menu at the top that enables you to specify the date range of the report (FIGURE 10.9).

FIGURE 10.9
Set the date range for the report with the Date Period menu.

2. Scroll down to see the data displayed in a chart and in a table format (FIGURE 10.10).

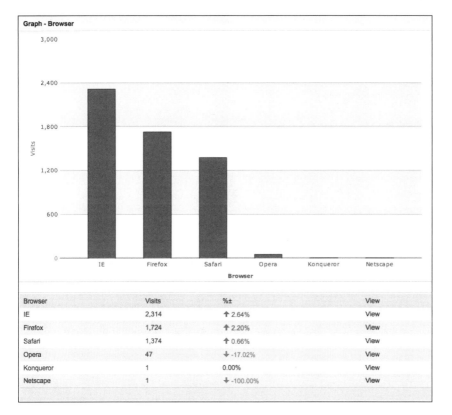

FIGURE 10.10
The data is displayed in a graph chart and listed in table rows.

3. Scroll down farther, below the charts, to see the Report Description. You can click the Export Report button to obtain a copy of the report in Excel, PDF, or CSV file formats to study the data (FIGURE 10.11).

   You can also run your own custom reports. The Reports section of the Admin Console includes custom report generators that allow you to view statistics regarding customers, the website, and e-commerce operations (FIGURE 10.12).

FIGURE 10.11
When you're exporting reports, use the menu to choose the desired file format.

FIGURE 10.12
The Reports tab includes several custom report areas.

In Chapter 8, "Marketing with E-mail Campaigns," you learned how to run a custom customer report to segment the customer database. Remember that in addition to creating a customer report and saving it, you can use the results of a custom report to add customers to a recipient list or a secure zone.

When you run a custom website report, you can sort the data and filter the results based on several fields. Use the options provided to slice the site data and determine how visitors are making their way to the site (FIGURE 10.13).

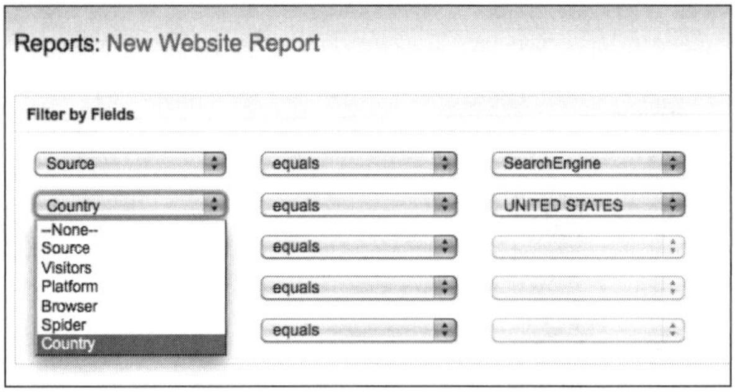

FIGURE 10.13
The Filter By Fields section includes menus you can use to define the report's parameters.

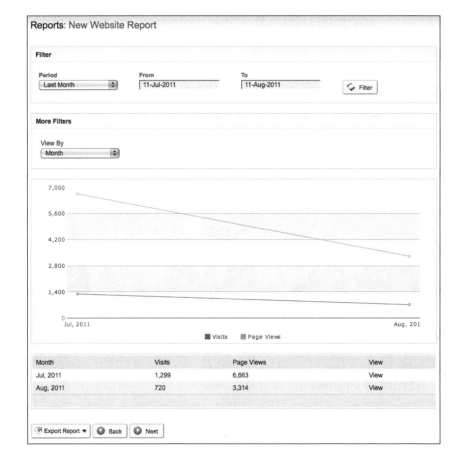

Site reports locate and display the website traffic that matches specific attributes and enable you to filter that data over time to identify trends (FIGURE 10.14).

FIGURE 10.14
Set date ranges to track site activity that occurs alongside business milestones such as hosting a recent promotional event or publishing an e-mail marketing campaign.

You can learn how the online store is performing by running a custom eCommerce report. Select the sections of the online store that you want to study (FIGURE 10.15).

FIGURE 10.15
Learn more about customer behavior by running reports to find specific details about the online store.

When running the reports, you can set the filters to access data about a specific segment of the market so that the business can learn more about the customers who purchase products (FIGURE 10.16).

FIGURE 10.16
Filter the eCommerce report criteria to drill down into specific sets of customers.

You can generate reports, and after evaluating them, you can reset the time range and specify additional filter settings using the menus at the top of the page. The data is displayed in several ways; the graph and table data are displayed underneath the filter menus (FIGURE 10.17).

FIGURE 10.17
Use the filter menus to define
the criteria for the statistics
to review report data more
efficiently.

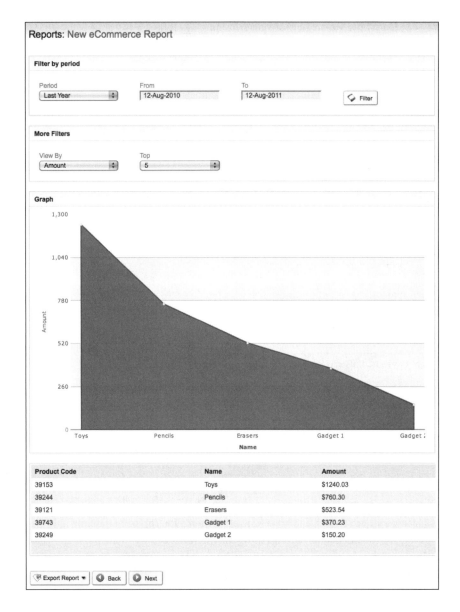

If you'd like to share the data with other systems or view it as a spreadsheet, click the Export Report button.

Whenever you create a report you want to run again in the future, you can save custom reports. That way, you can easily access the data again over time. In the right sidebar, click the Step 5: Save Report option. In the Report Details section, enter the name of the report in the Report Name field and click Save Report (**FIGURE 10.18**).

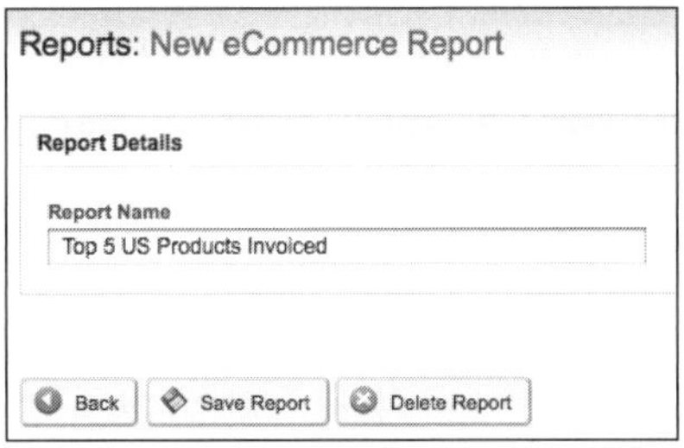

Reports: New eCommerce Report

Report Details

Report Name

Top 5 US Products Invoiced

Back Save Report Delete Report

FIGURE 10.18
After entering the report's name, click the Save Report button to save the report.

Later, when you return to the Reports tab and choose the customer, website, or eCommerce custom report areas, the custom reports you saved are listed on the corresponding page (FIGURE 10.19).

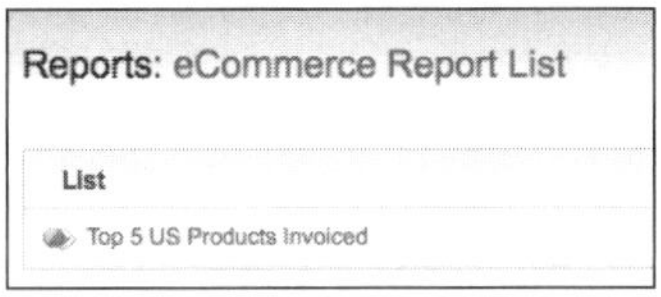

Reports: eCommerce Report List

List

Top 5 US Products Invoiced

FIGURE 10.19
The saved reports are listed by name in the customer, website, and eCommerce custom report pages.

The Business Catalyst Platform includes an integrated database that makes it easy for you and your clients to access the data in easy-to-consume formats. Take some time getting to know all the report options so that you can educate your clients on the features available. When you're pitching new projects, reports are one of the areas that make clients sit up and take notice. Business owners immediately recognize how much more effectively and efficiently they can run their business when they can see the macro and micro views of the site activity. This is one of the major selling points in Business Catalyst because the central database makes it possible to cross-reference and filter data across many different aspects.

Over time, as you become more familiar with analyzing reports, you can help clients by consulting with them and offering strategic ways to run custom reports. You can help them identify the weakest areas of a site and drive more traffic to the content you want visitors to access. You can also promote the online store in new ways after you learn the most popular site features and have a better understanding of the site's visitors.

Related Links

 Your Business Reporting & Analytics:
http://www.adobe.com/go/bc_reports_analytics

 Better Results with Business Insight:
http://www.adobe.com/go/bc_business_insight

Index

Numbers

1-Click Insert menu
  displaying, 59
  subscription forms, 165
  Suggestion Box form, 95
  using to add web forms, 94–96
  using with modules, 59–61
30-day trial, extending, online p13

Symbol

, (comma), using in module tags, 62

A

Ad Rotators module, 69
Admin Console
  Action Box sidebar, 18
  Admin menu, 11
  Administration Login page, online p9
  cases, 140–142
  Cases page for form data, 78
  catalog for online stores, 103–104
  charts, 212
  copying products, 110–112
  creating products, 106–108, 110
  creating templates, 33–35
  Customer Cases option, 78
  Customer Summary page, 78
  Customers tab, 10
  customizing modules with layouts, 52–56
  customizing system messages, 86
  Dashboard, 7–8
  Dashboard charts, 210–211
  Dashboard for form data, 77
  date range for statistics, 211
  deleting products, 105
  displaying, 3, 6
  displaying templates in, 33
  eCommerce tab, 9
  editing pages in Design view, 18–19
  editing source code in HTML view, 19–20
  editing Welcome text, 27
  Email Campaigns option, 168
  enabling access for clients, 6–7
  File Manager, 11
  form data, 77–79
  Geo Location chart, 212
  Home page, 77, 210–211
  Image Manager, 19
  inserting modules into web pages, 56–59
  listing products, 105
  Live Feed for form data, 77
  Manage Roles option, online p4
  Manage Users option, online p2–p3, online p6
  Manage Web Apps option, 198, 200
  managing products, 105–106
  managing sites with, 35
  marketing features, 9–10
  modules, 9, 48, 50–51
  New and Returning Visits chart, 212
  online-store workflow, 130
  Overview chart, 210–211
  Partner Portal, 11–14
  Reports tab, 10–11
  retrieving submitted messages, 77–78
  returning to, 14
  searching for cases in, 144
  Segment Customer Database, 178
  selecting products, 105
  Shipping Options, 125
  statistics in Dashboard, 210
  submenu options, 92
  Summary option, 212
  templates, 33–35
  Top Sources chart, 212
  updating images, 21
  updating sites, 20–21
  View All Products option, 106
  Visits and Page Views chart, 212
  Web Apps option, 186, 191
  Website area, 8
  Website tab, 16
Admin menu
  accessing, 11
  disabling, online p9
Administration List page, accessing, online p3
Administrator's role
  assigning to users, online p8
  explained, 137
  versus Users role, online p5
  warning about deletion of, 138
Adobe Business Catalyst. See Business Catalyst
Adobe Dreamweaver. See Dreamweaver
Ajax effect, setting, 61
Announcements module, 69
approvals, managing in workflow steps, 146–147
auto-responder e-mail, using, 164

B

backing up data, online p17–p18
billing options, 13, 131, online p14
Blog module, accessing, 5
Bookings module, 69, 71
Browsers report, 215
Business Catalyst
  features of, viii
  Impressum Online Store template, 2
  Site Details page, 2
  Site Option page, 2
  website, xii, 2, 14
business goals, facilitating with workflows, 148
business insight link, 221
Business plan, choosing, online p13
business reporting & analytics link, 221
Buy Now button, adding, 116–117

C

campaigns. See e-mail campaigns
CAPTCHA, 75, 98
case data, 135–138
cases
  accessing in Admin Console, 140–142
  adding notes and tasks for, 142–144
  creating, 139–142
  Details field, 141–142
  filtering, 144–145
  generating, 135–138
  searching for, 144–145
  Status menu, 141
  Thread Summary, 142
catalogs
  adding products to, 104, 108
  creating and managing, 9
  creating for online stores, 103–104
  listing in online store, 5
categories, using classify items, 60
charts, displaying statistics in, 210–211
client sites, managing, 12

clients
  evaluating potential of, xi
  invoicing, online p14
CMS (Content Management System), viii
coding link, 71
comma (,), using in module tags, 62
Comment form, selecting source code
  for, 55
commissions, accumulating, 13
contact data, managing, 79, 160–162
Contact Details page, accessing, 144
contact forms, managing, 6, 75–76. *See
  also* form data; web forms
contact records, adding notes and tasks,
  to, 144
Contact Us form
  displaying, 83
  editing for newsletter subscriptions,
   167–168
  selecting source code in, 86
  using to generate cases, 135–138
  workflow for, 80
Content Approval workflow, using, 148
content changes, making and saving, x,
  16, 18. *See also* web pages
Content Summary page, displaying, 213
copyright message, displaying in
  Dreamweaver, 40
CSS folder, all.css file in, 70
Custom Links menu, using, 51
custom reports. *See also* reports
  creating from customer database,
   178–182
  data fields, 179
  date ranges, 218
  display options, 219–220
  eCommerce, 219
  exporting, 220
  filtering, 180, 218–220
  generating, 181, 216–221
  saving, 182, 220–221
  types of, 179
customer behavior, running reports of, 219
Customer Cases option, choosing in Admin Console, 78, 141
customer cases, responding to, x
customer data links, 156
customer database
  generating custom reports, 178–182
  locating related customers, 180
  targeting segment of, 177–182
  using, 10
Customer Inquiry workflow, 80, 137–139

customer records
  adding notes and tasks to, 144
  contact data in, 79
Customer Summary page, displaying in
  Admin Console, 78
customer support workflow, creating, 148
customers
  communicating with, 74
  relating in database, 180
  sending messages to, 79
  subscribing to recipient lists, 163–164

D
Dashboard
  in Admin Console, 7–8
  links in, 8
  site statistics in, 7
data
  backing up, online p17–p18
  gathering with secure zones, 148–150
Design view, editing pages in, 18–19
DNS records link, online p18
domain names, managing, online p15,
  online p18
Dreamweaver
  accessing Business Catalyst from, 23
  accessing template files, 39–41
  adding placeholder content, 37–38
  adding web forms, 85–87
  applying templates to pages in, 35–38
  building templates in, 30
  Business Catalyst panel, 23–24
  connecting to sites, 23–25
  Contact Us form for newsletter subscriptions, 167–168
  copyright message, 40
  creating pages and using templates, 36
  CSS Rule Definition dialog box, 41
  deleting web-form source code, 85–87
  displaying template assets, 37
  downloading extension for, viii, 13
  DWT files, 30
  editing site content, 25–28
  editing store layouts, 122–123
  editing system messages, 86
  editing templates in, 39–44
  Files panel, 25
  Firebug add-on, 41
  inserting modules into web pages,
   63–65
  inserting Web Apps on pages, 193, 195
  Inspect mode, 40
  installing extension for, 22

Layouts folder, 67
Main template, 39
managing sites with, 35
Module Configure wizard, 87
module tags in template, 43–44
New CSS Rule button, 40
newsletter design, 174
Preview in Browser option, 28
product search form, 122–123
Put option, 38
Refresh option, 41
reinserting web-form source code,
  85–87
search functionality for Web Apps, 197
Select A Site menu, 23
Setup screen, 24
stylesheets folder, 41
Synchronize button, 63, 86
Tag Selector, 86
updating logo in template, 41–43
updating module Layout files, 66–68
updating page content, 37–38
updating slide show images, 25–27
updating template files, 41
uploading pages, 38
DWT files, using in Dreamweaver, 30
dynamic menus, 44–46

E
eCommerce. *See also* online stores
  link, 131
  report, 215, 219
  tab options, 9
editing site content, 25–28
e-mail addresses
  entering, online p16
  versus web forms, 75
e-mail campaigns
  Campaign Summary page, 176
  choosing recipients, 170, 172
  creating, 9–10, 168–170, 172–175
  design templates, 172–173
  publishing messages to lists, 175
  receiving messages, 175
  reporting system, 176
  Save Draft button, 174
  Send Verification Email button, 174
  sending, 168–170, 172–175
  targeting recipients, 176
  tracking statistics, 175–176
  verifying addresses, 170
e-mail etiquette, practicing, 177
e-mail marketing link, 182

e-mail messages
customizing, online p15
designing and sending, 9–10
receiving from clients, 134
e-mail newsletters link, 182
e-mail notifications. *See also* notification
messages
adding to web forms, 96
versus SMS notification, 147
using with cases, 147
e-mail versus HTML formats, 170

F
FAQ answers, customizing display of,
61–62
FAQ data items, inserting on pages, 57–59
FAQ items
Ajax behavior, 61–62
displaying in FAQs List page, 59
inserting, 62
inserting list of, 62
inserting with 1-Click Insert menu,
59–61
FAQ page
adding module tag to, 58
module tag, 56–57
refreshing, 51
FAQ questions
customizing, 53
displaying as numbered list, 68
FAQ search page, adding link to, 66
FAQs category, displaying in Module
Manager, 57
FAQs List page, displaying FAQs in, 50
FAQs module. *See also* modules
Back To FAQs link, 55–56
creating items in, 51
customizing layouts of, 53
features of, 69
formatting answer text, 51
sorting items in, 50
specifying, 62
storing guidelines in, 48–49
storing policies in, 48–49
using templates with, 51
file extensions, including, 17
File Manager, accessing, 11, 16
Firebug add-on, installing, 41
folders, displaying, 8
footer, sample in trial site, 32
footer menu items, displaying, 44
form data. *See also* contact forms
accessing in Admin Console, 77–79
case management workflow, 78–79

forms. *See* subscription forms; web forms
forums, 5–6, 155

G
Gallery, 13, online p11
Geo Location chart, displaying, 212
Geographic report, described, 215
graphs displaying statistics in, 210–211
guidelines, storing in FAQs module, 48–49

H
header area
sample in trial site, 31
updating for logout link, 154
home page
in trial site, 31–32
viewing for live site, 28
hosting plans, online p13–p14
HTML versus text e-mail formats, 170
HTML view, editing source code in, 19–20
HTTPS URL prefix, importance of, ix

I
Image Manager, displaying, 19
image verification, using on web forms, 75
images, updating in Admin Console, 21
Impressum Online Store template, 2
InContext Editing
accessing, 8
using to update sites, 20–21
Individual Catalog layout, 115
Individual Product layout, 116, 118
inquiries, displaying chart of, 211
Inspect mode, enabling in Dreamweaver, 40
inventory tracking, using with products, 109
invoices, generating, online p14

J
JPEG files, using for products, 106, 111

L
launch, preparing for, online p15–p16
layout files. *See also* store layouts
custom tags, 116
Individual Product, 118
in OnlineShop folder, 123
Reset To Original button, 112
leads and closing sales link, 98
Leads report, described, 215
Link Manager window, displaying, 44
List layout, editing for modules, 52–54
Literature module, 70
live site updates, testing, 28. *See also* sites

Local Favorites Web App, creating,
186–190
Log Out button, testing, 155
logging in, 2–3
Login area, editing text in, 27
login forms
including in secure zones, 149
sample in trial site, 32
logo, updating in template, 41
logout link, adding, 154
loyalty programs, using, 171

M
mail setup link, online p18
mailing lists, inviting subscriptions to, 177
Marketing area, using tools in, 9–10
Marketing report, described, 215
Marketing Summary page, displaying,
212–213
messages, sending to customers, 79
Miscellaneous report, described, 215
mobile devices, template for, 34
Module Configure wizard, accessing,
64–65, 87
module data, accessing in Admin Console,
50–51
Module Manager
closing, 58
FAQs category, 57
inserting web forms, 89
module tags, 89
opening, 57
Select Display Criteria menu, 58
module tags
adding to FAQ page, 58
attributes in, 62
commas (,) in, 62
identifying in templates, 43–44
using, 56–57
using with products, 118–120
modules. *See also* FAQs module
accessing in Admin Console, 48
accessing layouts, 53
AD Rotators, 69
adding site features, 69–70
Admin link, 52
Announcements, 69
Bookings, 69
CSS folder, 70
Customize link, 61
customizing with tag attributes, 62
designing features of, 52
displaying, 184
displaying options for, 52

editing data displayed in, 49–51
editing Detail layout, 54–56
editing List layout, 52–54
FAQ, 48–49
features of, 9, 47
inserting for web pages, 57–59
inserting into web pages, 56–59
inserting with 1-Click Insert menu, 59–61
inserting with Dreamweaver, 63–65
inserting with Module Manager, 57–59
Literature, 70
Photo Galleries, 70
Tag Insert menu, 56
updating layout files, 52, 66–68
using comments with CSS files, 70
Web Page Details page, 57

N

navigation links, sample in trial site, 31
New and Returning Visits chart, displaying, 212
Newsletter Signup forms, 159, 165–166
newsletter subscriptions, 166–168
newsletters, designing in Dreamweaver, 174
notes and tasks, adding to cases, 142–144
notification messages, using with cases, 147. See also e-mail notifications

O

online businesses
    analyzing models for, x–xi
    comparing, viii
    link, 14
    running, ix
    success of, ix–x
online sales, displaying chart of, 211
online stores. See also eCommerce; store
    layouts; trial sites
    accessing layouts, 114
    catalogs, 101, 103
    checking performance of, 219
    Detail view for products, 102
    DWT files, 112
    eCommerce tools, 130
    editing layouts in Admin Console, 112, 114–115
    layout files, 112
    listing catalogs in, 5
    managing, 131, 134
    moving products, 104
    Overall Layout, 114–115
    payment gateways, 102–103, 128–129
    product search form, 123–125

products, 101–102
returning to store layouts, 115
shipping options, 125–127
Shop link, 100–101
shopping cart, 102
template files, 112
View Cart link, 102
workflow in Admin Console, 130
OnlineShop folder, layout files in, 123
orders, managing, 144–145
Orders page, visiting, 149

P

page title, displaying, 17
pages. See web pages
paragraphs, typing, 18
Partner account, defining, 12
Partner Portal, 11–14, online p11
Partner settings, managing, online p12
Partners, referring, 13
Path report, described, 214
payment gateways, 103, 128–129
permissions, managing, online p4–p6
Photo Galleries module, 70
placeholder content, adding in Dreamweaver, 37–38
policies, storing in FAQs module, 48–49
Policy page, adding links to, 51
policy.htm file, selecting, 38
Premium Partners, features of, 13
pricing, getting information about, 13
Pro plan, choosing, online p14
Product Description Field, filling in, 107
Product Details page, displaying, 107
product images, displaying in Detail view, 120–122
product search form, adding to home page, 123–125
products
    adding to catalogs, 104, 108
    attribute groups, 121
    batch-importing, 112
    copying, 110–112
    creating, 106–108, 110
    deleting from online stores, 105
    grouping, 119, 121
    importing, 113
    inventory tracking, 109
    listing, 105
    managing with Admin Console, 105–106
    moving in online stores, 104
    moving tags for, 120
    pricing, 106–108

selecting, 105
Show More Options, 109
tagging, 118–120
Tax Codes option, 110
updating List view of, 116–117
uploading JPEG files for, 106, 111
View All Products option, 106
Weighting field, 111
profiles, creating for secure zones, 150

Q

Quick Subscribe feature, using, 161

R

recipient lists
    creating, 9, 160–161
    displaying, 161
    subscribing customers to, 163–164
    targeting in e-mail campaigns, 176
    targeting segments of, 177–182
recipients, importing with spreadsheets, 162
referral fee, earning, 13
registration forms, using, 149, 151
reports. See also custom reports
    Browsers, 215
    Content Summary page, 213
    customizing, 178–182
    eCommerce, 215
    exporting, 217
    generating, 212–215
    Geographic, 215
    Leads, 215
    Marketing, 215
    Marketing Summary page, 212–213
    Miscellaneous, 215
    Path, 214
    Search Engine, 215
    Visitors, 214
    Website Content, 215
Reports tab, options on, 10–11
Reset To Original button, 112
roles
    Administrators, 137–138
    managing, online p2–p6, online p15
    setting up for departments, 147
    tying to workflows, 138
    Users, 137–138
    warning about deletion of, 138

S

sales
  closing, 98
  displaying chart of, 211
Sales O Rama site project link, online p18
saving content changes, 18
search engine optimization (SEO), en-
    abling, online p16
Search Engine report, described, 215
search field, sample in trial site, 31
search page, setting up, 63–65
searches, creating, online p15
secure pages, considering, ix
secure zones
  benefits of, xi
  components of, 149
  creating profiles, 150
  Forums option, 153
  for gathering data, 148–150
  landing pages, 152–153
  link, 156
  listing, 152
  login forms, 149
  Members Only Area, 152
  registration forms, 149, 151
  testing, 155
SEO (search engine optimization), en-
    abling, online p16
shipping options
  choosing for products, 109
  setting up for online stores, 125–127
  User Defined, 126
Shipping Vendor Defined option, 126–127
shipping-options link, 131
signup form, sample in trial site, 32
site statistics, displaying in Dashboard, 7
site structure, displaying, 8
sitemap file, generating, online p16
sites. See also live site updates; trial sites
  Business Catalyst, xii, 2
  creating, 14
  listing in Clients section, online p12
  managing, 35
  sharing in Gallery, 13
  statistics, 210–211
  testing changes to, 155
  updating with InContext Editing, 20–21
slide show
  sample in trial site, 31
  updating images, 25–27
SMS (Short Message Service) notifica-
    tion, x
  adding to web forms, 96, 138–139
  versus e-mail notifications, 147

source code, editing in HTML view, 19–20
Starter plan, choosing, online p13
statistics, displaying in Dashboard, 7,
    210–211
store layouts. See also layout files;
    online stores
  accessing, 114
  Buy Now button, 116
  editing in Dreamweaver, 122–123
  Individual Catalog, 115
  Individual Product, 116
  Overall Layout file, 117
  returning to, 115
  Sales Price tag, 116
  updating List view of products,
    116–117
store purchases, testing, online p14
store-layouts link, 131
stores. See online stores
subscribers, managing, 161, 164
subscription activity, displaying, 160
subscription data, accessing, 160–161,
    163–164
subscription forms, using, 165–166
subscriptions, displaying chart of, 211
Suggestion Box form, 135–139, 146
Suggestion Box page, 91–96
support requests, managing, x
system emails, customizing, online p15
system messages
  customizing, online p15
  updating, 88

T

Table Wizard, using with Web Apps,
    189–190
tablets, template for, 34
Tag Insert menu
  displaying, 67–68
  using with modules, 56
  using with Web Apps, 190
Tag Selector, using in Dreamweaver, 86
tagging products, 119–120. See also mod-
    ule tags
tasks and notes, adding to cases, 142–144
tax codes
  adding for products, 110
  link, 131
template content, displaying, 34–35
Template Details page, displaying, 34
template files
  accessing in Dreamweaver, 39–41
  editing, 35
  updating in Dreamweaver, 41

templates
  accessing in Admin Console, 33–35
  adding, online p5
  applying in Admin Console, 33–35
  applying to pages in Dreamweaver,
    35–38
  benefits, 30
  building in Dreamweaver, 30
  creating in Admin Console, 33–35
  deleting, online p5
  displaying in Admin Console, 33
  editable regions, 30
  editing, 39–44, online p5
  e-mail campaigns, 172–173
  Enable Tablet & Phone Support, 34
  features of, 17, 30
  for importing products, 113
  Manage Site Wide Templates option,
    154
  mobile devices, 34
  module tags in, 43–44
  removing from sites, 34
  resetting for web page, 17
  setting default for, 34
  tablets, 34
  in trial site, 31–32
  updating logos in, 41
  using for online stores, 104
  using in Dreamweaver, 35
  using with FAQs module, 51
  using with products, 106–108
  viewing, online p5
test.htm page, creating, 17
text, adding to web pages, 8, 18–19
text e-mail versus HTML formats, 170
Top Sources chart, displaying, 212
Training area, features of, 13
trial sites. See also online stores; sites
  best practices, online p17
  billing options, online p14
  Blog page, 5
  Contact page, 6
  creating, 14, online p12
  domains for, 8
  footer, 32
  Forum page, 5–6
  header area, 31
  home page, 4–5, 31–32
  links, 14, online p18
  online p13
  login form, 32
  Main template, 34, 112
  navigation links, 31
  online store, 5

reviewing, 3–4
reviewing FAQs module in, 48–49
search field, 31
secure zones, 149
signup form, 2–3, 32
slide show, 31
Start From Scratch option, online p12
template in, 31–32
testing changes to, 155
upgrading to paid site, online p11–p14

U

upgrading trial sites, online p11–p14
URL redirects, managing, 16
user accounts
    creating, online p6–p9
    managing, online p16
    testing, online p9–p10
users
    assigning to roles, online p8
    managing, online p2–p6
Users List page, displaying, online p3
Users role
    versus Administrators role, online p5
    explained, 137
    warning about deletion of, 138

V

visitors
    gathering information from, 74
    ranking actions of, viii–ix
    thanking for feedback, 177
    tracking, 7
Visitors report, described, 214
visits, displaying chart of, 211
Visits and Page Views chart, displaying, 212

W

Web Apps
    About page update, 206–207
    Browse button, 200
    creating, 186–192
    Custom Fields page, 187
    description field, 191
    description tag, 189
    Detail layout, 188–189
    Edit layout file, 200
    editing layouts for, 188
    features built with, 184
    Field Name menu, 187–188
    Field Type menu, 187
    inserting on pages, 193–196
    Item Content field, 191–192

Item submission form, 200–205
layout files, 188
link, 208
link to submission form, 206–207
List layout, 188–189
managing, 198
mapping, 185
Name field, 186
populating items, 191–193
populating with visitor data, 198–200
processing transactions, 208
Requires Approval option, 198
search functionality, 196–198
Table Wizard, 189–190
Tag Insert menu, 190
using with web forms, 185
workflow, 207–208
Web Form Builder
    accessing, 80
    adding fields, 93–94
    adding form elements, 84
    auto-responder e-mail, 93
    creating forms, 93–94
    creating page for forms, 91
    Customer Inquiry Workflow, 80–81
    deleting elements, 84
    editing form elements, 84
    features of, 83
    listing forms, 83
    listing workflows, 80
    Manage Workflows, 80
    notification steps, 81
    notifications, 82
    returning to, 94
    Role Responsible menu, 81
    saving changes to forms, 84
    SMS notification, 82
    Suggestion Box page, 91
    using, 90
web forms. See also contact forms
    adding in Dreamweaver, 85–87
    asking for personal data, 75
    building, 97
    CAPTCHA, 75
    cases created for, 78
    creating, 97
    editing, 82–85
    editing for newsletter subscriptions,
        166–168
    versus e-mail addresses, 75
    e-mail notification, 96
    generating cases with, 135–138
    image verification, 75

inserting as module tags, 89–90
inserting on pages, 97
inserting with Module Manager, 89
questions on, 74
SMS notification, 96
styling, 97
triggering workflows, 79–82
updating, 97–98
updating pages after editing, 85
using, x
Web Page Details page, displaying, 57
web pages. See also content changes
    adding FAQ items to, 59
    adding text to, 18–19
    adding with 1-Click Insert menu, 94–96
    creating, 16–17
    creating in Dreamweaver, 35
    displaying, 16
    editing in Design view, 18–19
    header text, 18
    inserting modules into, 57–59
    making unavailable, 17
    manipulating, 16
    paragraph text, 18
    resetting templates for, 17
    saving in subfolders, 17
    setting publication dates for, 17
Website area, contents of, 8
Website Content report, described, 215
websites. See sites
Welcome text, updating, 27
workflows
    accessing for web forms, 80
    Approvals option, 137
    attaching, 148
    configuring for cases, 136–137
    Content Approval, 148
    Customer Inquiry, 137
    for customer support, 148
    Duration option, 137
    Escalations option, 137
    facilitating business goals, 148
    link, 156
    managing, online p15
    managing approvals in, 146–147
    notification messages, 147
    Reminders option, 137
    tying to roles, 138
    updating steps in, 138–139
    Web Apps, 207–208